T0407035

# KEY GOVERNMENT REPORTS

# VOLUME 16

# APRIL 2019

# MONTH IN REVIEW

Additional books and e-books in this series can be found
on Nova's website under the Series tab.

# KEY GOVERNMENT REPORTS

# VOLUME 16

## APRIL 2019

## ERNEST CLARK
### EDITOR

**NOTICE TO THE READER**

Additional color graphics may be available in the e-book version of this book.

**Library of Congress Cataloging-in-Publication Data**

ISBN: 978-1-53616-001-7

*Published by Nova Science Publishers, Inc.* † *New York*

# CONTENTS

# PREFACE

This book is a comprehensive compilation of all reports, testimony, correspondence and other publications issued by the GAO (Government Accountability Office) during the month of April, grouped according to topics. This book is focused on the following topics:

- Finance
- Government Operations
- Veterans

Chapter 1 - Concerns over efforts by U.S. taxpayers to use offshore accounts to hide income or evade taxes contributed to the passage of FATCA in 2010, which sought to create greater transparency and accountability over offshore assets held by U.S. taxpayers. House Report 114-624 included a provision for GAO to evaluate FATCA implementation and determine the effects of FATCA on U.S. citizens living abroad. GAO—among other things — (1) assessed IRS's efforts to use FATCA-related information to improve taxpayer compliance; (2) examined the extent to which Treasury administers overlapping reporting requirements on financial assets held overseas; and (3) examined the effects of FATCA implementation unique to U.S. persons living abroad. GAO reviewed applicable documentation; analyzed tax data;

and interviewed officials from IRS, other federal agencies and organizations, selected tax practitioners, and more than 20 U.S. persons living overseas.

Chapter 2 - American taxpayers spent at least half a billion dollars in 2017 on financial products—issued by banks, through paid tax return preparers—to help them file taxes and get advances or loans against tax refunds. GAO was asked to review tax-time financial products. Among other things, GAO (1) described market trends and examined IRS data, (2) described characteristics of product users and factors that influence product use, and (3) described product disclosure practices. GAO reviewed fee and product usage data; conducted a multivariate regression analysis to determine user characteristics; and analyzed disclosures of selected providers that are national chains and those of their bank partners. GAO conducted nongeneralizeable undercover visits of nine randomly selected tax preparers in the Washington, D.C. area to understand how they communicate fees and terms to taxpayers. Preparers were selected to ensure a mixture of regulatory jurisdictions, among other factors. GAO reviewed laws, regulations, and guidance on the products, and interviewed IRS and other government officials and a nongeneralizeable selection of product and service providers, tax preparation companies, consumer groups, and academics.

Chapter 3 - The Bureau, a component of the Department of Commerce (Commerce), is responsible for conducting a complete and accurate decennial census of the U.S. population. The decennial census is mandated by the Constitution and provides vital data for the nation. A complete count of the nation's population is an enormous undertaking as the Bureau seeks to control the cost of the census, implement operational innovations, and use new and modified IT systems. In recent years, GAO has identified challenges that raise serious concerns about the Bureau's ability to conduct a cost-effective count. For these reasons, GAO added the 2020 Census to its High-Risk list in February 2017. GAO was asked to testify about the reasons the 2020 Census remains on the High-Risk List and the steps the Bureau needs to take to mitigate risks to a successful census. To do so, GAO summarized its prior work regarding the Bureau's planning efforts for the 2020 Census. GAO also included preliminary observations from its ongoing work examining the IT systems readiness and cybersecurity for the 2020 Census. This information is related to, among other things, the Bureau's progress in developing and testing key systems and the status of cybersecurity risks.

Chapter 4 - The DATA Act required OMB or a designated federal agency to establish a pilot program to develop recommendations for reducing recipient reporting burden for federal grantees and contractors. The grants portion of the pilot tested six ways to reduce recipient reporting burden while the procurement portion focused on testing a centralized reporting portal for submitting reporting requirements. This chapter follows a 2016 GAO review on the design of the pilot. This chapter assesses the extent to which (1) the pilot met the statutory requirements set out in the DATA Act, (2) the grants portion of the pilot demonstrated changes in reporting burden, and (3) the procurement portion demonstrated changes in reporting burden. GAO reviewed statutory requirements, pilot plans, agency data and reports and interviewed OMB staff and officials from HHS and GSA.

Chapter 5 - For many of the approximately 612,000 spouses of active duty service members, the special conditions of military life may make it difficult to start or maintain a career. Military spouses may have to move frequently to keep families together when service members are relocated, or they may have to bear a larger share of family responsibilities. The My Career Advancement Account (MyCAA) program is one approach the Department of Defense (DOD) has taken to help military spouses improve their employment opportunities. The MyCAA program provides up to $4,000 in tuition assistance for education or training for eligible spouses of service members. The use of MyCAA funds is restricted to the attainment of certificates, licenses, or associate's degrees in a portable career field, which is defined by DOD and the Department of Labor as one that is high-growth, high-demand and most likely to have job openings in military duty locations. The John S. McCain National Defense Authorization Act for Fiscal Year 2019 includes a provision for GAO to review participation in and awareness of the MyCAA program. This chapter examines (1) what is known about participation rates among military spouses who are eligible for the MyCAA program, and (2) how DOD promotes awareness of and participation in the MyCAA program. To address the first objective, he United States Government Accountability Office (GAO) reviewed information on the number of spouses who received tuition assistance through MyCAA from annual DOD military family readiness reports for fiscal years 2011 through 2016, the years for which DOD reported MyCAA data. GAO also obtained data from DOD on military personnel and on the MyCAA program to determine the percentage of spouses who received tuition assistance under MyCAA for fiscal year 2017, the most recent data available at the time of our review. To understand potential reasons for trends in MyCAA participation, GAO interviewed DOD officials and reviewed 2015 data from its Survey of Active Duty Spouses (ADSS), the most recent available at the time of our review. GAO assessed the reliability of these data by conducting data checks, reviewing documentation, and interviewing knowledgeable DOD officials and researchers. GAO found these data to be sufficiently reliable to generally describe participation in the MyCAA program and have included caveats regarding what the data on the number of potentially eligible spouses represent and other limitations, as appropriate. To address the second objective, GAO reviewed DOD's MyCAA outreach materials and analyzed all of the pages on the MyCAA website as of February 2019 using an automated web-scraping program, which extracts and analyzes website data. GAO assessed the website's content against relevant standards on information quality of federal websites. GAO interviewed DOD officials about the agency's efforts to inform eligible spouses about the MyCAA program and promote participation in it. GAO also interviewed representatives from three military family advocacy organizations that they judgmentally selected on the basis of relevant research the organizations conducted on spouse employment; recommendations from other advocacy organizations; or involvement in DOD's Spouse Ambassador Network, which is composed of a variety of groups that are active in military spouse communities. GAO conducted this performance audit from September 2018 to April 2019 in accordance with generally accepted government auditing standards. Those standards require that GAO plan and perform the audit to obtain sufficient, appropriate evidence to provide a reasonable basis for our findings and conclusions based on our audit objectives. GAO believe that the evidence obtained provides a reasonable basis for our findings and conclusions based on our audit objectives.

Chapter 6 - VHA anticipates that it will provide care to more than 7 million veterans in fiscal year 2019. The majority of veterans using VHA health care services receive care in one or more of the 172 medical centers or at associated outpatient facilities. VHA collects an extensive amount of data that can be used to assess and manage the performance of medical centers. Many measures are publicly reported on VA web pages, allowing veterans the ability to compare medical centers' quality of care. GAO was asked to assess VHA's management of medical center performance. This chapter examines (1) the tools VHA uses to assess medical center performance; (2) VHA's use of medical center performance information to assess medical center directors; and (3) the extent to which VHA has evaluated the effectiveness of the SAIL system. GAO reviewed VHA policies, guidance, and performance information for medical centers and their associated directors. GAO also interviewed officials from VHA as well as from four VA medical centers, selected for variation in performance and geographic location.

Chapter 7 - In June 2018, Congress passed the VA MISSION Act of 2018, which requires VA to establish a permanent community care program. VA plans to consolidate the Choice Program and its other VA community care programs into one community care program—the VCCP. This legislation helps address some of the challenges faced by the Choice Program and VA's other community care programs. VA's implementation of the VCCP can benefit from the lessons learned under the Choice Program. Ignoring these lessons learned increases VA's risk for not being able to ensure that all veterans receive timely access to care in the community and that community providers are reimbursed in a timely manner. This testimony focuses on lessons learned from the Choice Program, including recommendations GAO has made to VA to help ensure (1) veterans' timely access to care under the VCCP (2) effective monitoring of veterans' access to care under the VCCP, and (3) timely payments to community providers under the VCCP. This testimony is based on GAO reports on the Choice Program that were issued in June 2018 and September 2018.

# FINANCE

In: Key Government Reports.  ISBN: 978-1-53616-001-7
Editor: Ernest Clark  © 2019 Nova Science Publishers, Inc.

*Chapter 1*

# FOREIGN ASSET REPORTING: ACTIONS NEEDED TO ENHANCE COMPLIANCE EFFORTS, ELIMINATE OVERLAPPING REQUIREMENTS, AND MITIGATE BURDENS ON U.S. PERSONS ABROAD*

## *Subcommittee on Financial Services*

### ABBREVIATIONS

| | |
|---|---|
| BSA | Bank Secrecy Act of 1970 |
| CDW | Compliance Data Warehouse |
| CRS | Common Reporting Standard |
| FATCA | Foreign Account Tax Compliance Act |

---

* This is an edited, reformatted and augmented version of United States Government Accountability Office; Report to Congressional Committees, Accessible Version, Publication No. GAO-19-180, dated April 2019.

| FBAR | Report of Foreign Banks and Financial Accounts |
| FBU | Federal Benefits Unit |
| FDB | FATCA Database |
| FFI | foreign financial institution |
| FinCEN | Financial Crimes Enforcement Network |
| Form 8938 | IRS Form 8938, Statement of Specified Foreign Financial Assets |
| Form 8966 | IRS Form 8966, FATCA Report |
| GIIN | Global Intermediary Identification Number |
| HCTA | Host Country Tax Authority |
| ICMM | International Compliance Management Model |
| ICMM-FIR | International Compliance Management Model-FATCA International Returns |
| IGA | intergovernmental agreement |
| IMF | Individual Master File |
| IPM | Integrated Production Model |
| IRC | Internal Revenue Code |
| IRS | Internal Revenue Service |
| IRTF | Individual Returns Transaction File |
| IT | Information Technology |
| MTRDB | Modernized Tax Return Database |
| NFE | Nonfinancial Entity |
| OECD | Organisation for Economic Co-operation and Development |
| RAAS | Research, Applied Analytics and Statistics |
| SSA | Social Security Administration |
| SSN | Social Security Number |
| State | Department of State |
| TIGTA | Treasury Inspector General for Tax Administration |
| TIN | Taxpayer Identification Number |
| Treasury | Department of the Treasury |

# WHY GAO DID THIS STUDY

Concerns over efforts by U.S. taxpayers to use offshore accounts to hide income or evade taxes contributed to the passage of FATCA in 2010, which sought to create greater transparency and accountability over offshore assets held by U.S. taxpayers.

House Report 114-624 included a provision for GAO to evaluate FATCA implementation and determine the effects of FATCA on U.S. citizens living abroad. GAO—among other things — (1) assessed IRS's efforts to use FATCA-related information to improve taxpayer compliance; (2) examined the extent to which Treasury administers overlapping reporting requirements on financial assets held overseas; and (3) examined the effects of FATCA implementation unique to U.S. persons living abroad.

GAO reviewed applicable documentation; analyzed tax data; and interviewed officials from IRS, other federal agencies and organizations, selected tax practitioners, and more than 20 U.S. persons living overseas.

# WHAT GAO RECOMMENDS

GAO is making one matter for congressional consideration to address overlap in foreign asset reporting requirements. GAO is making seven recommendations to IRS and other agencies to enhance IRS's ability to leverage FATCA data to enforce compliance, address unnecessary reporting, and better collaborate to mitigate burdens on U.S. persons living abroad. State and Social Security Administration agreed with GAO's recommendations. Treasury and IRS neither agreed nor disagreed with GAO's recommendations.

# WHAT GAO FOUND

Data quality and management issues have limited the effectiveness of the Internal Revenue Service's (IRS) efforts to improve taxpayer compliance using foreign financial asset data collected under the Foreign Account Tax Compliance Act (FATCA). Specifically, IRS has had difficulties matching the information reported by foreign financial institutions (FFI) with U.S. taxpayers' tax filings due to missing or inaccurate Taxpayer Identification Numbers provided by FFIs. Further, IRS lacks access to consistent and complete data on foreign financial assets and other data reported in tax filings by U.S. persons, in part, because some IRS databases do not store foreign asset data reported from paper filings. IRS has also stopped pursuing a comprehensive plan to leverage FATCA data to improve taxpayer compliance because, according to IRS officials, IRS moved away from updating broad strategy documents to focus on individual compliance campaigns. Ensuring access to consistent and complete data collected from U.S. persons—and employing a plan to leverage such data—would help IRS better leverage such campaigns and increase taxpayer compliance.

Due to overlapping statutory reporting requirements, IRS and the Financial Crimes Enforcement Network (FinCEN)—both within the Department of the Treasury (Treasury)—collect duplicative foreign financial account and other asset information from U.S. persons. Consequently, in tax years 2015 and 2016, close to 75 percent of U.S. persons who reported information on foreign accounts and other assets on their tax returns also filed a separate form with FinCEN. The overlapping requirements increase the compliance burden on U.S. persons and add complexity that can create confusion, potentially resulting in inaccurate or unnecessary reporting. Modifying the statutes governing the requirements to allow for the sharing of FATCA information for the prevention and detection of financial crimes would eliminate the need for duplicative reporting. This is similar to other statutory allowances for IRS to disclose return information for other purposes, such as for determining Social Security income tax withholding.

According to documents GAO reviewed, and focus groups and interviews GAO conducted, FFIs closed some U.S. persons' existing accounts or denied them opportunities to open new accounts after FATCA was enacted due to increased costs, and risks they pose under FATCA reporting requirements. According to Department of State (State) data, annual approvals of renunciations of U.S. citizenship increased from 1,601 to 4,449—or nearly 178 percent—from 2011 through 2016, attributable in part to the difficulties cited above.

Treasury previously established joint strategies with State to address challenges U.S. persons faced in accessing foreign financial services. However, it lacks a collaborative mechanism to coordinate efforts with other agencies to address ongoing challenges in accessing such services or obtaining Social Security Numbers. Implementation of a formal means to collaboratively address burdens faced by Americans abroad from FATCA can help federal agencies develop more effective solutions to mitigate such burdens by monitoring and sharing information on such issues, and jointly developing and implementing steps to address them.

April 1, 2019

The Honorable John Kennedy
Chairman

The Honorable Christopher Coons
Ranking Member
Subcommittee on Financial Services and General Government
Committee on Appropriations
United States Senate

The Honorable Michael Quigley
Chairman

The Honorable Tom Graves
Ranking Member

Subcommittee on Financial Services and General Government
Committee on Appropriations
House of Representatives

By law, U.S. individuals—regardless of whether they live in the United States or abroad—are required to report and pay applicable taxes on worldwide income to the Internal Revenue Service (IRS), including income from offshore accounts and other assets. While taxpayers can hold offshore accounts for a number of legitimate reasons, some taxpayers have also used such accounts to hide income and evade taxes. IRS does not have an estimate of the revenue loss due to offshore noncompliance. However, international tax policy experts believe that the losses are in the billions of dollars annually. These losses contribute to the tax gap—the difference between tax amounts that taxpayers should pay and what they actually pay voluntarily and on time—that has been a problem for decades. In 2016, IRS estimated that the average annual gross tax gap for tax years 2008 to 2010 was $458 billion, of which $319 billion was from individual taxpayers.

The passage of the Foreign Account Tax Compliance Act (FATCA) sought to reduce tax evasion by creating greater transparency and accountability with respect to offshore accounts and other assets held by U.S. taxpayers.[1] However, since FATCA's enactment in 2010, we and others have identified compliance burdens and other challenges FATCA has created for U.S. persons living abroad, foreign financial institutions, and other stakeholders.[2] For example, in our past work, we highlighted that some of the information reporting requirements for taxpayers subject to FATCA

---

[1] Subtitle A of Title V of the Hiring Incentives to Restore Employment Act is commonly referred to as FATCA. Pub. L. No. 111-147, §§ 501-541, 124 Stat. 71, 97-117 (2010).

[2] For example, see GAO, *Workforce Retirement Accounts: Better Guidance and Information Could Help Plan Participants at Home and Abroad Manage Their Retirement Savings*, GAO-18-19 (Washington, D.C.: Jan. 31, 2018); and *Reporting Foreign Accounts to IRS: Extent of Duplication Not Currently Known, but Requirements Can Be Clarified*, GAO-12-403 (Washington, D.C.: Feb. 28, 2012). See also National Taxpayer Advocate, *Fiscal Year 2018 Objectives Report to Congress, Volume 2: Foreign Account Tax Compliance Act (FATCA): The IRS's Approach to International Tax Administration Unnecessarily Burdens Impacted Parties, Wastes Resources, and Fails to Protect Taxpayer Rights* (Washington, D.C.: June 28, 2017), p. 122-130.

result in duplicative reporting to the Department of the Treasury (Treasury). This increases complexity and creates confusion for taxpayers.[3]

House Report 114-624 included a provision for us to evaluate IRS's implementation of FATCA and determine the effects of FATCA on U.S. citizens living abroad.[4] To address House Report 114-624, this chapter (1) assesses IRS's efforts to use information collected under FATCA to improve taxpayer compliance; (2) examines available foreign financial asset reports submitted by U.S. persons, including submissions that were below required filing thresholds; (3) examines the extent to which Treasury administers overlapping reporting requirements on foreign financial assets; (4) describes similarities and differences between FATCA and Common Reporting Standard (CRS) reporting requirements; and (5) examines the effects of FATCA implementation that are unique to U.S. persons living abroad.[5]

For our first objective, we identified criteria from our prior work identifying key practices for risk management.[6] We applied these criteria to assess steps IRS has taken to manage risks in not receiving complete and valid Taxpayer Identification Numbers (TIN) from foreign financial institutions (FFI). We also applied criteria from our prior work on use of documented frameworks to IRS documentation on FATCA compliance activities to determine the extent to which IRS implemented a comprehensive plan to maximize the use of collected data to enforce compliance with FATCA.[7]

For our second objective, we identified total maximum account values reported by individual filers of the Financial Crimes Enforcement Network (FinCEN) Form 114s (commonly known as the *Report of Foreign Bank and Financial Accounts*, or FBAR) in calendar year 2015 and 2016, using lower

---

[3] GAO-12-403.

[4] H.R. Rep. No. 114-624, at 22 (2016).

[5] The term "U.S. persons, " as used in this report, refers to specified individuals categorized in 26 C.F.R. § 1.6038D-1(2) as (1) U.S. citizens; (2) resident aliens of the United States for any portion of the taxable year; (3) nonresident aliens for whom an election under 26 C.F.R. §§ 6013(g)-(h) is in effect; or (4) nonresident aliens who are bona fide residents of Puerto Rico or a section 931 possession as defined in 26 C.F.R. § 1.931– 1(c)(1)).

[6] GAO, *Information Technology: IRS Needs to Take Additional Actions to Address Significant Risks to Tax Processing*, GAO-18-298 (Washington, D.C.: June 28, 2018).

[7] GAO, *Tax Preparer Regulation: IRS Needs a Documented Framework to Achieve Goal of Improving Taxpayer Compliance*, GAO-11-336 (Washington, D.C.: Mar. 31, 2011).

and upper bounds of foreign financial accounts reported for each year. See appendix III for more details on our methodology to evaluate these data. We summarized the numbers of IRS Forms 8938, *Statement of Specified Foreign Financial Assets* (Form 8938) filed in tax year 2016—the most recent year for which data were available—accounting for data limitations described in appendix I. We also identified Forms 8938 filed in tax year 2016 with available residency and asset information that reported specified foreign financial assets with aggregate values at or below end-of-year tax thresholds, which vary depending on the location of residence and filing status of such filers.

For our third objective, we reviewed IRS and FinCEN documentation, and applied criteria from *Fragmentation, Overlap, and Duplication: An Evaluation and Management Guide* to identify the extent to which IRS and FinCEN were engaged in overlapping activities, and collecting duplicative foreign financial asset information held by U.S. persons.[8] We assessed the extent to which individual filers who submitted a Form 8938 in 2015 and 2016 also submitted an FBAR for the same year.

For the three objectives described above, we assessed the reliability of data submitted on Forms 8938 filed by individuals for tax years 2015 and 2016, and FBARs for calendar years 2015 and 2016.

For our fourth objective, we reviewed documentation and interviewed officials from Treasury, IRS, and the Organisation for Economic Co-operation and Development (OECD) to compare and contrast FATCA and CRS reporting requirements.

For our fifth objective, we collected documentation and conducted focus groups and semi-structured interviews with Treasury, IRS, Department of State (State), and Social Security Administration (SSA) officials, and more than 20 U.S. persons subject to FATCA requirements, tax practitioners and various organizations in the United States and five other countries (Canada, Japan, Singapore, Switzerland, and the United Kingdom). We selected these countries based on geography, relatively high numbers of U.S. expatriates and Form 8938 filers, and tax information sharing agreements and other tax

---

[8] GAO, *Fragmentation, Overlap, and Duplication: An Evaluation and Management Guide*, GAO-15-49SP (Washington, D.C.: Apr. 14, 2015).

treaties with the United States. The findings from the focus groups and interviews are not generalizable to other U.S. persons, tax practitioners, or organizations.

We collected documentation from and interviewed Treasury, IRS, State, and SSA officials on steps to monitor and mitigate the effects of FATCA on U.S. persons living abroad. We also identified criteria from our prior work on key practices to enhance and sustain interagency collaboration and mechanisms to facilitate coordination.[9] We applied the criteria to agencies' collaborative efforts addressing issues U.S. persons living abroad faced from FATCA's implementation, and identified the extent to which agencies established effective collaborative mechanisms to identify, assess, and implement cross-agency solutions to such issues.

We conducted this performance audit from August 2017 to April 2019 in accordance with generally accepted government auditing standards. Those standards require that we plan and perform the audit to obtain sufficient, appropriate evidence to provide a reasonable basis for our findings and conclusions based on our audit objectives. We believe that the evidence obtained provides a reasonable basis for our findings and conclusions based on our audit objectives. See appendix I for more detailed information on our objectives, scope, and methodology.

## BACKGROUND

The United States has many international agreements that require treaty partners to provide certain information to IRS, which can help prevent the use of foreign bank accounts to facilitate tax evasion. FATCA goes much further, requiring FFIs to report more detailed information to IRS about their U.S. customers annually. These provisions are important developments in efforts to combat tax evasion by U.S. persons holding investments in

---

[9] GAO, *Managing for Results: Key Considerations for Implementing Interagency Collaborative Mechanisms,* GAO-12-1022 (Washington, D.C.: Sept. 27, 2012); and *Results-Oriented Government: Practices That Can Help Enhance and Sustain Collaboration among Federal Agencies,* GAO-06-15 (Washington, D.C.: Oct. 21, 2005).

offshore accounts. FATCA generally requires certain taxpayers to report foreign financial accounts and other specified foreign financial assets whose aggregate value exceeds specified thresholds to IRS on Form 8938.[10] These taxpayers must report these assets and income generated from such assets to IRS with their tax return on Form 8938. These thresholds vary by filing status—such as single or married filing jointly—and by domestic or foreign residency.[11]

FATCA also promotes third-party reporting of foreign financial assets by requiring a withholding agent to withhold 30 percent on certain payments to an FFI unless the FFI or the jurisdiction in which the FFI is located has entered into an agreement with the United States to report certain account information of their U.S. customers.[12] Under such an agreement, participating FFIs report detailed information to IRS annually about accounts held by their U.S. customers using an IRS Form 8966, *FATCA Report* (Form 8966).[13] According to IRS, FATCA improves visibility into taxable income from foreign sources, and enhances the agency's ability to identify and pursue taxpayer noncompliance. For example, FATCA allows IRS to compare information reported by FFIs on Forms 8966 to information reported by U.S. persons on Forms 8938. According to IRS, this comparison can be used to ensure taxpayers and FFIs are properly reporting foreign financial assets and income from international investments. This type of comparison is a common IRS enforcement technique.

---

[10] 26 U.S.C. § 6038D; 26 C.F.R. § 1.6038D-2. Taxpayers required to report specified foreign financial assets to IRS under IRC section 6038D include U.S. citizens, U.S. resident aliens (even if resident for only part of the year), nonresident aliens who elect to be treated as resident aliens for purposes of filing a joint tax return, and nonresident aliens who are bona fide residents of Puerto Rico, Guam, American Samoa, the Northern Mariana Islands, or the U.S. Virgin Islands.

[11] See appendix IV for thresholds of value of foreign assets making them reportable on Form 8938 by residency and filing status.

[12] 26 U.S.C. §§ 1471-1474.

[13] In general, information participating FFIs are required to report on the Form 8966 includes the name, address, and TIN of accountholders who are specified U.S. persons; and the account number, balance or value, gross receipts, and gross withdrawals or payments from each account held by such persons.

For example, IRS can directly compare information it receives from financial institutions' IRS Form 1099-INT, *Interest Income*, against a tax return to determine if the taxpayer reported income generated from interest earned.

To facilitate FATCA implementation for FFIs operating in jurisdictions with laws that would prohibit FFIs from complying with the terms of the FFI agreement, Treasury developed two alternative intergovernmental agreements (IGA)—Model 1 and Model 2—to facilitate the effective and efficient implementation of FATCA by removing partner jurisdictions' legal impediments to comply with FATCA reporting requirements, and reducing burdens on FFIs located in partner jurisdictions. FFIs from countries with Model 1 IGAs report information on U.S. persons' accounts to their respective host country tax authorities (HCTAs). The HCTAs, in turn, compile the information from FFIs and transmit it to IRS. In contrast, FFIs from countries with Model 2 IGAs, or countries treated as not having an IGA in effect, directly report information on U.S. persons' accounts to IRS.

Separate from the FATCA requirements, regulations implementing the Bank Secrecy Act of 1970 (BSA) also impose a separate self-reporting requirement for foreign accounts.[14] Specifically, certain taxpayers and residents are required to file an FBAR with FinCEN annually if they have financial interest or signature or other authority over one or more foreign financial accounts with a total of more than $10,000, regardless of whether they reside within or outside the United States.

Federal, state, and local law enforcement agencies can use information from these reports to combat financial crimes, including terrorist financing and tax evasion. Appendix IV provides a comparison of Form 8938 and FBAR reporting requirements.

Figure 1 depicts the flow of foreign financial account information from U.S. persons and FFIs to IRS and FinCEN through the FATCA and FBAR reporting processes.

---

[14] 31 C.F.R. § 1010.350.

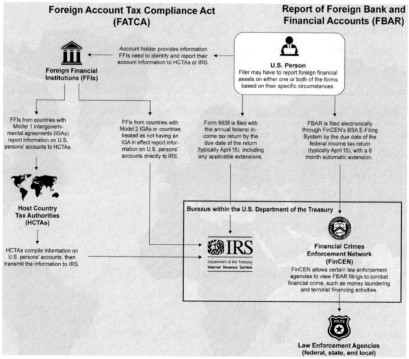

Source: GAO analysis of FATCA and FBAR reporting requirements. | GAO-19-180.

Figure 1. Illustration of Foreign Financial Account Reporting by U.S. Persons and Foreign Financial Institutions to Meet FATCA and BSA Reporting Requirements.

# FATCA DATA LIMITATIONS AND LACK OF A COMPREHENSIVE STRATEGY HAVE HAMPERED IRS EFFORTS TO INCREASE COMPLIANCE

## Incomplete and Inaccurate Reporting of Taxpayer Identification Numbers by FFIs Has Limited IRS's Efforts to Match Account Information for Compliance Purposes

As part of the FATCA reporting requirements, IRS collects information on financial accounts through forms and reports submitted by both taxpayers and FFIs. As part of this effort, IRS requires taxpayers to identify their TINs on Forms 8938 they submit. IRS also requires participating FFIs to report the TINs of each account holder who is a specified U.S. person on Forms 8966. IRS intends to use reported TINs to link Form 8938 data filed by taxpayers to Form 8966 data filed by the FFIs to ensure that taxpayers and FFIs are properly reporting foreign financial assets.

However, IRS often could not link account information collected from FFIs to the account's owner because of incorrect or missing TINs.[15] In July 2018, the Treasury Inspector General for Tax Administration (TIGTA) found that almost half of new Forms 8966 filed by FFIs did not include a TIN or included an invalid TIN.[16] A consulting firm working with FFIs to implement FATCA reporting requirements told us that FFIs encountered significant challenges obtaining accurate TINs from U.S. persons as part of the self-certification process. For instance, FFIs encountered situations where U.S. persons provided incomplete or inaccurate TINs—such as Social Security Numbers (SSN) with less than nine digits—on forms used to self-certify their status as U.S. persons. FFIs also encountered situations where U.S. persons may not have obtained TINs or were unwilling to provide them to FFIs.[17]

Additionally, banking associations told us that it has taken time, effort, and expense for FFIs to report TINs, as they had to upgrade computer systems to collect and record TINs from U.S. customers. Finally, Treasury told us that jurisdictions that have an IGA with the United States but no legal

---

[15] For individuals filing taxes, a TIN would be a Social Security Number (SSN), Individual Taxpayer Identification Number, or Adoption Taxpayer Identification Number.

[16] See Treasury Inspector General for Tax Administration, *Despite Spending Nearly $380 Million, the Internal Revenue Service Is Still Not Prepared to Enforce Compliance With the Foreign Account Tax Compliance Act*, 2018-30-040 (Washington, D.C.: July 5, 2018). As of September 30, 2017, IRS had received approximately 8.8 million new Form 8966 records on files stored in its International Compliance Management Model database, of which more than 4.3 million had either lacked a TIN or had an invalid TIN.

[17] Officials from two organizations representing Americans living overseas said that U.S. persons living abroad might not possess an SSN because their parents did not obtain one for them as a minor. Often, this may have been due to the parents leaving the United States when the child was young. Additionally, State officials said that U.S. citizens applying for U.S. passports while overseas frequently forget their SSN or do not know if their parents ever applied for an SSN on their behalf. See below for challenges U.S. persons living abroad encountered when applying for an SSN.

requirement to collect TINs are not in compliance with the requirements of the IGA.

Treasury and IRS determined that some FFIs reporting from countries with Model 1 IGAs needed additional time to implement procedures to obtain and report required U.S. TINs for preexisting accounts that are U.S. reportable accounts. Consequently, IRS provided a transition period, through the end of 2019, for compliance with the TIN requirements for FFIs under Model 1 IGAs. Specifically, in September 2017, IRS issued a notice modifying procedures for FFIs reporting from countries with Model 1 IGAs to become compliant with TIN reporting requirements for preexisting accounts. For calendar years 2017-2019, IRS will not determine that certain FFIs in countries with Model 1 IGAs are significantly noncompliant with their obligations under the IGA solely as a result of a failure to report U.S. TINs associated with the FFI's U.S. reportable accounts, providing they (1) obtain and report the date of birth of each account holder and controlling person whose TIN is not reported, (2) make annual requests for missing TINs from each account holder, and (3) search electronically searchable data maintained by such FFIs for missing required U.S. TINs before reporting information that relates to calendar year 2017 to a partner jurisdiction.[18] As a result, even without any further extensions, calendar year 2020 is the earliest IRS will be enforcing requirements for FFIs from countries with Model 1 IGAs to provide accurate and complete information on U.S. account holders' TINs to IRS.

Without valid TINs on Forms 8966 submitted by FFIs, according to IRS officials, IRS faces significant hurdles in matching accounts reported by FFIs to those reported by individual tax filers on their Forms 8938. As a result, IRS must rely on information such as names, dates of birth, and addresses that the filers and/or FFIs may not consistently report. Without

---

[18] The U.S. reportable accounts covered under the IRS notice include those accounts maintained as of the determination date specified in the applicable Model 1 IGA. Under this rule, according to Treasury officials, many accounts would still be subject to U.S. TIN reporting because (1) they are not preexisting accounts, or (2) the FFI obtains the U.S. TIN through the annual request process. In addition, date of birth reporting is required; Treasury anticipates the date of birth may be used by IRS (along with other available information) to help to identify a taxpayer, even in the absence of a TIN.

data that can be reliably matched between Forms 8938 and 8966, IRS's ability to identify taxpayers not reporting accurate or complete information on specified foreign financial assets is hindered, interfering with its ability to enforce compliance with FATCA reporting requirements, and ensure taxpayers are paying taxes on income generated from such assets.

In July 2018, TIGTA reported that IRS lacked success in matching FFI and individual taxpayer data because reports FFIs filed did not include or included invalid TINs. This, in turn, affected IRS's ability to identify and enforce requirements for individual taxpayers.[19] TIGTA recommended, among other things, that IRS initiate compliance efforts to address and correct missing or invalid TINs on Form 8966 filings from FFIs from countries with Model 2 IGAs or without any IGAs with the United States. IRS management said it disagreed with this recommendation because a system to ensure validation of every TIN upon submission of a Form 8966 would be cost prohibitive. However, IRS management said that IRS would address invalid TINs as they are uncovered on other compliance efforts, such as initiating development of a data product to automate risk assessments across the FATCA filing population. IRS also said it continues efforts to systematically match Form 8966 and Form 8938 data to identify nonfilers and underreporting related to U.S. holders of foreign accounts. However, IRS management told us they are waiting until they have a full set of data, including TINs, before doing analysis to develop a compliance strategy. According to TIGTA, IRS management believed that having the FFI's Global Intermediary Identification Number (GIIN) on Form 8938, which is filed by the taxpayer, would help with matching records. However, Form 8938 instructions identify that the field is optional for taxpayers to complete.[20] TIGTA recommended that to reduce taxpayer burden in obtaining GIINs from FFIs, IRS add guidance to Form 8938 instructions to inform taxpayers on how to use the FFI List Search and Download Tool on the IRS's website to obtain an FFI's GIIN.[21] IRS agreed with this

---

[19] TIGTA, 2018-30-040.
[20] As part of FATCA, all relevant FFIs located in partner jurisdictions with Model 2 IGAs— and most FFIs located in jurisdictions with model 1 IGAs—must obtain a GIIN.
[21] TIGTA, 2018-30-040. TIGTA also made several recommendations to improve Model 2 IGA FFI reporting.

recommendation. However, even if an individual taxpayer provided GIINs, IRS may continue to have difficulty matching accounts with U.S. taxpayers if the TIN and name of the account holder reported on the Form 8966 do not match the TIN and name of the taxpayer on the Form 8938.

IRS officials said they are aware of these difficulties and have attempted to match Forms 8938 and 8966 based on other criteria such as dates of birth. In its response to our draft report, IRS said that all financial institutions and foreign tax authorities that file required account information receive a notification listing administrative and other minor errors contained in their reporting. According to IRS, its Large Business and International division follows up with foreign tax authorities regarding these errors to ensure the tax authorities are working with financial institutions to correct these errors in compliance with the countries' IGAs. IRS added it has initiated a campaign addressing FFIs that do not meet their compliance responsibilities with respect to account opening requirements. Additionally, IRS drafted a risk acceptance form and tool addressing risks in implementing FATCA compliance and business process capabilities. This risk assessment focused on the limitations IRS faces due to budget constraints, but did not address the specific risks it faces from not receiving complete and valid TINs on U.S. account holders. We previously reported that risk management could help stakeholders make decisions about assessing risk, allocating resources, and taking actions under conditions of uncertainty.[22] Key management practices for risk management we identified from our prior work include identifying, analyzing, and prioritizing risks; developing a mitigation plan to address identified risks; implementing the plan; and monitoring, reporting, and controlling risks.[23] Without developing a risk mitigation plan to address risks IRS faces from not receiving complete and valid TINs moving forward, IRS may lose opportunities to adjust its compliance programs to better identify U.S. persons who are not fully reporting specified foreign financial assets as required under FATCA.

---

[22] GAO, *DOD Financial Management: Ineffective Risk Management Could Impair Progress toward Audit-Ready Financial Statements*, GAO-13-123 (Washington, D.C.: Aug. 2, 2013).
[23] GAO-18-298.

## IRS Databases Lack Consistent and Complete FATCA and Taxpayer Data Useful for Compliance Enforcement and Research

Several IRS databases store data collected from individuals' electronic and paper filings of Form 8938 and/or elements of parent individual tax returns to which the Form 8938 is attached—the filer's country of residence and filing status—used to determine specified reporting thresholds for Form 8938 filers.[24] Additionally, data from these databases and other sources are transferred downstream to IRS's Compliance Data Warehouse (CDW)—a database used for research and analytical purposes.[25]

We extracted data from copies of Individual Return Transaction File (IRTF) and Modernized Tax Return Database (MTRDB) data copied into CDW to obtain information reported on Forms 8938 and relevant information from parent tax returns, such as filing status and filers' country of residence. We found that IRTF and MTRDB had inconsistent and incomplete data. For example, neither database had consistent and complete information on foreign financial account and other asset information submitted by Form 8938 filers. While IRS officials told us that IRTF is the authoritative source for filers of Form 8938, it does not store account and other asset information submitted on Forms 8938.

Additionally, IRS officials said MTRDB is not designed to store information submitted on paper filings of Forms 8938 and parent tax returns. Officials from IRS's Research, Applied Analytics and Statistics (RAAS) division also noted that CDW did not have reliable information from Form 8938 paper filings. Because of the lack of foreign financial asset information

---

[24] Databases storing data collected from Form 8938 filings and related elements of parent individual tax returns include the Individual Master File (IMF), IRTF, MTRDB, International Compliance Management Model-FATCA International Returns, FATCA Database, and Integrated Production Model. Appendix II includes descriptions of the purposes of each database.

[25] CDW includes a copy of IMF data and provides access to a variety of other tax return, enforcement, compliance, and other data.

from such filings, we could not report complete information on assets reported by Form 8938 filers.[26]

Further, IRS does not provide instructions to CDW users on how to extract appropriate data from CDW—such as data copied from IRTF and MTRDB—leading to confusion on which databases to use for extracting Form 8938 and relevant parent tax return data. For example, five distinct tables within CDW are required to identify the TIN, parent form, filing status, country of residence, and amount of foreign assets accurately. Without clear explanations of how data in each of these tables relate to each other and to the underlying filings, errors could be introduced into CDW users' analyses of foreign asset information.

*Standards for Internal Control in the Federal Government* notes that management should use quality information to achieve the entity's objectives.[27] One attribute of this principle includes processing data into quality information that is appropriate, current, complete, accurate, accessible, and provided on a timely basis. Additionally, the Internal Revenue Manual states that IRS needs to measure taxpayer compliance so that customer-focused programs and services can be enhanced or developed so that compliance information and tools can be improved.[28]

According to IRS officials, IRS researchers have been taking additional steps to obtain and review Form 8938 and parent tax return data stored in the Integrated Production Model (IPM) database. They said IPM is the only database that contains complete data from individuals' electronic and paper filings of Forms 8938 and relevant elements of parent tax returns. IRS officials said that RAAS has been working with IRS's information technology (IT) division to obtain read-only access to IPM, and import Forms 8938 and 8966 data from IPM into CDW for analysis. However, as of February 2019, this effort has been delayed due to budget constraints.

---

[26] See appendix II for more detailed information on problems we identified with the consistency and completeness of Form 8938 and relevant parent tax return data stored in IRS databases.

[27] GAO, *Standards for Internal Control in the Federal Government*, GAO-14-704G (Washington, D.C.: September 2014).

[28] Internal Revenue Service, Internal Revenue Manual, IRM § 4.22.1.2(4). Accessed November 11, 2018, https://www.irs.gov/irm/. The Internal Revenue Manual is an official compendium of internal guidelines for IRS personnel.

In its response to our draft report, IRS said that obtaining read-only access would require a new technical process and plans to continue working with IT on the feasibility and timeframe for enabling this access. Enabling access to consistent and complete Form 8938 and parent tax return data for compliance staff and researchers from RAAS and other IRS business units would help IRS strengthen its efforts to enforce compliance with FATCA reporting requirements and conduct research to bolster enforcement efforts. However, such efforts may be hampered until IRS can ensure readily available access to such data.

## IRS Stopped Pursuing a Comprehensive Plan to Leverage FATCA Data to Improve Taxpayer Compliance

We previously recommended that IRS develop a broad strategy, including a timeline and performance measures, for how IRS intends to use FATCA information to improve tax compliance.[29] IRS agreed with this recommendation and developed a strategy for FATCA in July 2013. IRS updated the strategy in 2016 by creating the FATCA Compliance Roadmap as a comprehensive plan to articulate IRS's priorities to facilitate compliance with FATCA reporting requirements. The roadmap also provided an overview of compliance activities used solely for enforcing FATCA reporting requirements or enhancing existing compliance efforts. However, in July 2018, TIGTA reported that IRS had not updated the FATCA Compliance Roadmap since 2016, and had taken limited or no action on a majority of the planned activities outlined in it.[30]

We also found that IRS had not yet evaluated the effects of FATCA, including the effects on voluntary tax compliance. IRS documentation states that only 7 of 31 capabilities outlined in the FATCA Compliance Roadmap were delivered due to funding constraints. As of October 2018, IRS has stopped using the FATCA Compliance Roadmap and has not developed a

---

[29] GAO, *Foreign Account Reporting Requirements: IRS Needs to Further Develop Risk, Compliance, and Cost Plans*, GAO-12-484 (Washington, D.C.: Apr.16, 2012).
[30] TIGTA, 2018-30-040.

revised comprehensive plan to manage efforts to leverage FATCA data to improve taxpayer compliance. According to IRS officials, IRS moved away from updating broad strategy documents, such as the FATCA Compliance Roadmap, to focus on individual compliance campaigns. These include a campaign to match individual tax filers to the reports from FFIs, and another campaign to identify FFIs with FATCA reporting requirements who are not meeting all of their obligations.

According to what IRS told us, with the passage of time and as FATCA is becoming more integrated into agency operations, it has moved from updating the broad strategy documents focused on FATCA to working on compliance campaigns that incorporate FATCA into overall tax administration. Additionally, IRS and outside researchers plan to study the role of enforcement in driving overall patterns in reporting offshore assets and income generated from such assets. Though IRS maintains that FATCA is more integrated into its operations, TIGTA's 2018 report concluded that IRS was still unprepared to enforce compliance with FATCA in part because it took limited or no action on the majority of planned activities outlined in the FATCA Compliance Roadmap.[31]

Documenting a framework for using FATCA reporting requirements to improve taxpayer compliance and measure their effect is consistent with three steps we found leading public sector organizations take to increase the accountability of their initiatives: (1) define clear missions and desired outcomes; (2) measure performance to gauge progress; and (3) use performance information as a basis for decision-making.[32] We also previously reported that it is important for IRS to use a documented framework that defines a clear strategy, timeline, and plans for assessment.[33] Having such a framework in place can help IRS better allocate resources and avoid unnecessary costs resulting from not having the necessary or appropriate data available to execute its objectives.

---

[31] TIGTA, 2018-30-040.
[32] See GAO-12-484 and GAO-11-336.
[33] GAO-11-336.

In light of the challenges IRS faces to collect, manage, and use FATCA data to improve compliance in a resource-constrained environment, employing a comprehensive plan would help IRS maximize the use of collected data and better leverage individual campaigns to increase taxpayer compliance. Without such a plan, IRS's ability to collect and leverage data collected under FATCA for compliance enforcement and other purposes is constrained.

## ANALYSIS OF FBAR AND FATCA DATA PROVIDE INSIGHTS, INCLUDING THE POSSIBILITY THAT TENS OF THOUSANDS OF FORMS 8938 MAY HAVE BEEN FILED UNNECESSARILY

### More than 900,000 Individual FBAR Filers Reported about $1.5 Trillion or More in Foreign Accounts in Both Calendar Years 2015 and 2016

We could not report on total values of foreign financial assets on Forms 8938 in tax years 2015 and 2016. However, we could provide a range of total maximum account values reported on FBARs during the same period. Specifically, we determined that more than 900,000 individuals filed FBARs in calendar years 2015 and 2016, and declared total maximum values of accounts ranging from about $1.5 trillion to more than $2 trillion each year.[34]

---

[34] The lower bound of individual FBAR filings from calendar years 2015 and 2016 includes those filings reporting total maximum values of accounts of less than $1 billion. The upper bound of such filings includes those filings that reported total values of less than $5 billion. We are providing a range of estimates because we found a large number of filings made potentially in error—such as reporting more than $100 trillion in foreign assets. Additionally, we could not independently verify the accuracy of all self-reported FBAR data, as we have only limited means to determine which filings have errors and which filings have accurate information. See appendix III for more detailed information on the ranges of estimates of total maximum account values reported by FBAR filers for both 2015 and 2016, and our methodology for developing the range of estimates.

## Table 1. Tax Year 2016 Form 8938 Electronic and Paper Filings Stored in IRS's IRTF

| Residence and filing status | Electronic filings | Paper filings | Total filings |
|---|---|---|---|
| U.S. persons living in the United States | | | |
| Married filing jointly | 191,220 | 27,953 | 219,173 |
| Other[a] | 78,939 | 18,764 | 97,703 |
| Total—U.S. persons living in the United States | 270,159 | 46,717 | 316,876 |
| U.S. persons living abroad | | | |
| Married filing jointly | 16,237 | 8,871 | 25,108 |
| Other[a] | 33,568 | 29,239 | 62,807 |
| Total—U.S. persons living abroad | 49,805 | 38,110 | 87,915 |
| Total—all U.S. persons | 319,964 | 84,827 | 404,791 |

Source: GAO analysis of IRS data. | GAO-19-180.
[a]Filers in this category include those who identify as single, married filing separately, "head of household" or "qualifying widow(er)."

A little more than one in five—or about 21.7 percent—of the approximately 404,800 Forms 8938 filed with IRS in tax year 2016 were done so from U.S. persons living abroad, with the other 78.3 percent living in the United States.

Table 1 shows that a higher proportion of Form 8938 filings from U.S. persons living abroad for tax year 2016 were filed on paper (43.3 percent) than Form 8938 filings from U.S. persons living in the United States during the same period (14.7 percent). We extracted these data from IRTF, which IRS officials said is the authoritative source for filers of Form 8938. However, we could not report complete information on foreign financial assets reported by Form 8938 filers because such data are incomplete; as noted above, IRS databases we used to extract Form 8938 data—IRTF and MTRDB—do not include asset information reported on paper filings of Forms 8938.

## Tens of Thousands of Forms 8938 May Have Been Filed Unnecessarily in Tax Year 2016

Of the approximately 404,800 Forms 8938 filed by individuals for tax year 2016—the most recent data available—we could access information on residency of filers and reported foreign financial assets from about 277,600 Forms 8938 that did not indicate that foreign financial assets and values were declared on other forms besides the Form 8938.[35] Of the subset of these Forms 8938, more than one quarter—or about 73,500— reported foreign financial assets in amounts that indicate the Form 8938 may have been filed unnecessarily, since they reported specified foreign financial assets with aggregate values at or below reporting thresholds as of the last day of the tax year.36 Based on available Form 8938 data from tax year 2016, table 2 shows that about 61,900 filings from U.S. persons living in the United States and about 11,600 filings from U.S. persons living abroad during the same tax year reported specified foreign financial assets with aggregate values at or below end of tax year thresholds. These totals likely understate the total number of Forms 8938 that U.S. persons may have filed unnecessarily in tax year 2016; due to data limitations, these totals exclude Forms 8938 without asset information stored in IRS's databases, including most Forms 8938 filed on paper and Forms 8938 where filers identified that they declared foreign financial assets on other forms besides the Form 8938.

There is no clear explanation as to why some U.S. persons may have filed Forms 8938 unnecessarily. However, we identified a number of potential reasons from focus groups and other interviews with stakeholder groups. In focus groups we conducted, participants expressed confusion about IRS's instructions for completing the Form 8938 and information provided on IRS's website.

---

[35] Under Part IV of the Form 8938, filers may identify that they declared specified foreign financial assets on other forms besides the Form 8938. In these instances, filers do not need to include these assets on the Form 8938 for the tax year.

[36] FATCA generally requires certain taxpayers to report to IRS on Form 8938 foreign financial accounts and other specified foreign financial assets whose aggregate value exceeds specified thresholds, which vary by residency and filing status. See appendix IV for more detailed information on these thresholds.

**Table 2. Number of Available Tax Year 2016 Form 8938 Individual Filings at or below, or above End-of-Year Asset Reporting Thresholds, Excluding Filers Who Used Other Forms**

| Residence and filing status | Threshold for reporting aggregate asset value as of the last day of the tax year | Number of filings reporting at or below threshold | Number of filings reporting above threshold |
|---|---|---|---|
| U.S. persons living in the United States | | | |
| Married filing jointly | Exceeds $100,000 | 46,747 | 121,090 |
| Other[a] | Exceeds $50,000 | 15,154 | 54,861 |
| Total—U.S. persons living in the United States | | 61,901 | 175,951 |
| U.S. persons living abroad | | | |
| Married filing jointly | Exceeds $400,000 | 4,937 | 8,279 |
| Other[a] | Exceeds $200,000 | 6,630 | 19,906 |
| Total—U.S. persons living abroad | | 11,567 | 28,185 |
| Total—all U.S. persons | | 73,468 | 204,136 |

Source: GAO analysis of IRS data. | GAO-19-180.

Note: Table does not include 50,538 filings from U.S. persons living in the United States and 39,672 Form 8938 filings from U.S. persons living abroad without asset information stored in IRS's databases. Table also does not include information from Form 8938 filings where filer(s) identified on part IV of Form 8938 that they declared foreign financial assets on other forms besides the Form 8938. Table also does not include information on any other filings for which the residence of the filer could not be determined.

[a]Filers in this category include those who identify as single, married filing separately, "head of household" or "qualifying widow(er)."

In the instructions for completing Form 8938, IRS described the specific types of foreign financial assets that are to be reported on Form 8938, and the asset value thresholds that must be met for required reporting, depending on the location of residence and filing status of the taxpayer. IRS also posted responses to frequently asked questions on meeting FATCA reporting requirements on its website, and established a separate page on its website comparing foreign financial assets that must be reported on Form 8938 and/or FBAR.

Nonetheless, focus group participants reported confusion on whether and how to report investment and retirement accounts and compulsory savings plans managed by their country of residence.[37] In a meeting we convened with an organization representing tax attorneys, they told us taxpayers are unsure about what account values to report on the Form 8938.

Tax practitioners participating in another focus group added that they filed Forms 8938 regardless of the aggregate value of the assets because it was too cumbersome for them to identify whether the assets exceeded reporting thresholds as of the end of the year or at any time during the year.

IRS officials also cited a number of possible reasons why U.S. persons may be filing Forms 8938 unnecessarily. For example, it may be easier for U.S. persons to report all specified foreign financial assets they hold on the Form 8938, rather than determine whether the value of such assets met applicable thresholds. IRS officials also said that U.S. persons might complete a Form 8938 for reasons besides meeting tax-filing requirements, such as providing evidence of assets for a loan application.

IRS's Taxpayer Bill of Rights states that taxpayers are entitled to clear explanations of the laws and IRS procedures in all tax forms, instructions, publications, notices, and correspondence. Furthermore, one of IRS's strategic goals is to empower taxpayers by making it easier for them to understand and meet their filing, reporting, and payment obligations.[38] IRS officials said they hosted sessions for tax practitioners at IRS Nationwide Tax Forums to address FATCA reporting requirements.

However, they said IRS has not taken direct steps to identify or implement actions to further clarify instructions and related guidance on IRS's website for completing Form 8938, such as information on which foreign financial assets to report, how to calculate asset values, and

---

[37] According to IRS instructions, Form 8938 filers may generally rely on periodic account statements for the tax year to report a financial account's maximum value. For most other specified foreign financial assets, filers may generally use the value of such assets as of the last day of the tax year if the assets (1) are not financial accounts, and (2) are held for investment and not held in accounts maintained by financial institutions. However, filers cannot use the aforementioned sources of asset values if they know or have reason to know—based on readily accessible information—that the values identified in such sources do not reflect reasonable estimates of the maximum value of the asset during the tax year.

[38] IRS Strategic Plan, Fiscal Years 2018-2022.

determine whether such values exceed required reporting thresholds. Additionally, IRS officials said they have not conducted additional outreach to educate taxpayers on required reporting thresholds under FATCA, or notify Form 8938 filers of instances where aggregate values of specified foreign financial assets reported on Forms 8938 were below reporting thresholds.

IRS officials said they have not made efforts to determine whether there is a pattern of unnecessary Form 8938 filings that they could address. Rather, they said they believed resources should be devoted to FATCA implementation in general. However, as shown above, we have identified many tens of thousands of instances where U.S. persons may have filed Forms 8938 unnecessarily. Without assessing factors contributing to unnecessary Form 8938 reporting—and identifying or implementing actions to further clarify and educate taxpayers on FATCA reporting requirements—IRS is missing opportunities to help taxpayers understand their filing and reporting obligations and minimize their compliance burdens while properly meeting their tax obligations. Additionally, IRS may be missing opportunities to reduce costs in processing forms that taxpayers did not need to file.

Because of overlapping statutory reporting requirements, IRS and FinCEN—both bureaus within Treasury—collect duplicative foreign financial asset data using two different forms (Form 8938 and FBAR). Our evaluation and management guide for fragmentation, overlap, and duplication states that overlap occurs when multiple agencies or programs have similar goals, engage in similar activities or strategies to achieve them, or target similar beneficiaries.[39] Table 3 shows that individuals required to report foreign financial assets on Form 8938, in many cases, also must meet FBAR reporting requirements.

---

[39] GAO-15-49SP.

# DIFFERENT LAWS ESTABLISHED OVERLAPPING FOREIGN FINANCIAL ASSET REPORTING REQUIREMENTS AND COMPOUNDED TAXPAYER COMPLIANCE BURDEN

## Table 3. Illustrative Examples of Overlap in Form 8938 and FBAR Reporting Requirements

| | IRS Form 8938 (Form 8938), Statement of Specified Foreign Financial Assets (To meet FATCA reporting requirements under IRC Section 6038D and implementing regulations)[a] | FinCEN Form 114, Report of Foreign Bank and Financial Accounts (FBAR) (To meet FBAR reporting requirements under section 5314 of title 31, United States Code, and implementing regulations)[b] | Explanation of Overlapping Requirements |
|---|---|---|---|
| Type of filer | Any specified person that has an interest in a specified foreign financial asset during the taxable year. Specified persons include:<br><br>• specified individuals, including U.S. citizens, resident aliens, and certain nonresident aliens; and<br><br>• specified domestic entities including certain domestic corporations, partnerships, and trusts.[c] | U.S. persons, which include U.S. citizens, residents and domestic entities—such as corporations, partnerships or trusts—that have an interest in foreign financial accounts and meet the reporting threshold. | A specified individual for FATCA purposes, such as a U.S. citizen or resident, in many cases will also be a U.S. person for FBAR purposes. Specified domestic entities for FATCA purposes—such as corporations, trusts, and estate—in many cases can also be classified as a U.S. person for FBAR purposes. |

**Table 3. (Continued)**

| | IRS Form 8938 (Form 8938), Statement of Specified Foreign Financial Assets (To meet FATCA reporting requirements under IRC Section 6038D and implementing regulations)[a] | FinCEN Form 114, Report of Foreign Bank and Financial Accounts (FBAR) (To meet FBAR reporting requirements under section 5314 of title 31, United States Code, and implementing regulations)[b] | Explanation of Overlapping Requirements |
|---|---|---|---|
| Type of interest in foreign financial assets[d] | A U.S. person has a specified interest in a foreign financial asset if he or she realizes any income, gains, losses, deductions, credits, gross proceeds, or distributions from holding or disposing of the account or asset that are or would be required to be reported, included, or otherwise reflected on the person's income tax return. A U.S. person can have a specified interest in a foreign financial asset in certain other circumstances as well. | A U.S. person has a financial interest in each bank, securities or other financial account in a foreign country (1) for which he or she is the owner of record or has legal title whether the account is maintained for his or her own benefit or for the benefit of others, (2) the legal owner has a certain specified relationship with the U.S. person, or (3) has signature or other authority to control the disposition of the assets in a financial account. | In many cases, specified interests as defined in Form 8938 instructions will be the same as financial interests under FBAR. |

| | IRS Form 8938 (Form 8938), Statement of Specified Foreign Financial Assets (To meet FATCA reporting requirements under IRC Section 6038D and implementing regulations)[a] | FinCEN Form 114, Report of Foreign Bank and Financial Accounts (FBAR) (To meet FBAR reporting requirements under section 5314 of title 31, United States Code, and implementing regulations)[b] | Explanation of Overlapping Requirements |
|---|---|---|---|
| Threshold of value of foreign assets making them reportable (individuals) | The minimum threshold for required reporting is more than $50,000 in total value of assets on the last day of the tax year, or more than $75,000 of such assets at any time during the year. However, the thresholds may be higher depending on the filing status and address of specified individuals | This is an aggregate balance, meaning if a person has two accounts, both accounts must be reported if the maximum account values of each (determined separately), when combined exceed $10,000. | Assets required to be reported on both Form 8938 and FBAR include foreign financial accounts. Therefore, foreign financial accounts whose aggregate value exceeds $50,000 as of the last day of the tax year have to be reported on both forms if such values also exceed the minimum Form 8938 thresholds; these thresholds depend on the filing status and address of specified individuals. However, Form 8938 filers do not have to file an FBAR for the same reporting year in cases where aggregate value of assets required to be reported on the FBAR—including assets also required to be reported on Form 8938—are below FBAR's $10,000 reporting threshold.[e] |

**Table 3. (Continued)**

| | IRS Form 8938 (Form 8938), Statement of Specified Foreign Financial Assets (To meet FATCA reporting requirements under IRC Section 6038D and implementing regulations)[a] | FinCEN Form 114, Report of Foreign Bank and Financial Accounts (FBAR) (To meet FBAR reporting requirements under section 5314 of title 31, United States Code, and implementing regulations)[b] | Explanation of Overlapping Requirements |
|---|---|---|---|
| Foreign financial assets reportable on both forms (including maximum value of asset)[f] | • financial (deposit and custodial) accounts held at foreign financial institutions.<br>• foreign financial account for which a person has signature authority and a financial interest in the account (subject to exceptions).[g]<br>• foreign stock or securities held in a financial account at a foreign financial institution.[h]<br>• foreign mutual funds.<br>• foreign accounts held by a foreign or domestic grantor trust for which the specified individual is the grantor.<br>• foreign-issued life insurance or annuity contract with a cash-value. | | Banks, securities, and other financial accounts as defined under FBAR would include financial assets maintained by a foreign financial institution as defined for Form 8938 as listed in this row. |
| Foreign financial assets reportable on only one form (including maximum value of asset)[f] | • foreign stock or securities not held in a financial account.<br>• foreign nonaccount investment assets held by a foreign or domestic grantor trust for which the specified individual is the grantor.<br>• foreign partnership interests.<br>• foreign hedge funds and foreign private equity funds. | • financial account held at a foreign branch of a U.S. financial institution.<br>• foreign financial account for which a person has signature authority, but no financial interest in the account (subject to exceptions).[g]<br>• indirect interests in foreign financial assets through an entity.[i] | Not applicable. |

| | IRS Form 8938 (Form 8938), Statement of Specified Foreign Financial Assets (To meet FATCA reporting requirements under IRC Section 6038D and implementing regulations)[a] | FinCEN Form 114, Report of Foreign Bank and Financial Accounts (FBAR) (To meet FBAR reporting requirements under section 5314 of title 31, United States Code, and implementing regulations)[b] | Explanation of Overlapping Requirements |
|---|---|---|---|
| Penalties | Up to $10,000 for failure to disclose and an additional $10,000 for each 30 days of nonfiling after IRS notice of a failure to disclose, for a potential maximum penalty of $50,000.[j] Criminal penalties may also apply. | For civil penalty assessment prior to August 2, 2016, if nonwillful, up to $10,000 per violation; if willful, the greater of $100,000 or 50 percent of account balances per violation.[k] Civil monetary penalties are adjusted for inflation. Criminal penalties may also apply. | A U.S. person may be liable for civil and criminal penalties under two different penalty regimes unless he or she discloses specified foreign financial assets to IRS and FinCEN using two separate forms—Form 8938 and FBAR. |

Source: GAO analysis of IRS and FinCEN information. | GAO-19-180. [a]26 U.S.C. § 6038D; 26 C.F.R. §§ 1.6038D-1 to 1.6038D-8., [b]31 U.S.C. § 5314; 31 C.F.R. § 1010.350.

[c]26 C.F.R. § 1.6038D-6. A domestic corporation, a domestic partnership, or a trust described in IRC section 7701(a)(30)(E) can be classified as a specified domestic entity, if such corporation, partnership, or trust is formed or availed of for purposes of holding, directly or indirectly, specified foreign financial assets.

[d]See appendix IV for a complete definition of specified and financial interests covered under Form 8938 and FBAR reporting requirements, respectively.

[e]As an example, a single taxpayer living in the U.S. possesses a foreign bank account with a maximum annual value of $5,000 and foreign partnership interests valued at $80,000. The single taxpayer must file an IRS Form 8938 since total specified foreign financial assets held exceed the $75,000 maximum aggregate annual reporting threshold for U.S. persons living in the United States and not married filing jointly. However, the taxpayer does not have to file an FBAR since the maximum value of the foreign bank account is below FBAR's $10,000 reporting threshold.

[f]Includes maximum value of specified foreign financial assets (Form 8938) or maximum value of financial accounts maintained by a financial institution physically located in a foreign country (FBAR).

[g]Under FATCA, any income, gains, losses, deductions, credits, gross proceeds, or distributions from holding or disposing of the account are or would be required to be reported, included, or otherwise reflected on a person's income tax return. Under FBAR reporting requirements, a person has signature or other authority if he or she has the authority (alone or in conjunction with another) to control the disposition of money, funds or other assets held in a financial account by direct communication (whether in writing or otherwise) to the person with whom the financial account is maintained.

[h]The account itself is subject to reporting, but the contents of the account do not have to be separately reported.

[i] Assets only must be reported if a person has sufficient ownership or beneficial interest (i.e., a greater than 50 percent interest) in the entity.

[j] 26 U.S.C. § 6038D; 26 C.F.R. § 1.6038D-8. In addition to the penalty for failure to file Form 8938, taxpayers who fail to report income from such assets on their tax returns are subject to a penalty of 40 percent of the tax due on that income (in addition to the tax on the income). There is no differentiation in the penalty based on willfulness of the failure to file.

[k] For penalties assessed after August 1, 2016, whose associated violations occurred after November 2, 2015, the maximum penalties for negligent, nonwillful, and willful violations are adjusted for inflation. 31 C.F.R. § 1010.821.

For example, specified individuals with foreign financial accounts exceeding $50,000 in aggregate value on the last day of the tax year must file both Form 8938 and FBAR if such values exceed the minimum Form 8938 thresholds; these thresholds depend on the filing status and address of specified individuals.[1] Table 3 also shows that, in many cases, specified interests in foreign financial assets as defined in Form 8938 instructions are the same as the financial interest in such assets under FBAR. Further, as noted in Table 3, the overlapping requirements lead to IRS and FinCEN collecting the same information on certain types of foreign financial assets. For example, both Form 8938 and FBAR collect information on foreign financial accounts for which a person has signature authority and a financial interest in the account. Form 8938 and FBAR also both collect duplicative information on several other types of foreign financial assets, such as foreign mutual funds and accounts at a foreign financial institution that include foreign stock or securities.

Overlapping reporting requirements result in most Form 8938 filers also filing an FBAR during the same reporting year. Table 4 shows that close to 75 percent of Form 8938 filers in tax years 2015 and 2016 percent also filed an FBAR for the same year using the same TIN.

**Table 4. Number and Percentage of Individual 2015 and 2016
Form 8938 Filings from Filers who also Submitted
an FBAR for 2015 and 2016**

| Year | Number of Form 8938 filings | Number of Form 8938 filers who also submitted an FBAR | Percentage of Form 8938 filers who also submitted an FBAR |
|------|------|------|------|
| 2015 | 365,540 | 272,684 | 74.6% |
| 2016 | 404,791 | 295,236 | 72.9% |

Source: GAO analysis of IRS and FinCEN data. | GAO-19-180.

---

[1] See appendix IV for thresholds of value of foreign assets making them reportable on Form 8938 by residency and filing status.

Overlapping requirements to file both Form 8938 and FBAR increases the compliance burden on U.S. persons and adds complexity that can create confusion, potentially resulting in inaccurate or unnecessary reporting. Focus group participants in all five countries included in our study affirmed that U.S. persons experienced confusion and frustration with having to report duplicative foreign financial asset information on both forms. Focus group participants and others we interviewed also noted that U.S. persons incurred additional financial costs to complete and file both Form 8938 and FBAR. For instance, one tax practitioner in Canada said the charge was about $190 to report four-to-five accounts on an FBAR in addition to charging about $540 for basic tax return packages. An accounting firm based in Japan typically charged between $300 and $800 to complete a Form 8938 and between $150 and $500 to complete an FBAR, depending on the number of accounts reported on the forms. Proposed revisions to regulations implementing BSA proposed by FinCEN may also increase the number of duplicative foreign financial accounts reported on Form 8938 and FBAR. Currently, U.S. persons must report detailed information on all foreign financial accounts on Form 8938 if the value of such accounts and other specified foreign financial assets reaches applicable reporting thresholds.[2] In contrast, U.S. persons are generally exempted from reporting detailed account information on FBARs if they report having signature or other authority over 25 or more foreign financial accounts. FinCEN's proposed revisions to BSA regulations would eliminate the exemption, requiring U.S. persons to report detailed information on all foreign financial accounts in which he or she has a financial interest if the value of such accounts exceed FBAR's $10,000 reporting threshold. FinCEN estimated that it will receive account information for the first time on about 5.4 million foreign financial accounts if it finalizes the proposed revisions.[3] In turn, these revisions may

---

[2] See appendix IV for thresholds of value of foreign assets making them reportable on Form 8938 by residence and filing status.

[3] See Department of the Treasury, Financial Crimes Enforcement Network; Amendment to the Bank Secrecy Act Regulations—Reports of Foreign Financial Accounts, 81 Fed. Reg. 12,613 (Mar. 10, 2016). FinCEN's estimate of additional foreign financial accounts reported based on proposed revisions to the regulations are based on the number of accounts reported on FBARs in 2013, in which the filers had 25 or more foreign financial accounts and noted the

lead to increased filings of duplicative asset data on both Form 8938 and FBAR, as U.S. persons may have to report detailed information on all foreign financial accounts using both forms.

U.S. persons also face exposure to two different penalty regimes for any failures in accurately and completely reporting foreign financial asset information to two bureaus within Treasury—IRS and FinCEN.[4] Officials from one organization representing U.S. persons living abroad said penalties due to failure to report certain accounts on one or both forms can be significant, even if little or no taxes are owed on those accounts. The duplicative reporting of foreign financial asset data on two different forms also creates additional costs to the government to process and store the same or similar information twice, and enforce reporting compliance with both requirements.

In 2012, we recommended that Treasury direct the Office of Tax Policy, IRS, and FinCEN to determine whether the benefits of implementing a less duplicative reporting process exceed the costs and, if so, implement that process.[5] Treasury did not implement our recommendation. While we continue to believe that the agencies should have considered whether less duplicative reporting could have been implemented, we do recognize that FATCA and FBAR were enacted under two different statutes to serve different purposes.[6] As mentioned above, according to IRS, FATCA improves visibility into taxable income from foreign sources and enhances the agency's ability to identify and pursue taxpayer noncompliance. In contrast, the information reported on the FBAR is collected to identify money laundering and other financial crimes; law enforcement agencies can use BSA information—including information collected from FBARs— to

---

number of such accounts. FinCEN is currently drafting a final rule, which will go through a formal clearance process including intra departmental review within Treasury.

[4] 26 U.S.C. § 6038D(d); 31 U.S.C. § 5321(a)(5); 31 C.F.R. § 1010.840.

[5] GAO-12-403.

[6] FATCA was enacted as subtitle A of title V of the Hiring Incentives to Restore Employment Act. Pub. L. No. 111-147, §§ 501-541, 124 Stat. 71, 97-117 (2010). FBAR reporting requirements were imposed by section 1010.350 of title 31, Code of Federal Regulations, promulgated under the authority of the Bank Secrecy Act of 1970. Pub. L. No. 91-508, 84 Stat. 1114 (1970), as amended, *codified as* 12 U.S.C. §§ 1730d, 1829b, 1951–1959; 18 U.S.C. § 6002; 31 U.S.C. §§ 321, 5311–5322.

aid regulatory and criminal investigations. Additionally, data collected from Form 8938 and FBAR are used in different systems for use by different bureaus within Treasury. Fully addressing issues stemming from overlapping reporting requirements and the resulting collection of duplicative information—while at the same time ensuring that such information can be used for tax compliance and law enforcement purposes—can only be done by modifying the statutes governing the requirements.

Further, IRS and FinCEN have varying degrees of access to foreign financial asset information collected from Form 8938 and FBAR to enforce tax compliance and financial crime laws. FATCA was enacted, in part, to improve visibility into taxable income from foreign sources. However, information provided on Forms 8938 is taxpayer return information protected by section 6103 of the Internal Revenue Code (IRC), which generally prohibits IRS from disclosing information provided on Forms 8938.[7] IRS can share return information with other government agencies and others when it is allowed by statute. For example, under section 6103, IRS may disclose return information related to taxes imposed under the IRC—such as self-employment income tax, Social Security and Medicare tax and income tax withholding—to the Social Security Administration (SSA) as needed to carry out its responsibilities under the Social Security Act.[8] However, according to FinCEN officials, FinCEN, law enforcement, and regulators often cannot access information submitted on Forms 8938. While section 6103 provides other exceptions to disclosure prohibitions—such as allowing IRS to share return information with law enforcement agencies for investigation and prosecution of nontax criminal laws—such information is generally only accessible pursuant to a court order.[9]

As noted above, information reported on the FBAR can be used by law enforcement agencies to aid regulatory and criminal investigations. This includes IRS, which has been delegated responsibility from FinCEN to enforce compliance with FBAR reporting requirements. IRS has used FBAR

---

[7] 26 U.S.C. § 6103(a). For example, according to IRS officials, IRS, FinCEN, law enforcement, and regulators cannot utilize Forms 8938 in FBAR enforcement without a determination that a potential BSA violation was in furtherance of a potential violation of the IRC.

[8] 26 U.S.C. § 6103(l)(1).

[9] 26 U.S.C. § 6103(i)(1).

information in addressing taxpayer noncompliance with reporting and paying taxes on foreign assets and income. For example, taxpayers accepted into one of IRS's offshore voluntary disclosure programs must have filed amended or late FBARs as part of their program applications.[10] Investigators from IRS's Criminal Investigation division generally reviewed applications to determine if the taxpayer has made a complete and truthful disclosure. IRS examiners can also use information from case files of program participants—such as information disclosed on FBARs— to identify new groups of taxpayers suspected of hiding income offshore. IRS can then choose to continue offering offshore programs and encourage these newly identified groups of taxpayers, as well as all taxpayers with unreported offshore accounts, to disclose their accounts voluntarily.

In addition to eliminating overlapping reporting requirements, harmonizing statutes governing foreign financial asset reporting and use of information collected on such assets to make such statutes fully consistent could yield additional benefits to both IRS and the law enforcement community. Specifically, and as shown in appendix IV, there are specified foreign financial assets reported on Form 8938—such as foreign hedge funds and foreign private equity funds—that are not required to be reported on an FBAR. In contrast, there are other specified foreign financial assets reported on an FBAR—such as indirect interests in foreign financial assets through an entity—that are not required to be reported on Form 8938. Without congressional action to address overlap in foreign financial asset reporting requirements, IRS and FinCEN will neither be able to coordinate efforts to collect and use foreign financial asset information, nor reduce unnecessary burdens faced by U.S. persons in reporting duplicative foreign financial asset information.

---

[10] Between 2003 and 2018, IRS carried out five offshore disclosure programs that offered incentives for taxpayers to disclose their offshore accounts and pay delinquent taxes, interest, and penalties. Generally, the programs offered somewhat reduced penalties and no risk of criminal prosecution of eligible taxpayers who fully disclosed their previously unreported offshore accounts, and paid taxes due plus interest. The fifth program, which started in 2014, closed on September 28, 2018.

# FFIs FACE OVERLAPPING FOREIGN ACCOUNT REPORTING SYSTEMS, BUT ALIGNMENT WOULD ENTAIL SIGNIFICANT CHANGES IN LAW

Two reporting systems for sharing foreign account information from foreign financial institutions are in operation globally—FATCA and the Common Reporting Standard (CRS). According to officials from banking associations and a consulting firm, FFIs in the countries where we examined FATCA implementation encountered challenges implementing and now maintaining two overlapping reporting systems for collecting and transmitting account information to other countries for a seemingly similar purpose, and collecting sufficient information from customers to ensure they meet the requirements of both systems. As noted above, we previously identified overlap as occurring when multiple agencies or programs have similar goals, engage in similar activities or strategies to achieve them, or target similar beneficiaries.[11]

According to an IRS official, collecting account information under FATCA ushered in an era of greater transparency; as noted above, FATCA's passage sought to reduce tax evasion by creating greater transparency and accountability with respect to offshore accounts and other assets held by U.S. taxpayers. When FATCA was first introduced, there was no international platform to share account information between countries. The United States and other countries worked together to reach an agreement on the electronic formatting that would be used to share the information.

Other countries tax authorities' became more interested in understanding the financial assets held abroad by their residents through an exchange of account information among themselves.

---

[11] GAO-15-49SP.

In response, the Organisation for Economic Co-operation and Development (OECD) established the CRS reporting system for automatic exchange of information among member countries. According to the OECD, CRS was developed with a view to maximize efficiency and reduce cost for financial institutions. Thus, CRS drew extensively on the intergovernmental approach used to implement FATCA reporting requirements for FFIs. Countries participating in CRS exchange account information with each other using OECD's Common Transmission System, which was modeled on FATCA's International Data Exchange System.[12] Figure 2 depicts the flow of account information between countries under FATCA and CRS.

CRS reporting requirements are in many ways similar to FATCA, including required reporting of the account holders' name and address, taxpayer identification number, account number, account balance, and income and sales proceeds. However, the requirements differ in significant ways. The biggest differences in requirements are driven by the nature of the U.S. tax system. The United States, like many countries, generally taxes citizens and resident aliens on their worldwide income regardless of where that income is earned.

However, the United States differs from other countries because it generally subjects U.S. citizens who reside abroad to U.S. taxation in the same manner as U.S. residents. In contrast to U.S. policy, most other countries do not tax their citizens if they reside in a country other than their country of citizenship. Further, IGAs implementing FATCA require FFIs to report the foreign-held accounts of U.S. citizens and residents—including resident aliens—while CRS requires financial institutions in jurisdictions participating in CRS to report on almost all accounts held by nonresidents of the reporting country. Appendix V provides more detailed information on differences in reporting requirements, due diligence requirements, and definitions under FATCA and CRS.

---

[12] CRS is implemented through legislation by each participating jurisdiction.

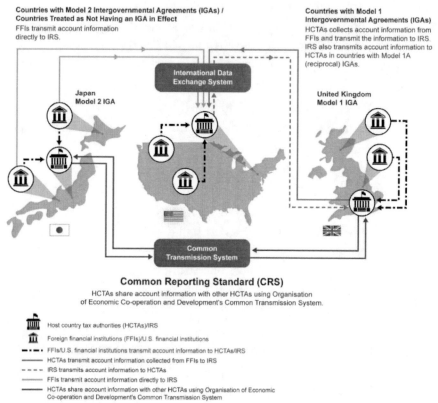

**Foreign Account Tax Compliance Act (FATCA)**
Host country tax authorities (HCTAs) and foreign financial institutions (FFIs) share account information with IRS using IRS's International Data Exchange System.

Countries with Model 2 Intergovernmental Agreements (IGAs) /
Countries Treated as Not Having an IGA in Effect
FFIs transmit account information directly to IRS.

Countries with Model 1
Intergovernmental Agreements (IGAs)
HCTAs collects account information from FFIs and transmit the information to IRS. IRS also transmits account information to HCTAs in countries with Model 1A (reciprocal) IGAs.

International Data Exchange System

Japan
Model 2 IGA

United Kingdom
Model 1 IGA

Common Transmission System

**Common Reporting Standard (CRS)**
HCTAs share account information with other HCTAs using Organisation of Economic Co-operation and Development's Common Transmission System.

Host country tax authorities (HCTAs)/IRS
Foreign financial institutions (FFIs)/U.S. financial institutions
FFIs/U.S. financial institutions transmit account information to HCTAs/IRS
HCTAs transmit account information collected from FFIs to IRS
IRS transmits account information to HCTAs
FFIs transmit account information directly to IRS
HCTAs share account information with other HCTAs using Organisation of Economic Co-operation and Development's Common Transmission System

Source: GAO. | GAO-19-180.

Figure 2. Flow of Account Information under FATCA and CRS Reporting Systems.

These differences in tax systems drive variations in due diligence procedures between FATCA and CRS. For example, FATCA aims to identify whether an account holder at a foreign institution is a U.S. person based on citizenship and tax residency information.[13] In contrast, CRS aims to identify the tax residency of all account holders of a financial institution, and does not consider citizenship.

---

[13] Pub. L. No. 111-147, §§ 501-541, 124 Stat. 71, 97-117 (2010).

Due to the multilateral nature of CRS, if an account holder is determined on the basis of the due diligence procedures to have residency in two or more countries, information would be exchanged with all jurisdictions in which the account holder is determined a resident for tax purposes.

Under CRS rules, information about foreign accounts held by a U.S. citizen with a tax residence abroad would not be reported to IRS, but rather to the jurisdiction in which they were a resident for tax purposes. Because the United States taxes the worldwide income of U.S. citizens, CRS rules would need to require identification of account holders' citizenship in member countries where they are residents if FATCA were to be aligned with CRS. Table 5 shows a comparison of individuals reported to IRS under FATCA and hypothetically under CRS.

Treasury and IRS, as part of its 2017-2018 Priority Guidance Plan, are considering modifying certain elements of the existing FATCA regulations. For instance, Treasury and IRS are considering coordinating certain documentation requirements for participating FFIs with the requirements under IGAs. In December 2018, Treasury and IRS also proposed regulations intended, in part, to reduce the burdens of FATCA.[14] The proposed regulations included a clarification of the definition of an investment entity that is similar to the guidance published by OECD interpreting the definition of a "managed by" investment entity under CRS.[15]

---

[14] 83 Fed. Reg. 64,757 (Dec. 18, 2018).

[15] Under 26 C.F.R. § 1.1471-5(e)(4)(i)(B), an entity is an investment entity (and therefore a financial institution) if the entity's gross income is primarily attributable to investing, reinvesting, or trading in financial assets and the entity is "managed by" another entity that is a depository institution, custodial institution, insurance company, or an investment entity described in 26 C.F.R. § 1.1471-5(e)(4)(i)(A). The proposed regulations clarify that an entity is not "managed by" another entity for purposes of 26 C.F.R. § 1.1471–5(e)(4)(i)(B) solely because the first-mentioned entity invests all or a portion of its assets in such other entity, and such other entity is a mutual fund, an exchange traded fund, or a collective investment entity that is widely held and is subject to investor-protection regulation.

**Table 5. Comparison of FFI Reporting to IRS under FATCA and Hypothetically under CRS**

| Citizenship | FATCA (on basis of U.S. citizenship and tax residency) | CRS (on basis of tax residency) |
|---|---|---|
| U.S. citizen living in the United States with a U.S. account | Reported via IRS Form 1099 | Reported via IRS Form 1099 |
| U.S. citizen living in the United States with a foreign account | Account reported | Account reported |
| U.S. citizen with a tax residence abroad and a foreign account | Account reported | Account not reported |
| Permanent resident alien with a tax residence abroad and a U.S. account[a] | Reported via IRS Form 1099 | Account not reported |
| Permanent resident alien living in the United States with a U.S. account[a] | Reported via IRS Form 1099 | Reported via IRS Form 1099 |
| Permanent resident alien living in the United States with a foreign account[a] | Account reported | Account reported |
| Nonresident alien living in the United States with a U.S. account | Reported via IRS Form 1099 | Reported via IRS Form 1099 |
| Nonresident alien living in the United States with a foreign account | Account not reported | Account not reported |

Source: GAO. | GAO-19-180.

Note: Information in this table assumes that all applicable reporting thresholds are met.

[a]A person is a resident alien of the United States for tax purposes if he or she is lawfully admitted for permanent residence (the green card test), meets the substantial presence test, or makes a first year election. 26 U.S.C. § 7701(b)(1).

If the United States wanted to adopt CRS, some of the key differences between FATCA and CRS—as outlined above and in appendix V—could be aligned through regulation while others would require legislation. According to Treasury officials, to align FATCA and CRS, Congress would need to revise statutes to:

- provide for the collection of information for accounts that residents of partner jurisdictions maintain at U.S. financial institutions;
- require certain U.S. financial institutions to report the account balance (including, in the case of a cash value insurance contract or annuity contract, the cash value or surrender value) for all financial accounts maintained at a U.S. office and held by foreign residents;
- expand the current reporting required with respect to U.S. source income paid to accounts held by foreign residents to include similar non-U.S. source payments;
- require financial institutions to report the gross proceeds from the sale or redemption of property held in, or with respect to, a financial account; and
- require financial institutions to report information with respect to financial accounts held by certain passive entities with substantial foreign owners.

While better aligning FATCA and CRS to some extent is possible, anything short of the United States fully adopting CRS would not fully eliminate the burdens of overlapping requirements that FFIs must currently meet under the two different systems.

While having the United States adopt the CRS reporting system in lieu of FATCA could benefit FFIs that may otherwise have to operate two overlapping reporting systems, it would result in no additional benefit to IRS in terms of obtaining information on U.S. accounts. Additionally, it could generate additional costs and reporting burdens to U.S. financial institutions that would need to implement systems to meet CRS requirements. The extent of these costs is unknown.

Further, adoption of CRS would create the circumstance where foreign accounts held by U.S. citizens with a tax residence in partner jurisdiction— including U.S. citizens who have a U.S. tax obligation—would not be reported to IRS.

## AGENCIES COORDINATED EFFORTS TO ADDRESS CHALLENGES U.S. PERSONS LIVING ABROAD ENCOUNTERED FROM FATCA IMPLEMENTATION, BUT OPPORTUNITIES EXIST TO ENHANCE COLLABORATION

### Some U.S. Persons Living Abroad Encountered Reduced Access to Financial Services Due in Part to Costs and Risks FFIs Faced from Implementing FATCA

Tax practitioners and others we interviewed said that U.S. persons living abroad—whether or not they are required to complete a Form 8938—risk being denied access to foreign financial services. U.S. persons and tax practitioners located in four of the five countries where we conducted focus groups and interviews reported that some U.S. persons and U.S.- owned businesses encountered difficulties opening bank accounts with FFIs after FATCA was enacted, with some FFIs closing U.S. persons' existing accounts or denying them opportunities to open new accounts. One focus group participant, for example, said that the financial institution closed down all accounts including business checking, savings, and money market accounts after FATCA was implemented, requiring this individual to find a local resident who could co-sign on a new account.

Costs FFIs would incur from implementing FATCA were cited as a significant factor in increasing barriers faced by U.S. persons in accessing foreign financial services. Officials from one organization representing tax attorneys said that as a result of costs associated with FATCA implementation, FFIs have found it less burdensome to close accounts of U.S. persons or require the accounts to be moved to a Securities and Exchange Commission registered affiliate than comply with FATCA. Tax practitioners and an official from a bankers association added that because FFIs may gain only small margins of profit from U.S. persons, FFIs may believe it is too troublesome to do business with them.

Additionally, officials from a foreign government agency told us that because FATCA is expensive for FFIs to continue implementing, banks in their country might charge U.S. persons seeking access to financial services additional fees to account for FATCA implementation costs. Tax practitioners, consultants working with FFIs to implement FATCA reporting requirements, and the National Taxpayer Advocate told us that FFIs with smaller asset sizes such as smaller trust companies were more prone to decline business with U.S persons.[16] Officials from an advocacy group representing U.S. persons living abroad told the National Taxpayer Advocate that some smaller banks declined U.S. persons as customers as a business decision, believing it would cost more for them to comply with FATCA reporting requirements than maintain U.S. expatriates' accounts.

Banking associations we interviewed said that decisions made by FFIs on whether to accept U.S. persons as customers also depends on the overall risks and benefits of taking on individual U.S. persons, shaped in part from risks in not meeting FATCA reporting requirements. Representatives of a banking association and an advocacy group told us that some FFIs decided to avoid doing business with U.S. persons after they became concerned about potential penalties for failure to comply—either willfully or in error—with FATCA reporting requirements. One banking association added that such errors could affect other aspects of FFIs' relationships with the U.S. government, such as nonprosecution agreements made with the U.S. Department of Justice.

Officials from one consulting firm that helped FFIs meet FATCA reporting requirements added that FFIs' determination of risk depends on many layers, such as the value of clients' assets or the country in which clients reside or possess citizenship. After FATCA's implementation, according to officials from the consulting firm, FFIs decided to turn away U.S. persons in some cases because the benefits of doing business with U.S. persons were less than the potential risks. For example, if a U.S. person only maintained a payroll account, the FFI may determine it would not make enough money to account for risks in incorrectly identifying the status of the customer as a U.S. or non-U.S. person. However, focus group participants

---

[16] The National Taxpayer Advocate leads the Taxpayer Advocate Service, an independent organization inside IRS that helps taxpayers resolve problems and works for systemic change to mitigate problems experienced by groups of taxpayers.

from two countries said that FFIs may agree to accept U.S persons as customers if they have higher account balances that offset risks from FATCA reporting requirements. One focus group participant, for instance, said banks in his country will do business with a U.S. person if he or she has more than $500,000 in assets. Additionally, U.S. persons and tax practitioners we interviewed said that other factors such as language barriers and U.S. regulations designed to prevent money laundering may also inhibit U.S. persons' access to brokerage accounts while overseas.

## Form 8938 Reporting Requirements for Individuals with Signature Authority on and Financial Interest in Accounts May Have Contributed to Employment and Promotion Denials Overseas

Focus group participants and others we interviewed said that Form 8938 reporting requirements contributed to denials of employment and promotion opportunities for U.S. persons living abroad. Treasury officials noted that requirements imposed by FATCA do not directly hinder U.S. persons from gaining employment or promotion opportunities overseas. However, focus group participants, a consulting firm, and a foreign government agency noted that foreign-owned companies and nonprofit organizations such as churches did not want to hire or promote U.S. persons because they wanted to avoid exposing information to the U.S. government on their organizations' accounts and client trust accounts where the U.S. person would have signature authority. As noted above, a U.S. person is generally required to report on the Form 8938 foreign financial accounts for which the person has signature authority if he or she has a financial interest in the account.[17]

Focus group participants and others noted that such requirements have adversely affected the ability of U.S. persons to serve on a corporate board

---

[17] Under FATCA, any income, gains, losses, deductions, credits, gross proceeds, or distributions from holding or disposing of the account are or would be required to be reported, included, or otherwise reflected on a person's income tax return.

or in a nonprofit organization, or maintain business relationships. Treasury and Department of Commerce officials stationed in one country included in our review added that FATCA implementation has played a role in dissuading foreign-owned corporations in some Asian countries from considering U.S. persons for corporate leadership positions such as directorships. This is in part because FATCA has triggered additional paperwork burden and operating costs for onboarding U.S. employees since they have had to help them meet Form 8938 reporting requirements. Two advocacy groups representing U.S. persons living abroad added that it is also harder for U.S.-based companies to justify relocating U.S. persons overseas and paying for such relocations since they also have had to help their U.S. employees meet Form 8938 reporting requirements in addition to meeting other tax filing requirements.

## U.S. Persons Living Abroad Encounter Challenges Obtaining Social Security Numbers Necessary to Meet U.S. Tax Obligations and Obtain Financial Services

U.S. embassy documents indicate there was increased demand for Social Security Numbers (SSN) since FATCA's passage in 2010, driven in part by U.S. citizens applying for an SSN to gain access to foreign financial services or resolve outstanding U.S. tax obligations before completing renunciation. However, officials from two organizations representing Americans living abroad cited significant challenges faced by some U.S. persons living abroad in obtaining SSNs required to meet their U.S. tax obligations or obtain financial services. U.S. persons living abroad might not possess an SSN because their parents did not obtain one for them as a minor. Often, this may have been due to the parents leaving the United States when the child was young. State officials also said that U.S. citizens applying for U.S. passports while overseas frequently forget their SSNs or do not know if their parents ever applied for an SSN on their behalf.

Officials from organizations representing U.S. persons living abroad added that without an SSN, these persons are unable to claim refunds or other tax benefits when filing their tax returns, or participate in IRS programs to voluntarily disclose previously unreported tax liabilities and assets. Additionally, some might be unable to gain or maintain access to financial accounts or other assets in their countries of residence without an SSN. According to these officials and tax practitioners we interviewed, U.S. persons living abroad face greater challenges in obtaining SSNs than those living in the United States. For instance, they faced difficulties obtaining documentation from the United States that the Social Security Administration (SSA) requires with SSN applications; traveling to Social Security offices and U.S. embassies or consulates to certify documents or submit applications in person; and receiving valid SSNs from SSA in a timely manner to file tax returns or participate in offshore disclosure programs.[18]

SSA officials also identified several challenges U.S. persons experience when applying for an SSN from abroad. For instance, SSA officials said that efforts to authenticate documents submitted with SSN applications can cause delays for U.S. persons living abroad in obtaining an SSN. Additionally, SSN applicants living abroad face significantly longer wait times than applicants living in the United States once their applications are processed.

---

[18] SSN applicants must properly complete the application for a Social Security Card and provide at least two documents to prove age, identity, and U.S. citizenship. SSA can only accept original documents or documents certified by the custodian of the original record. The applicant can submit the completed application and evidence at any Social Security office or U.S. embassy or consulate with a Federal Benefits Unit (FBU). A Regional Federal Benefits Officer may also specifically authorize a U.S. embassy or consulate without an FBU to accept an application. Additionally, first-time SSN applicants over age 12 may submit their applications at any U.S. embassy or consulate, regardless of whether there is an FBU or whether there is Regional Federal Benefits Officer authorization. Military dependents or U.S. citizens working on a U.S. military post may also go to a Post Adjutant or Personnel Office. If the applicant is age 12 or older, he or she must participate in a mandatory in-person interview, and must submit satisfactory evidence explaining why he or she did not have an SSN prior to age 12. U.S. persons in Canada who are required to submit an SSN application in person are referred the appropriate SSA domestic border field office in the United States. Once the SSN application is processed and approved, the applicant will receive a Social Security Card in the mail.

According to SSA officials, after an application is processed, it can take 3 to 6 months—depending on the country's mail service—for an individual to receive a Social Security Card.

This is significantly longer than the 2-week period it takes SSN applicants to receive a card after mailing in their applications from within the United States.

## FATCA Implementation Contributed to Increased Renunciations of U.S. Citizenship, but the Extent of the Effect is Unclear

According to Department of State (State) data, the annual number of approvals of requests for renunciations of U.S. citizenships increased nearly 178 percent during a 6-year period, from 1,601 in 2011—the year after FATCA was enacted—to 4,449 in 2016, the most recent year to which full data on renunciations were available.

According to U.S. embassy documents and information provided by focus group participants and interviewees across all the countries we examined, FATCA was the reason or a contributing factor in some of these decisions and the resulting increase in total renunciations. Specific effects of FATCA implementation contributing to decisions to renounce U.S. citizenship included reduced access to foreign financial services and employment or promotion opportunities in a foreign-owned company—as identified above from our document reviews, focus groups, and interviews—and burdens in meeting FATCA reporting requirements.

However, the extent to which FATCA implementation contributed to increased renunciations is unclear. State officials said that data are unavailable to determine the extent to which these renunciation decisions were the direct result of FATCA because State has no legal obligation to collect information on the motivation behind renunciation of citizenship.

**Treasury, State, and SSA Initially Collaborated to Remedy FATCA-Related Issues for U.S. Persons Abroad, but Problems Persist without Cross-Agency Efforts to Address Them**

In response to concerns about the availability of foreign financial services, Treasury implemented regulations that allow certain low-risk local FFIs to be deemed compliant with FATCA, but only if the FFIs do not implement policies or practices that discriminate against opening or maintaining accounts for specified U.S. persons.[19] Treasury and State also previously established joint strategies to address these challenges. For instance, Treasury and State developed guidance on FATCA that was posted on embassy websites to educate U.S. persons and others. Additionally, Treasury and State officials conducted outreach events and workshops through U.S. embassies and American chambers of commerce worldwide to provide information on FATCA and other tax filing requirements, According to State officials, the U.S. embassies in at least two countries— Switzerland and France—also worked with foreign officials and/or FFIs to increase access to financial services for U.S. citizens residing in those countries. For instance, Treasury and State officials reached agreements with FFIs in Switzerland to provide a wider range of financial services to U.S. persons. Similarly, in 2017, SSA and State implemented an interagency agreement to streamline processes for providing SSNs to U.S. persons living abroad after FATCA's implementation in 2010. SSA officials said they are also in discussions with State on improving SSA's website to include more transparent, specific information for SSN overseas applicants about SSA documentation requirements.

Tax practitioners, advocacy groups, and Treasury officials we interviewed said FFIs have become more willing to accept U.S. persons as customers compared to when FATCA was enacted in 2010. However, U.S. persons living abroad continue to face issues gaining access to foreign financial services. For example, in a September 2018 letter sent by the Chair of the Finance Committee of the Netherlands House of Representatives to a

---

[19] 26 C.F.R. § 1.1471-5(f)(1)(i)(A)(9).

member of Congress, U.S. citizens born outside the United States and who have never lived, studied, or worked in the United States are effectively being denied access to financial services in the Netherlands. Focus group participants added that some banks will reject U.S. clients or charge heavy fees for them to open an account.

Agencies have ongoing efforts to address FATCA-related issues, as listed below, but some are ad hoc, fragmented, or otherwise not part of a broader effort between Treasury and other agencies such as State or SSA to use ongoing collaborative mechanisms to monitor and share information on such issues, and jointly develop and implement steps to address them:

- Treasury officials said they are participating in discussions with FFIs to address residual issues with access to foreign financial services. However, they said they have not involved other agencies in these discussions.

- IRS officials, in response to concerns from the French government, said they are developing a program to help streamline foreign asset-related tax compliance requirements for a small group of U.S. born citizens that have been French residents most of their lives without an SSN, and—according to State officials—did not wish to take the necessary steps to renounce their citizenship. However, no effort has been made to address these issues more broadly.

- State encouraged U.S. citizens to alert the nearest U.S. embassy of any practices they encounter with regard to the provision of financial services. State documents noted that some Americans have been turned away by banks or required to meet a higher deposit threshold in part because of FATCA reporting requirements. State documentation also noted that there have been cases of U.S. citizens with existing bank accounts who have been asked to close them. However, State documentation we reviewed does not highlight collaborative efforts currently underway with Treasury or other agencies to address banking access issues U.S. persons living abroad are presently encountering worldwide.

- As described above, SSA and State streamlined processes and policies for U.S. persons abroad seeking to obtain SSNs. However, SSA officials said they have not been involved in any ongoing efforts involving Treasury to identify systemic issues and related solutions involving SSNs for the purposes of tax compliance and citizenship renunciations. Treasury officials said they spoke with SSA officials about problems U.S. persons living abroad face in obtaining SSNs, but SSA believed that cycle times for processing SSN applications submitted by U.S. persons living abroad were not significantly greater than for applications submitted by U.S. persons living in the United States, although mailing times could vary significantly and take up to 3 to 6 months.

We have previously identified key practices to enhance and sustain interagency collaboration, including

- defining and articulating a common outcome,
- establishing mutually reinforcing or joint strategies, and
- developing mechanisms to monitor, evaluate, and report on results.[20]

One goal in IRS's strategic plan is to collaborate with external partners proactively to improve tax administration, while objectives in SSA's strategic plan include improving service delivery and expanding service delivery options. Additionally, according to State's Bureau of Consular Affairs website, one of State's key priorities is to protect the interests of U.S. citizens overseas, such as through ensuring responsive and efficient provision of consular services overseas. As noted above, there are a host of ongoing issues and challenges for U.S. persons living abroad from implementation of FATCA, such as loss of access to foreign financial

---

[20] See GAO-06-15 for additional examples of key practices to enhance and sustain interagency collaboration. We broadly define collaboration as any joint activity that is intended to produce more public value than could be produced when the agencies act alone. See GAO-12-1022 for a list of selected mechanisms for interagency collaboration.

services, denial of employment and promotion opportunities overseas, and difficulty obtaining SSNs from abroad. However, Treasury currently lacks a collaborative mechanism to coordinate efforts with other agencies to address these issues, and Treasury officials said they do not plan to establish them. Without effective collaborative mechanisms to monitor and share information and implement cross-agency solutions, future efforts to address such issues will continue to be fragmented and less effective than they otherwise could be.

## CONCLUSION

In enacting FATCA, Congress sought to reduce tax evasion by creating greater transparency and accountability over offshore assets held by U.S. taxpayers. Because of FATCA, IRS receives information on foreign financial assets from hundreds of thousands of filers annually. IRS could use this information to help ensure taxpayers holding offshore assets report and pay taxes owed on income generated from such assets. However, to take full advantage of the information, IRS must address key challenges. Specifically, Taxpayer Identification Numbers (TIN) reported by FFIs are often inaccurate or incomplete, which makes it difficult for IRS to match information reported by FFIs to individual taxpayers. As such, IRS must develop a plan to mitigate the risks that these data issues pose to agency efforts to identify and combat taxpayer noncompliance.

Lack of consistent, complete, and readily available Form 8938 and related parent individual tax return data also affects IRS's compliance activities, making it more difficult for IRS business units to extract and analyze FATCA data to improve tax compliance efforts and reduce tax revenue loss from income generated from offshore assets. At the same time, IRS has stopped following its FATCA Compliance Roadmap it developed in 2016 because, according to IRS officials, IRS moved away from updating broad strategy documents to focus on individual compliance campaigns. However, in light of the challenges IRS continues to face in fully integrating FATCA information into its compliance programs, it will not maximize use of such information and effectively leverage individual compliance campaigns unless it employs a comprehensive plan that enables IRS to better leverage such campaigns to improve taxpayer compliance.

Our analysis of available data indicates that many of the Forms 8938 filed in tax year 2016 may have been filed unnecessarily. Factors that are contributing to this unnecessary reporting are unclear. While IRS has provided instructions and guidance on its website for completing Form 8938, focus group participants and tax practitioners reported confusion on whether and how to report investments in foreign accounts. Taking steps to identify and address factors contributing to unnecessary Form 8938 reporting would help reduce taxpayer burden and reduce processing costs for IRS.

Reporting requirements for foreign financial assets under FATCA overlap with reporting requirements under FBAR. These overlapping requirements—implemented under two different statutes—have resulted in most taxpayers filing Forms 8938 also filing FBARs with FinCEN. Duplicative filings on foreign financial assets cause confusion, frustration, and compliance burdens for taxpayers. Duplicative filings also increased costs to the government to process and store the same or similar information. Modifying the statutes governing the requirements can fully address the issues outlined above, and can allow for the use of FATCA information for prevention and detection of financial crimes. This is similar to other statutory allowances for IRS to disclose return information for other purposes, such as for determining Social Security income tax withholding.

Lastly, FATCA has created challenges for some U.S. persons living abroad that go beyond increasing their tax compliance burdens. Some U.S. persons living abroad are still facing issues accessing financial services and employment and obtaining SSNs. Treasury, State, and SSA have taken some steps to address these issues both separately and in coordination with each other. However, Treasury, as the agency ultimately responsible for effective administration of FATCA, currently lacks a collaborative mechanism with State and SSA to address ongoing issues. Establishing a formal means to collaboratively address burdens faced by Americans abroad from FATCA can help agencies develop effective solutions to mitigate such burdens.

## MATTER FOR CONGRESSIONAL CONSIDERATION

We are making the following matter for congressional consideration:

- Congress should consider amending the Internal Revenue Code, Bank Secrecy Act of 1970, and other statutes, as needed, to address overlap in foreign financial asset reporting requirements for the purposes of tax compliance and detection, and prevention of financial crimes, such as by aligning the types of assets to be reported and asset reporting thresholds, and ensuring appropriate access to the reported information.

## RECOMMENDATIONS FOR EXECUTIVE ACTION

We are making the following four recommendations to IRS:

- The Commissioner of Internal Revenue should develop a plan to mitigate risks with compliance activities due to the lack of accurate and complete TINs of U.S. account holders collected from FFIs. (Recommendation 1)
- The Commissioner of Internal Revenue should ensure that appropriate business units conducting compliance enforcement and research have access to consistent and complete data collected from individuals' electronic and paper filings of Form 8938 and elements of parent individual tax returns. As part of this effort, the Commissioner should ensure that IRS provides clear guidance to the business units for accessing such data in IRS's Compliance Data Warehouse. (Recommendation 2)
- The Commissioner of Internal Revenue should employ a comprehensive plan for managing efforts to leverage FATCA data in agency compliance efforts. The plan should document and track activities over time to

o   ensure individuals and FFIs comply with FATCA reporting requirements;

o   assess and mitigate data quality risks from FFIs;

o   improve the quality, management, and accessibility of FATCA data for compliance, research, and other purposes; and

o   establish, monitor, and evaluate compliance efforts involving FATCA data intended to improve voluntary compliance and address noncompliance with FATCA reporting requirements. (Recommendation 3)

- The Commissioner of Internal Revenue should assess factors contributing to unnecessary Form 8938 reporting and take steps, as appropriate, to address the issue. Depending on the results of the assessment, potential options may include:

o   identifying and implementing steps to further clarify IRS Form 8938 instructions and related guidance on IRS's website on determining what foreign financial assets to report, and how to calculate and report asset values subject to reporting thresholds; and

o   conducting additional outreach to educate taxpayers on required reporting thresholds, including notifying taxpayers that may have unnecessarily filed an IRS Form 8938 to reduce such filings. (Recommendation 4)

We are also making the following recommendation to Treasury:

- The Secretary of the Treasury should lead efforts, in coordination with the Secretary of State and Commissioner of Social Security, to establish a formal means to collaboratively address ongoing issues— including issues accessing financial services and employment and obtaining SSNs—that U.S. persons living abroad encounter from implementation of FATCA reporting requirements. (Recommendation 5)

We are also making the following recommendation to State:

- The Secretary of State, in coordination with the Secretary of the Treasury and Commissioner of Social Security, should establish a formal means to collaboratively address ongoing issues—including issues accessing financial services and employment and obtaining SSNs—that U.S. persons living abroad encounter from implementation of FATCA reporting requirements. (Recommendation 6)

We are also making the following recommendation to SSA:

- The Commissioner of Social Security, in coordination with the Secretaries of State and Treasury, should establish a formal means to collaboratively address ongoing issues—including issues accessing financial services and employment and obtaining SSNs—that U.S. persons living abroad encounter from implementation of FATCA reporting requirements. (Recommendation 7)

## AGENCY COMMENTS AND OUR EVALUATION

We provided a draft of this chapter to the Secretaries of State and the Treasury, Commissioner of Internal Revenue, and Acting Commissioner of Social Security.

IRS provided written comments that are summarized below and reprinted in appendix VI. IRS did not state whether it agreed or disagreed with our four recommendations but otherwise provided responses.

Regarding our recommendation to develop a plan to mitigate risks with compliance activities due to the lack of accurate and complete TINs of U.S. account holders collected from FFIs (recommendation 1), IRS reiterated that it provided a transition period, through the end of 2019, for compliance with the TIN requirements for FFIs in countries with Model 1 IGAs with the United States. IRS also said that it continued to make progress on improving

FATCA filing compliance, citing efforts such as initiating a campaign addressing FFIs that do not meet their compliance responsibilities. While these efforts may help IRS obtain more accurate and complete information from financial accounts, IRS did not specify how it will mitigate the ongoing hurdles it faces in matching accounts reported by FFIs without valid TINs to accounts reported by individual tax filers and ensure compliance.

Regarding our recommendation that appropriate business units have access to consistent and complete data collected from Forms 8938 and tax returns filed by individuals (recommendation 2), IRS reiterated that RAAS has been working to obtain read-only access to the IPM database but that limited budgetary resources are delaying implementation. Enabling access to consistent and complete Form 8938 and tax return data would help IRS better target compliance initiatives and leverage limited available enforcement resources. While IRS continues to work on enabling access to IPM, it could still provide clear guidance to its business units for accessing Form 8938 and tax return data in IRS's Compliance Data Warehouse, as we recommended.

Regarding our recommendation to employ a comprehensive plan for managing efforts to leverage FATCA data in agency compliance efforts (recommendation 3), IRS said the resources that would be required to develop a comprehensive plan would be better spent on enforcement activities. While implementing enforcement activities could increase compliance with FATCA reporting requirements, it risks not maximizing the value of such efforts without a comprehensive plan to manage and address the myriad of challenges discussed in this chapter. Further, it is our belief that IRS's failure to execute the FATCA roadmap is not justification for abandoning a strategic approach going forward.

Regarding our recommendation to assess factors contributing to unnecessary Form 8938 reporting and take appropriate steps to address the issue (recommendation 4), IRS said it will continue to observe filings of Form 8938 and, to the extent that there are unnecessary filings, assess options to inform account holders to reduce reporting and filing burdens followed by appropriate steps to implement any selected options.

Our analysis of available data indicates that many Forms 8938 may have been filed unnecessarily. Implementing our recommendation reduces the risk that taxpayers file—and IRS processes—forms unnecessarily.

Treasury provided written comments but did not state whether it agreed or disagreed with our recommendation that it lead efforts, in coordination with State and SSA, to establish a formal means to collaboratively address ongoing issues that U.S. persons living abroad encounter from implementation of FATCA reporting requirements (recommendation 5). Treasury said it will work collaboratively with State and SSA to answer questions that Americans abroad have regarding their tax obligations and, where appropriate, to direct U.S. citizens to resources that will help them understand the procedures applied by SSA to apply for an SSN.

However, Treasury said it is not the appropriate agency to lead coordination efforts involving foreign employment issues and issues regarding access to foreign financial services and obtaining SSNs. As we noted above, Treasury is ultimately responsible for effective administration of FATCA. As such, it is in a better position than State or SSA to adjust regulations and guidance implementing FATCA to address burdens FFIs and foreign employers face from FATCA implementation while ensuring tax compliance. Additionally, Treasury has an interest in helping U.S. persons receive valid SSNs from SSA in a timely manner to meet their tax obligations. Treasury's written response is reprinted in appendix VII.

State and SSA also provided written comments in which they concurred with our recommendations to establish a formal means to address collaboratively together with Treasury ongoing issues that U.S. persons living abroad encounter with FATCA (recommendations 6 and 7). State and SSA's written comments are reprinted in appendices VIII and IX, respectively.

Treasury, State, and SSA provided technical comments, which we incorporated as appropriate.

We are sending copies of this chapter to the appropriate congressional committees, the Secretaries of State and the Treasury, Commissioner of Internal Revenue, Acting Commissioner of Social Security, and other interested parties.

James R. McTigue, Jr.
Director, Tax Issues Strategic Issues Team

# APPENDIX I: OBJECTIVES, SCOPE, AND METHODOLOGY

The objectives of this chapter are to (1) assess the Internal Revenue Service's (IRS) efforts to use information collected under the Foreign Account Tax Compliance Act (FATCA) to improve taxpayer compliance; (2) examine available foreign financial asset reports submitted by U.S. persons, including submissions that were below required filing thresholds; (3) examine the extent to which the Department of the Treasury (Treasury) administers overlapping reporting requirements on foreign financial assets; (4) describe similarities and differences between FATCA and Common Reporting Standard (CRS) reporting requirements; and (5) examine the effects of FATCA implementation that are unique to U.S. persons living abroad.[21]

For our first objective, we reviewed Treasury Inspector General for Tax Administration reports and collected information from Treasury and IRS to summarize efforts to collect complete and valid Taxpayer Identification Numbers (TIN) from foreign financial institutions (FFI).

We identified criteria from our prior work identifying key practices for risk management.[22] The key practices are derived from the Software Engineering Institute's Capability Maturity Model® Integration for Development and Office of Management and Budget guidance.[23]

---

[21] Subtitle A of Title V of the Hiring Incentives to Restore Employment Act is commonly referred to as FATCA. Pub. L. No. 111-147, §§ 501-541, 124 Stat. 71, 97-117 (2010).

[22] GAO, *Information Technology: IRS Needs to Take Additional Actions to Address Significant Risks to Tax Processing*, GAO-18-298 (Washington, D.C.: June 28, 2018).

[23] Software Engineering Institute, Capability Maturity Model® Integration for Development (CMMI-DEV), Version 1.3 (Pittsburgh, Pa.: November 2010); Office of Management and Budget, *Managing Information as a Strategic Resource*, OMB Circular No. A-130 (Washington, D.C.: revised 2016); Office of Management and Budget, *Management's Responsibility for Enterprise Risk Management and Internal Control*, OMB Circular No. A-123 (Washington, D.C.: 2016).

We applied these criteria to assess steps IRS has taken to manage risks in not receiving complete and valid TIN information from FFIs. We also applied criteria from our prior work on use of documented frameworks to IRS documentation on FATCA compliance activities to determine the extent to which IRS implemented a comprehensive plan to maximize use of collected data to enforce compliance with FATCA.[24]

For our second objective, we identified total maximum account values reported by individual filers of Financial Crimes Enforcement Network (FinCEN) Form 114s (commonly known as the *Report of Foreign Bank and Financial Accounts*, or FBAR) in calendar years 2015 and 2016. See appendix III for more details on our methodology to evaluate these data. We also summarized the numbers of IRS Forms 8938, *Statement of Specified Foreign Financial Assets* (Form 8938) filed in tax year 2016, accounting for the data limitations described below. We also identified Forms 8938 filed in tax year 2016—the most recent year for which data were available—with available residency and asset information that reported specified foreign financial assets with aggregate values at or below end-of-year tax thresholds, which vary depending on the location of residence and filing status of such filers.

For our third objective, we reviewed IRS and FinCEN documentation, and applied criteria from *Fragmentation, Overlap, and Duplication: An Evaluation and Management Guide* to identify the extent to which IRS and FinCEN were engaged in overlapping activities, and collecting duplicative information on foreign financial assets held by U.S. persons.[25] We assessed the extent to which individual filers who submitted a Form 8938 in 2015 and 2016 also submitted an FBAR for the same year by determining the number and percentage of Forms 8938 with TINs that also match the TIN listed on the corresponding FBAR for the same year.

---

[24] GAO, *Tax Preparer Regulation: IRS Needs a Documented Framework to Achieve Goal of Improving Taxpayer Compliance*, GAO-11-336 (Washington, D.C.: March 31, 2011).

[25] GAO, *Fragmentation, Overlap, and Duplication: An Evaluation and Management Guide*, GAO-15-49SP (Washington, D.C.: April 14, 2015).

For the three objectives described above, we assessed the reliability of data submitted on Forms 8938 filed by individuals for tax years 2015 and 2016, the most recent data available. These data were extracted from IRS's Individual Return Transaction File (IRTF) and Modernized Tax Return Database (MTRDB) through IRS's Compliance Data Warehouse (CDW). We also assessed the reliability of data from FBARs for calendar years 2015 and 2016 by (1) reviewing documentation about the data and the systems that produced them; (2) conducting electronic tests, such as identifying data with significant numbers of missing Form 8938 or FBAR records, or values of foreign financial assets reported outside an expected range; (3) tracing selections or random samples of data to source documents; and (4) interviewing IRS and FinCEN officials knowledgeable about the data. We also reviewed Form 8938 and relevant parent tax return data stored in IRS databases to determine whether IRS management is using quality information collected from Forms 8938 to achieve its objectives, as defined in our *Standards for Internal Control in the Federal Government*.[26] We determined that data extracted from IRTF on characteristics of Form 8938 filers and from FBAR filings was sufficiently reliable for our purposes, subject to caveats identified in this chapter.[27] However, we determined we could not obtain complete data on foreign financial assets reported on Forms 8938 filed on paper.

For our fourth objective, we reviewed model international agreements and other documentation, and interviewed officials from Treasury, IRS, and the Organisation for Economic Co-operation and Development to compare and contrast FATCA and CRS reporting requirements.

---

[26] GAO, *Standards for Internal Control in the Federal Government*, GAO-14-704G (Washington, D.C.: September 2014).

[27] We required each FBAR filing to contain data on (1) the filer, (2) the transmitter of the report, and (3) the transmitter contact. Due to the likelihood that filings without these required data elements contained other errors, we dropped these from our analysis. Additionally, we dropped FBAR filings that (1) were missing data on the reporting year; (2) did not report information on any foreign accounts; or (3) declared more than $100 trillion in assets.

We also used the collected information to identify what changes, if any, the United States and other countries could implement to align FATCA and CRS reporting requirements.

For our fifth objective, we collected documentation and conducted focus groups and semi-structured interviews with 21 U.S. persons living abroad that were subject to FATCA reporting requirements. We also conducted focus groups and interviews with tax practitioners, banking and CPA organizations, government agencies, advocacy groups representing Americans living abroad, and other organizations from the United States and five other countries (Canada, Japan, Singapore, Switzerland, and the United Kingdom). We selected these countries based on geography, relatively high numbers of U.S. expatriates and Form 8938 filers, tax information sharing agreements, and other tax treaties with the United States.

The findings from the focus groups and interviews are not generalizable to other U.S. persons, tax practitioners or organizations, but were selected to represent the viewpoints of U.S. persons, FFIs, and host country tax authorities required to transmit information on foreign accounts and other specified foreign financial assets to IRS.

We conducted a thematic analysis of the focus groups and interviews, and reviewed cables from U.S. embassies to identify the unique effects of FATCA implementation on U.S. persons living abroad. We collected documentation from and interviewed Treasury, IRS, Department of State, and Social Security Administration officials on steps to monitor and mitigate such effects.

We also identified criteria from our prior work on key practices to enhance and sustain interagency collaboration and mechanisms to facilitate coordination.[28]

---

[28] GAO, *Managing for Results: Key Considerations for Implementing Interagency Collaborative Mechanisms,* GAO-12-1022 (Washington, D.C.: September 27, 2012); and *Results-Oriented Government: Practices That Can Help Enhance and Sustain Collaboration among Federal Agencies,* GAO-06-15 (Washington, D.C.: October 21, 2005).

We applied the criteria to agencies' collaborative efforts addressing issues U.S. persons living abroad faced from FATCA's implementation, and identified the extent to which agencies established effective collaborative mechanisms to identify, assess, and implement cross-agency solutions to such issues.

We conducted this performance audit from August 2017 to April 2019 in accordance with generally accepted government auditing standards. Those standards require that we plan and perform the audit to obtain sufficient, appropriate evidence to provide a reasonable basis for our findings and conclusions based on our audit objectives. We believe that the evidence obtained provides a reasonable basis for our findings and conclusions based on our audit objectives.

## APPENDIX II: IRS DATA MANAGEMENT SYSTEMS STORING DATA FROM IRS FORMS 8938 AND RELATED ELEMENTS OF INDIVIDUAL TAX RETURNS

The following IRS databases store data collected from individuals' electronic and paper filings of Forms 8938 and/or elements of individual parent tax returns—the filer's address and filing status—used to determine specified reporting thresholds for Form 8938 filers:[29]

- Individual Master File (IMF), which serves as IRS's system for processing individual taxpayer account data. Using this system, accounts are updated, taxes are assessed, and refunds are generated as required during each tax-filing period.

---

[29] FATCA generally requires certain taxpayers to report to IRS on Form 8938 foreign financial accounts and other specified foreign financial assets whose aggregate value exceeds specified thresholds, which vary by residency and filing status. See appendix IV for more detailed information on these thresholds.

- Individual Returns Transaction File (IRTF), which stores edited, transcribed, and error-corrected data from the Form 1040 series and related forms for the current processing year and two prior years.

- Modernized Tax Return Database (MTRDB), which serves as the official repository of all electronic returns processed through IRS's Modernized e-File system. Tax return data is stored immediately after returns are processed.

- International Compliance Management Model (ICMM)-FATCA International Returns (ICMM-FIR), which collects, parses, and stores data from incoming form reports–such as Forms 8938 and 8966–into the FATCA Database (FDB), which serves as the repository where ICMM-FIR stores data and from which downstream applications can pull data.

- Integrated Production Model (IPM), which is a downstream data repository that houses IMF data, information returns, and other data. According to IRS officials, data from IPM are consolidated and made available to a variety of downstream, security certified, systems for use in conducive analysis, case selection, and report preparation.

Additionally, data from these and other IRS databases are copied to IRS's Compliance Data Warehouse (CDW) periodically, which captures data from multiple production systems and organizes the data in a way that is conductive to analysis.[30]

Table 6 highlights several problems with the consistency and completeness of Form 8938 and relevant parent tax return data stored across the listed databases.

---

[30] CDW also includes a copy of IMF and Business Master File data, and provides access to a variety of other tax return, enforcement, compliance, and other data.

## Table 6. Comparison of Individual IRS Form 8938 and Related Parent Tax Return Data Stored in Selected IRS Databases

| Contained Information | IMF | IRTF | MTRDB | ICMM-FIR | FDB | IPM |
|---|---|---|---|---|---|---|
| Contains complete records of individual tax returns? | Yes | Yes Contains 404,791 records of individual tax returns for tax year 2016. | Incomplete Contains 314,573 records of individual tax returns filed in tax year 2016 also stored in IRTF. However, MTRDB is not designed to store records of returns submitted on paper. Rather, it is intended to be a repository only for electronically filed returns processed through IRS's Modernized e-File program. | Incomplete Contains information from Form 8938 electronic and paper filings and all Form 8938 data contained in IPM. Contains information from some elements from parent tax returns submitted with Forms 8938, such as taxpayer identification numbers and document locator numbers. | Yes | Yes |
| Contains country code from where Form 8938 was filed? | No | Incomplete | Yes | Incomplete | Incomplete FDB stores country codes from electronic filings, but not paper filings. | Yes |
| Contains filing status of Form 8938 filers? | Yes | Yes | Yes | No | No | Yes |
| Contains summary account and other asset information from Form 8938, Parts I and II? | No | No | Yes | Yes | Yes | Yes |
| Contains detailed account and other asset information from Form 8938, Parts V and VI? | No | No | Yes | Yes | Yes | Yes |

Source: GAO analysis of IRS information. | GAO-19-180.

Note: Data from these and other databases are copied to IRS's CDW periodically.

- Inconsistent and incomplete data on address and filing status of Form 8938 filers: As noted above, elements of parent tax returns—specifically the filer's country of residence and filing status—are used to determine specified reporting thresholds for Form 8938 filers. However, IRTF and MTRDB have inconsistent and incomplete data on addresses linked to Form 8938 filers, and report inconsistent numbers of Forms 8938 filed from a U.S. residence.

- For example, the variable identified as containing data on foreign countries of residence in IRTF shows approximately 8,100 foreign filers in tax years 2015 and 2016, whereas a similar variable in MTRDB shows approximately 89,000 foreign filers for those same years. Additionally, FDB does not contain country codes from paper filings of Form 8938. ICCM-FIR stores information from some elements from parent tax returns—such as TINs and document locator numbers.

- According to IRS officials, however, ICMM-FIR lacks data on country codes and filing status of Form 8938 filers. IRS officials said that ICMM-FIR was not designed or intended to store data on Form 8938 filers; rather, it was designed to be a database for use in comparing Form 8938 and 8966 data. In general, IRS officials indicated that they would like to adjust the way ICMM-FIR stores data, but that would require modifying the way the database was established.

- Incomplete data on assets reported on Forms 8938: MTRDB contains detailed information on specified foreign financial assets submitted on electronic filings of Form 8938 and the country code from which the Form 8938 was filed. IRS officials said it is not designed to store information submitted on paper filings of Forms 8938 and parent tax returns. IRS officials said that while IMF processes information transcribed from individual income tax returns, there is no requirement to cross-reference information from the tax return with information submitted with an accompanying Form 8938. Additionally, while IRS officials told us that IRTF is the authoritative source for filers of Form 8938, it does not store account and other asset information submitted from Forms 8938. When asked whether there is any move to store account and other asset information collected from Forms 8938 into IRTF, IRS officials said that the decision on what returns or portions of returns are transcribed are subject to resource constraints and are prioritized from year to year.


# APPENDIX III: METHODOLOGY AND DETAILED INFORMATION ON 2015 AND 2016 INDIVIDUAL FBAR FILINGS

Table 7 shows that more than 900,000 individuals filed Financial Crimes Enforcement Network (FinCEN) Form 114s (commonly known as the *Report of Foreign Bank and Financial Accounts*, or FBAR) in calendar years 2015 and 2016, and declared total maximum values of accounts ranging from about $1.5 trillion to more than $2 trillion each year.[1] We are providing a range of estimates because we found a large number of filings made potentially in error. In some cases, for instance, FBAR filers reported more than $100 trillion in foreign financial accounts. We assume many of these filings are likely made in error, but have only limited means to determine which filings have errors, and which filings have accurate information.

Because we cannot independently verify the accuracy of all self-reported FBAR data, we decided to present a range of data with (1) a lower bound discarding all FBAR filings reporting total values of reported foreign financial accounts at or above $1 billion; and (2) an upper bound discarding all filings reporting total values of such accounts at or above $5 billion.[2]

---

[1] The lower bound of individual FBAR filings from calendar years 2015 and 2016 includes those filings reporting total maximum values of accounts of up to $1 billion. The upper bound of such filings includes those filings reported total values of up to $5 billion.

[2] Of the 683 individual FBAR filers reporting $1 billion or more in total maximum account values in calendar years 2015 or 2016, 447 (or about 65.4 percent) of filers (1) did not file an FBAR for the other year, or (2) reported total maximum account values of $500 million or less on the FBAR for the other year. The number of individual FBAR filers reporting total maximum account values of $5 billion or more increased by about 55.8 percent between calendar years

Table 2 excludes amended and duplicated FBAR filings. This table also excludes FBAR filings that reported a financial interest in 25 or more financial accounts, but reported total maximum account values of $0 from parts II and III of the FBAR.[3] Although we identified problems with the data, we determined they were reliable enough to provide an estimated range of asset values to report the scale of foreign financial accounts held by U.S. persons.

Table 8 shows a detailed breakdown of 2015 and 2016 FBAR filings by residence and categories of total maximum account values reported on the FBARs.

**Table 7. Number of Individuals Filing FBARs and Total Maximum Value of Accounts Reported by Such Individuals, Calendar Years 2015 and 2016**

| | Lower bound (FBAR filings reporting total maximum values of accounts of less than $1 billion) | | Upper bound (FBAR filings reporting total maximum values of accounts less than$5 billion) | |
|---|---|---|---|---|
| Calendar year | Number of individual FBAR filers | Total maximum value of accounts (dollars in trillions)[a] | Number of individual FBAR filers | Total maximum value of accounts (dollars in trillions)[a] |
| 2015 | 928,813 | 1.55 | 929,123 | 2.26 |
| 2016 | 949,167 | 1.50 | 949,510 | 2.19 |

Source: GAO analysis of FinCEN data. | GAO-19-180.
Note: This table excludes amended and duplicated FBAR filings. This table also excludes FBAR filings that reported a financial interest in 25 or more financial accounts but reported total maximum account values of $0 from parts II and III of the FBAR.
[a]Includes total maximum value of accounts reported on parts II and III of the FBAR.

2015 and 2016. In contrast, individual FBAR filers reporting account values of $5 billion or less increased only about 2.2 percent during the same period.
[3] Under the "special rules" provisions at 31 CFR 1010.350(g)(1)–(2), when a person or entity has a financial interest in, or signature authority over, 25 or more foreign financial accounts, the filer is required to report the number of accounts and the filer's identifying information (name, address, taxpayer identification number, and for individual filers date of birth). However, these filers are exempted from providing detailed account information on each of their foreign financial accounts. For instance, filers submitting FBARs covered by the special rules are not required to provide the account number, the name of the foreign financial institution that holds the account, the address of the foreign financial institution, the maximum value of the account during the calendar year, or the type of account.

# Table 8. Individual FBAR Filings by Location of Residence and Categories of Total Maximum Account Values, Calendar Years 2015 and 2016

| Location of residence | Category of total maximum value of accounts[a] | Individual FBAR filers-calendar year 2015 | | Individual FBAR filers-calendar year 2016 | |
|---|---|---|---|---|---|
| | | Number | Percent | Number | Percent |
| U.S. address | $0-$10,000 | 31,552 | 4.4 | 34,672 | 4.7 |
| | $10,001-$50,000 | 239,508 | 33.3 | 250,031 | 33.6 |
| | $50,001-$100,000 | 120,593 | 16.7 | 125,058 | 16.8 |
| | $100,001-$250,000 | 135,872 | 18.9 | 140,992 | 19.0 |
| | $250,001-$500,000 | 73,346 | 10.2 | 75,342 | 10.1 |
| | $500,001-$1,000,000 | 46,741 | 6.5 | 47,203 | 6.4 |
| | $1,000,001-$5,000,000 | 48,269 | 6.7 | 47,006 | 6.3 |
| | $5,000,001-$10,000,000 | 9,011 | 1.3 | 8,265 | 1.1 |
| | $10,000,001-$50,000,000 | 10,331 | 1.4 | 9,722 | 1.3 |
| | $50,000,001-$100,000,000 | 2,170 | 0.3 | 1,932 | 0.3 |
| | $100,000,001-$500,000,000 | 2,120 | 0.3 | 2,099 | 0.3 |
| | $500,000,001-$1,000,000,000 | 388 | 0.1 | 342 | 0.0 |
| | $1,000,000,001-$5,000,000,000 | 287 | 0.0 | 315 | 0.0 |
| | More than $5,000,000,000 | 71 | 0.0 | 112 | 0.0 |
| | Total—all categories | 720,259 | 100 | 743,091 | 100 |
| Foreign address | $0-$10,000 | 5,470 | 2.6 | 5,260 | 2.6 |
| | $10,001-$50,000 | 57,667 | 27.9 | 55,864 | 27.4 |
| | $50,001-$100,000 | 33,420 | 16.1 | 32,858 | 16.1 |
| | $100,001-$250,000 | 42,845 | 20.7 | 42,297 | 20.7 |
| | $250,001-$500,000 | 26,682 | 12.9 | 26,885 | 13.2 |
| | $500,001-$1,000,000 | 19,060 | 9.2 | 19,192 | 9.4 |

| Location of residence | Category of total maximum value of accounts[a] | Individual FBAR filers-calendar year 2015 | | Individual FBAR filers-calendar year 2016 | |
|---|---|---|---|---|---|
| | | Number | Percent | Number | Percent |
| Foreign address | $1,000,001-$5,000,000 | 17,556 | 8.5 | 17,530 | 8.6 |
| | $5,000,001-$10,000,000 | 2,071 | 1.0 | 2,019 | 1.0 |
| | $10,000,001-$50,000,000 | 1,693 | 0.8 | 1,609 | 0.8 |
| | $50,000,001-$100,000,000 | 250 | 0.1 | 237 | 0.1 |
| | $100,000,001-$500,000,000 | 227 | 0.1 | 191 | 0.1 |
| | $500,000,001-$1,000,000,000 | 49 | 0.0 | 41 | 0.0 |
| | $1,000,000,001-$5,000,000,000 | 23 | 0.0 | 26 | 0.0 |
| | More than $5,000,000,000 | (b) | (b) | (b) | (b) |
| | Total—all categories | 207,013[c] | 100[c] | 204,009[c] | 100[c] |
| Total—all residences and categories | | 927,272[c] | 100[c] | 947,100[c] | 100[c] |

Source: GAO analysis of FinCEN data. | GAO-19-180.

Note: This table excludes 4,444 FBAR filings from calendar years 2015 and 2016 that are missing a country of residence. This table excludes amended and duplicated FBAR filings. This table also excludes FBAR filings that reported a financial interest in 25 or more financial accounts but reported total maximum account values of $0 from parts II and III of the FBAR.

[a]Includes total maximum account values reported on parts II and III of FBAR.

[b]Fewer than 20 filers living abroad reported total maximum account values of more than $5 billion, so they are masked to avoid disclosing federal tax information.

[c]The total does not include individual FBAR filers with foreign addresses who reported total maximum account values of more than $5 billion.

# Appendix IV: Detailed Comparison of Individual Foreign Financial Asset Reporting Requirements

## Table 9. Detailed Comparison of Form 8938 and FBAR Reporting Requirements

| | Internal Revenue Service (IRS) Form 8938 (Form 8938), Statement of Specified Foreign Financial Assets<br><br>(To meet Foreign Account Tax Compliance Act (FATCA) reporting requirements under Internal Revenue Code (IRC) Section 6038D and implementing regulations.)[a] | Financial Crimes Enforcement Network (FinCEN) Form 114, Report of Foreign Bank and Financial Accounts(FBAR)<br><br>(To meet FBAR reporting requirements under section5314 of title 31, United States Code, and implementing regulations.)[b] |
|---|---|---|
| Who Must File? | A specified person that has any interest in a specified foreign financial asset during the taxable year must file a Form 8938 attached to the annual return if the aggregate value of all such assets exceeds certain thresholds.[c]<br><br>A specified person is a specified individual or a specified domestic entity.[d]<br><br>A specified individual is an individual who is a<br><br>• U.S. citizen;<br>• resident alien of the United States for any portion of the taxable year;[e]<br>• nonresident alien for whom an election under IRC Section 6013(g) or (h) is in effect; for<br><br>    • nonresident alien who is a bona fide resident of a U.S. possession, including bona fide residents of Puerto Rico, Guam, American Samoa, the Northern Mariana Islands, or the U.S. Virgin Islands.[d] | Each U.S. person having a financial interest in, or signature or other authority over, a bank, securities, or other financial account in a foreign country shall report such relationship for each year in which such relationship exists, subject to a threshold.[b] A U.S. person is<br><br>• U.S. citizen; or<br>• resident of the United States;[g] or an entity, including but not limited to, a corporation, partnership, trust, or LLC, created, organized, or formed under the laws of the United States, any state, the District of Columbia, any U.S. possession or territory, or Indian tribe.[b] |

| | Internal Revenue Service (IRS) Form 8938 (Form 8938), Statement of Specified Foreign Financial Assets (To meet Foreign Account Tax Compliance Act (FATCA) reporting requirements under Internal Revenue Code (IRC) Section 6038D and implementing regulations.)[a] | Financial Crimes Enforcement Network (FinCEN) Form 114, Report of Foreign Bank and Financial Accounts(FBAR) (To meet FBAR reporting requirements under section5314 of title 31, United States Code, and implementing regulations.)[b] |
|---|---|---|
| Who Must File? (Continued) | In general, a specified individual who is a dual resident and is treated as a nonresident alien for purposes of computing the U.S. tax liability is not required to report on assets held with respect to the portion of the year the person is considered a dual resident taxpayer.[c] A specified domestic entity is a domestic corporation, a domestic partnership, or a trust described in IRC section 7701(a)(30)(E), if such corporation, partnership, or trust is formed or availed of for purposes of holding, directly or indirectly, specified foreign financial assets. | |
| Type of interest in foreign financial accounts/assets | Specified interest in a foreign financial asset: A U.S. person has a specified interest if he or she <br><br>• realizes any income, gains, losses, deductions, credits, gross proceeds, or distributions from holding or disposing of the account or asset that are or would be required to be reported, included, or otherwise reflected on the person's income tax return.[c] <br>• has an interest in property transferred in connection with the performance of services on the first date that the property is substantially vested.[c] | Financial interest: A U.S. person has a financial interest in each bank, securities, or other financial account in a foreign country for which he or she is the owner of record or has legal title whether the account is maintained for his or her own benefit or for the benefit of others. If an account is maintained in the name of more than one person, each U.S. person in whose name the account is maintained has a financial interest in that account.[i] A U.S. person also has a financial interest in each bank, securities or other financial |

**Table 9. (Continued)**

| | Internal Revenue Service (IRS) Form 8938 (Form 8938), Statement of Specified Foreign Financial Assets (To meet Foreign Account Tax Compliance Act (FATCA) reporting requirements under Internal Revenue Code (IRC) Section 6038D and implementing regulations.)[a] | Financial Crimes Enforcement Network (FinCEN) Form 114, Report of Foreign Bank and Financial Accounts(FBAR) (To meet FBAR reporting requirements under section5314 of title 31, United States Code, and implementing regulations.)[b] |
|---|---|---|
| Type of interest in foreign financial accounts/assets (Continued) | • elects to include unearned income of a child from a specified foreign financial asset held by their child on the person's income tax return.[c] <br><br> In general, a specified person is not treated as having an interest in any specified foreign financial asset held by a corporation, partnership, trust, or estate solely because of the person's status as a shareholder, partner, or beneficiary of such entity. However, there are exceptions for certain trusts and estates and assets held by a disregarded entity.[c] | account in a foreign country for which the owner of record or holder of legal title is: <br><br> • a person acting as an agent, nominee, attorney, or in some other capacity on behalf of the U.S. person with respect to the account; <br><br> • a corporation in which the U.S. person owns directly or indirectly more than 50 percent of the voting power or the total value of the shares, a partnership in which the U.S. person owns directly or indirectly more than 50 percent of the interest in profits or capital, or any other entity (other than an entity in paragraphs (e)(2)(iii) through (iv) of this section) in which the U.S. person owns directly or indirectly more than 50 percent of the voting power, total value of the equity interest or assets, or interest in profits; <br><br> • a trust, if the U.S. person is the trust grantor and has an ownership interest in the trust for United States Federal tax purposes; or <br><br> • a trust in which the U.S. person either has a present beneficial interest in more than 50 percent of the assets or from which such person receives more than 50 percent of the current income.[j] |

| | Internal Revenue Service (IRS) Form 8938 (Form 8938), Statement of Specified Foreign Financial Assets (To meet Foreign Account Tax Compliance Act (FATCA) reporting requirements under Internal Revenue Code (IRC) Section 6038D and implementing regulations.)[a] | Financial Crimes Enforcement Network (FinCEN) Form 114, Report of Foreign Bank and Financial Accounts(FBAR) (To meet FBAR reporting requirements under section5314 of title 31, United States Code, and implementing regulations.)[b] |
|---|---|---|
| Type of interest in foreign financial accounts/assets (Continued) | | • Signature authority: A person has signatory or other authority if he or she has the authority (alone or in conjunction with another) to control the disposition of money, funds, or other assets held in a financial account by direct communication (whether in writing or otherwise) to the person with whom the financial account is maintained, subject to certain exceptions.[k] |
| Threshold of value of foreign assets making them reportable (individuals) | By statute, the threshold is $50,000 in the aggregate or a higher amount prescribed by the Department of the Treasury (Treasury).[a] The thresholds may be higher depending on the residence and filing status of specified individuals. Thresholds for specified individuals living in the United States: <br><br> • married filing jointly: Total value of assets was more than $100,000 on the last day of the tax year, or more than $150,000 at any time during the year. <br> • other filers: Total value of assets was more than $50,000 on the last day of the tax year, or more than $75,000 at any time during the year.[c] <br><br> Thresholds for specified individuals living abroad: <br><br> • married filing jointly: Total value of assets was more than $400,000 on the last day of the tax year, or more than $600,000 at any time during the year. | This is an aggregate balance, meaning if a person has two accounts, both accounts must be reported if the maximum account values of each (determined separately), when combined exceed $10,000. |

## Table 9. (Continued)

| | Internal Revenue Service (IRS) Form 8938 (Form 8938), Statement of Specified Foreign Financial Assets (To meet Foreign Account Tax Compliance Act (FATCA) reporting requirements under Internal Revenue Code (IRC) Section 6038D and implementing regulations.)[a] | Financial Crimes Enforcement Network (FinCEN) Form 114, Report of Foreign Bank and Financial Accounts(FBAR) (To meet FBAR reporting requirements under section5314 of title 31, United States Code, and implementing regulations.)[b] |
|---|---|---|
| Threshold of value of foreign assets making them reportable (individuals) (Continued) | • other filers: Total value of assets was more than $200,000 on the last day of the tax year, or more than $300,000 at any time during the year.[c]<br><br>Joint owners have an interest in the full value of the jointly owned foreign financial asset when determining whether they meet a reporting threshold.[h] | |
| Foreign financial assets reportable on both Form 8938 and FBAR (including maximum value of asset)[l] | • financial (deposit and custodial) accounts held at foreign financial institutions.<br>• foreign financial account for which a person has signature authority and a financial interest in the account (subject to exceptions).[m]<br>• foreign stock or securities held in a financial account at a foreign financial institution.[n]<br>• foreign mutual funds.<br>• foreign accounts held by a foreign or domestic grantor trust for which the specified individual is the grantor.<br>• foreign-issued life insurance or annuity contract with a cash value. | • foreign financial account for which a person has signature authority and a financial interest in the account (subject to exceptions).[n]<br>• foreign stock or securities held in a financial account at a foreign financial institution.[n]<br><br><br>• foreign accounts held by a foreign or domestic grantor trust for which the specified individual is the grantor. |
| Foreign financial assets reportable only on one form (including maximum value of asset) | • foreign stock or securities not held in a financial account.<br>• foreign partnership interests.<br>• foreign nonaccount investment assets held by a foreign or domestic grantor trust for which the specified individual is the grantor. .<br><br>• foreign hedge funds and foreign private equity funds. | • financial account held at a foreign branch of a U.S. financial institution.[n]<br>• foreign financial account for which a person has signature authority, but no financial interest in the account (subject to exceptions).[m]<br>• indirect interests in foreign financial assets through an entity.[o] |

| | Internal Revenue Service (IRS) Form 8938 (Form 8938), Statement of Specified Foreign Financial Assets (To meet Foreign Account Tax Compliance Act (FATCA) reporting requirements under Internal Revenue Code (IRC) Section 6038D and implementing regulations.)[a] | Financial Crimes Enforcement Network (FinCEN) Form 114, Report of Foreign Bank and Financial Accounts(FBAR) (To meet FBAR reporting requirements under section5314 of title 31, United States Code, and implementing regulations.)[b] |
|---|---|---|
| When and where form is reported | Filed with the annual federal income tax return by the due date of the return (typically April 15), including any applicable extensions.[c] | Filed electronically through FinCEN's Bank Secrecy Act E-Filing System or paper filed with IRS (with FinCEN granted exemption) by the due date of federal income tax returns (typically April 15), with a 6-month automatic extension.[p] |
| Penalties | Up to $10,000 for failure to disclose, and an additional $10,000 for each 30 days of non-filing after IRS notice of a failure to disclose for a potential maximum penalty of $50,000.[q] Criminal penalties may also apply. | Civil penalties for each FBAR violation can be up to $500 for a negligent FBAR violation and up to $10,000 for nonwillful violation. In addition, a person with a willful FBAR violation may be subject to a civil monetary penalty equal to the greater of $100,000 or 50 percent of the amount in the account at the time of the violation, and be subject to possible criminal sanctions.[r] These penalties are per person, per account, and per year. |

Source: GAO analysis of IRS and FinCEN information. | GAO-19-180.

[a]26 U.S.C. § 6038D; 26 C.F.R. §§ 1.6038D-1 to 1.6038D-8.

[b]31 U.S.C. § 5314; 31 C.F.R. § 1010.350.

[c]26 C.F.R. § 1.6038D-2. Filers in this category include those who identify as single, married filing separately, "head of household," or "qualifying widow(er)."

[d]26 C.F.R. § 1.6038D-6.

[e]Resident aliens of the United States are defined at 26 U.S.C. § 7701(b) and the regulations thereunder. The United States does not include possessions and territories for this purpose.

[f]Under 26 U.S.C. § 6013(g), in cases where married couples where one spouse is a U.S. taxpayer and the other is not, the spouse who is a nonresident alien for U.S. income tax classification purposes can elect to be a U.S. taxpayer so the married couple can file a joint tax return. Under 26 U.S.C. § 6013(h), in cases where married couples where one spouse is a U.S. taxpayer and the other is not, the nonresident alien spouse can elect to be a U.S. taxpayer for the full year in which he or she immigrates to the United States so the couple can file a joint income tax return.

[g] 26 U.S.C. § 7701(b) and the regulations thereunder. 31 C.F.R. § 1010.350(b)(2) states: "A resident of the United States is an individual who is a resident alien under 26 U.S.C. 7701(b) and the regulations thereunder." Resident aliens of the United States are defined at 26 C.F.R. § 301.7701(b)- 1, but the definition of the United States is modified to include possessions and territories.

[h] 26 C.F.R. § 1.6038D-2(c)(2). Married individuals filing jointly need only report each jointly owned asset once. If filing separately and other spouses are specified individuals, each includes half of the value when calculating whether the value exceeds the threshold for reporting. If filing separately and only one spouse is a specified individual, the specified individual must include the entire value calculating whether the value exceeds the threshold for reporting.

[i] 31 C.F.R. § 1010.350(e)(1).

[j] 31 C.F.R. § 1010.350(e)(2).

[k] 31 C.F.R. § 1010.350(f). Certain officers or employees of certain federally regulated financial institutions and investment companies and entities with certain listed or registered classes of securities need not report signature or other authority over a foreign account if the officer or employee has no financial interest in the account.

[l] Includes maximum value of specified foreign financial assets (Form 8938) or maximum value of financial accounts maintained by a financial institution physically located in a foreign country (FBAR).

[m] Under FATCA, any income, gains, losses, deductions, credits, gross proceeds, or distributions from holding or disposing of the account are or would be required to be reported, included, or otherwise reflected on a person's income tax return. Under FBAR reporting requirements, a person has signature or other authority if he or she has the authority (alone or in conjunction with another) to control the disposition of money, funds or other assets held in a financial account by direct communication (whether in writing or otherwise) to the person with whom the financial account is maintained.

[n] The account itself is subject to reporting, but the contents of the account do not have to be separately reported.

[o] Assets only must be reported if a person has sufficient ownership or beneficial interest (i.e., a greater than 50 percent interest) in the entity.

[p] Pub. L. No. 114-41, § 2006(b)(11), 129 Stat. 443, 458–459 (2015).

[q] 26 U.S.C. § 6038D; 26 C.F.R. § 1.6038D-8. In addition to the penalty for failure to file Form 8938, taxpayers who fail to report income from such assets on their tax returns are subject to a penalty of 40 percent of the tax due on that income (in addition to the tax on the income). There is no differentiation in the penalty based on willfulness of the failure to file.

[r] For penalties assessed after August 1, 2016, whose associated violations occurred after November 2, 2015, the maximum penalties for negligent, nonwillful, and willful violations are adjusted for inflation. 31 C.F.R. § 1010.821.

# APPENDIX V: KEY DIFFERENCES BETWEEN FATCA INTERGOVERNMENTAL AGREEMENTS AND CRS

## Table 10. Comparison of Key Differences between Foreign Account Tax Compliance Act Intergovernmental Agreements and the Common Reporting Standard

| | Intergovernmental agreements (IGAs) implementing Foreign Account Tax Compliance Act (FATCA) | Common Reporting Standard (CRS) |
|---|---|---|
| Participating jurisdictions(as of October 2018) | 99 —Model 1 IGA jurisdictions<br>14 —Model 2 IGA jurisdictions | 102 —participating jurisdictions |
| Reporting differences | | |
| Reporting nexus for financial institutions | FATCA Model 1 IGA reporting can be based either where the residence of the financial institution is located, or where the financial institution is organized. Under Model 2 IGA reporting, the financial institution reports directly to IRS. | CRS reporting is based only on the laws of the residence of the financial institution. |
| Financial institution registration | IRS generally requires financial institutions to register to obtain a Global Intermediary Identification Number. | No financial institution registration is required. |
| Non-reporting financial institutions | FATCA includes exempt beneficial owners, deemed compliant foreign financial institutions and other categories not in CRS, including:<br><br>• treaty qualified retirement funds.<br>• investment entities wholly owned by exempt beneficial owners.<br>• local banks.<br>• financial institutions with a local client base or only low-value accounts.<br>• sponsored investment entity and controlled foreign corporations. | Similar categories are not present in CRS. CRS does include other non-reporting financial institutions such as:<br><br>• governmental entities.<br>• certain retirement funds.<br>• collective investment vehicles. |

**Table 10. (Continued)**

| | Intergovernmental agreements (IGAs) implementing Foreign Account Tax Compliance Act (FATCA) | Common Reporting Standard (CRS) |
|---|---|---|
| | • sponsored closely held investment vehicles. <br> • investment advisors and investment managers. | |
| Persons subject to reporting | Foreign accounts of U.S. citizens, resident aliens (green card holders), and U.S. residents. | Accounts held by nonresidents of the reporting country. For reporting purposes, a taxpayer may be a resident for more than one country for tax purposes. |
| Nonreportable persons | FATCA has a detailed list setting out each category of nonreportable U.S. persons. The categories are drawn from the FATCA statute and contain U.S.-specific definitions with references to U.S. domestic law. | CRS contains a shorter list of nonreportable persons with nonjurisdiction specific descriptions. |
| Information reported | Financial institutions report the following information only on account holders who are U.S. persons: <br> • name of taxpayer. <br> • address of taxpayer. <br> • taxpayer identification number. <br> • account number. <br> • name and identifying number of financial institution. <br> • account balance. <br> • income and sales proceeds (phased in from 2017). | Financial institutions report on all foreign account holders to the country where they are resident. CRS requires financial institutions to report the same information on account holders as does FATCA, but also requires reporting of information on tax residency, date, and place of birth for all account holders. |
| Due diligence differences | | |
| Due diligence process | Identify whether an account holder is a U.S. person using citizenship and tax residency. Information is required for account holders who are U.S. persons. | Identify the tax residency of each of its account holders. Information is required for all account holders. |

| | Intergovernmental agreements (IGAs) implementing Foreign Account Tax Compliance Act (FATCA) | Common Reporting Standard (CRS) |
|---|---|---|
| Double or multiple residency | This situation is not contemplated under FATCA. | Due to the multilateral context of CRS, in case of double or multiple residency of an account holder (determined on the basis of the due diligence procedures), information will be exchanged with all jurisdictions in which the account holder is found to be resident for tax purposes. |
| Definitional differences | | |

Examples include:

- Debt or equity interests in an investment entity

  - FATCA: Excludes debt or equity interests in an investment entity if the interests are publicly traded, unless the interests are registered on the books of the investment entity (with exceptions).

  - CRS: Does not exclude equity or debt interests in an investment entity from the definition of financial account where the interests are regularly traded on an established securities market, unless the interest is held by a custodial institution.

- Dormant accounts

  - FATCA: A dormant account is reviewed, identified, and reported like any other account.

  - CRS: A dormant account may be treated as an excluded account and thus would not require reporting.

- Financial asset

  - FATCA: IGAs do not provide a definition of financial assets that must be reported by financial institutions.

  - CRS: Financial assets that must be reported by financial institutions include securities, partnership interest, commodities, swaps, insurance or annuity contract, or any interest in such assets.

- Passive nonfinancial entity (NFE)

  - FATCA: Model 1 IGAs do not cover passive NFE investment entities in non-participating jurisdictions, which are subject to a 30-percent withholding tax.

CRS: A passive NFE includes investment entities not resident in participating jurisdictions.

# APPENDIX VI: COMMENTS FROM THE INTERNAL REVENUE SERVICE

DEPARTMENT OF THE TREASURY
INTERNAL REVENUE SERVICE
WASHINGTON, D.C. 20224

DEPUTY COMMISSIONER

February 28, 2019

James R. McTigue
Director, Tax Issues
Strategic Issues Team
U.S. Government Accountability Office
441 G Street N.W.
Washington, DC 20548

Dear Mr. McTigue:

Thank you for the opportunity to review and comment on the draft report, Foreign Asset Reporting: Actions Needed to Enhance Compliance Efforts, Eliminate Overlapping Requirements, and Mitigate Burdens on U.S. Persons Abroad (GAO-19-180).

The information reporting regime for the Foreign Account Tax Compliance Act (FATCA) was enacted in 2010 and, since that time, the filings of the Foreign Bank Account Reporting form have more than doubled. FATCA, combined with enforcement efforts on the part of the IRS and Department of Justice, has drawn attention to the requirements to disclose foreign accounts and report income generated by those accounts. The increased disclosure and reporting demonstrates improved voluntary compliance thus heightening fairness and integrity in the tax system. Specifically, the implementation of FATCA has led to reporting from more than 30,000 foreign financial institutions and 80 tax jurisdictions and made it much harder for U.S. taxpayers to hide assets in offshore accounts and evade U.S. tax on the income generated by those accounts. Indeed, aggregate income statistics suggest that reported foreign-source income increased significantly for individuals disclosing offshore wealth under the FATCA regime.

The enactment and implementation of FATCA also triggered the development of a world-wide data exchange platform and the Organization for Economic Cooperation and Development's Common Reporting Standard (CRS). The account documentation due diligence and reporting rules imposed by CRS on financial institutions mirror those required by FATCA and fortify a global commitment to reduce cross-border tax evasion and create greater tax transparency.

The IRS's implementation of FATCA has been informed by, and is responsive to, stakeholder feedback. Our forms were developed and revised in close coordination with stakeholders, including our FATCA form user group. The collecting and reporting of taxpayer identification numbers (TINs) as part of FATCA reporting posed some challenges for foreign financial institutions and their U.S. taxpayer customers. In response to these concerns, the IRS provided several transition periods and rules to facilitate gathering reliable TIN information.

Throughout these transitions, we have continued to make progress on improving FATCA filing compliance. For example, the FATCA Filing Accuracy campaign will address those entities that have FATCA reporting obligations but do not meet all their compliance responsibilities. Likewise, we are currently in our first foreign financial institution certification cycle, where we are reviewing information submitted by responsible officers regarding their entity's efforts to meet their FATCA obligations.

As part of FATCA implementation, the IRS developed a FATCA Compliance Roadmap in 2013 – a broad strategy document. FATCA is now integrated into our operations and has evolved. Our going-forward strategy for FATCA compliance is part of the Large Business & International (LB&I) Division's overall portfolio management strategy. This is a strategic approach used to manage the compliance efforts and projects under LB&I's jurisdiction through a variety of workstreams, including campaigns and other compliance programs.

Sincerely,

Kirsten B. Wielobob
Deputy Commissioner for
Services and Enforcement

**GAO Recommendations and the IRS Responses to the Draft Report on Foreign Asset Reporting: Actions Needed to Enhance Compliance Efforts, Eliminate Overlapping Requirements, and Mitigate Burdens on U.S. Persons Abroad (GAO-19-180).**

### Recommendation 1:
The Commissioner of Internal Revenue should develop a plan to mitigate risks with compliance activities due to the lack of accurate and complete Taxpayer Identification Numbers of U.S. account holders collected from foreign financial institutions.

### Comment:
The IRS provided a transition period, through the end of 2019, for compliance with the TIN requirements for foreign financial institutions under Model 1 Intergovernmental Agreements (IGAs). During this transition period, we continue to make progress on improving FATCA filing compliance. All financial institutions and foreign tax administrations that file forms reporting accounts as required by FATCA receive a notification listing errors contained in their reporting. The Large Business & International (LB&I) Division follows up with foreign tax administrations regarding these errors to ensure the tax administrations are working with their financial institutions to correct these errors as their governments agreed in the IGAs. We also initiated a campaign addressing foreign financial institutions that do not meet their compliance responsibilities with respect to account opening requirements.

**Recommendation 2:**

The Commissioner of Internal Revenue should ensure that appropriate business units conducting compliance enforcement and research have access to consistent and complete data collected from individuals' electronic and paper filings of Form 8938 and elements of parent individual tax returns. As part of this effort, the Commissioner should ensure that IRS provides clear guidance to the business units for accessing such data in IRS's Compliance Data Warehouse.

**Comment:**

IRS Research, Applied Analytics, and Statistics (RAAS) has been working to obtain read-only access to the Integrated Production Model (IPM) database. The IPM contains the electronic and paper filing information that is the subject of this recommendation. Obtaining read-only access requires Information Technology (IT) resources, as it is a new technical process. We continue to work with IT on the feasibility and timeframe for enabling this access, but limited budgetary resources are delaying implementation.

**Recommendation 3:**

The Commissioner of Internal Revenue should employ a comprehensive plan for managing efforts to leverage Foreign Account Tax Compliance Act (FATCA) data in agency compliance efforts. The plan should document and track activities over time to

- ensure individuals and foreign financial institutions (FFIs) comply with FATCA reporting requirements;
- assess and mitigate data quality risks from FFIs;
- improve the quality, management and accessibility of FATCA data for compliance, research and other purposes; and
- establish, monitor and evaluate compliance efforts involving FATCA data intended to improve voluntary compliance and address noncompliance with FATCA reporting requirements.

**Comment:**

The resources that would be dedicated to update a comprehensive plan unique to FATCA (akin to the FATCA Roadmap) are better spent on the enforcement activities. Plans are underway. Enforcement resources are being used to implement this plan, rather than updating a comprehensive plan to address the four activities identified in this recommendation. LB&I has overall responsibility for these activities and their approach is expected to achieve the broader objective of improving financial institution and U.S. account holder compliance with FATCA.

**Recommendation 4:**

The Commissioner of Internal Revenue Service should assess factors contributing to unnecessary Form 8938 reporting and take appropriate steps to address the issue. Depending on the results of the assessment, potential options may include:

- identifying and implementing steps to further clarify IRS Form 8938 instructions and related guidance on IRS's website on determining what foreign financial assets to report, and how to calculate and report asset values subject to reporting thresholds; and
- conducting annual outreach to educate taxpayers on required reporting thresholds, including notifying taxpayers that may have unnecessarily filed an IRS Form 8938 to reduce such filing.

**Comment:**

The IRS will continue to observe filings of Form 8938 and, to the extent that there are unnecessary filings, assess options to inform account holders to reduce reporting and filing burdens followed by appropriate steps to implement any selected options.

# APPENDIX VII: COMMENTS FROM THE DEPARTMENT OF THE TREASURY

DEPARTMENT OF THE TREASURY
WASHINGTON, D.C. 20220

March 8, 2019

James R. McTigue
Director, Tax Issues
Strategic Issues Team
U.S. Government Accountability Office
441 G Street N.W.
Washington, DC 20548

Dear Mr. McTigue:

We appreciate the opportunity to review the draft report, *Foreign Assets Reporting: Actions Needed to Enhance Compliance Efforts, Eliminate Overlapping Requirements, and Mitigate Burdens on U.S. Persons Abroad (GAO-19-180).*

The Treasury Department and the Internal Revenue Service (IRS) have been leading the implementation of the Foreign Account Tax Compliance Act (FATCA) since its enactment in 2010, with the goal of ensuring the information reporting regime is effective at detecting non-compliance of U.S. persons using offshore accounts or entities while minimizing the burdens on financial institutions and account holders. It is important to note that all U.S. citizens are required to comply with U.S. tax laws, whether resident in the United States or abroad, and that FATCA is a tool to ensure compliance with the existing tax laws and to improve the integrity of our voluntary tax system.

To further reduce the burdens of FATCA compliance, the Treasury Department has worked collaboratively with foreign jurisdictions to implement FATCA through intergovernmental agreements (IGAs). The United States has signed IGAs with 101 jurisdictions, under which partner governments facilitate the collection of financial account information of U.S. persons. An additional 12 jurisdictions have reached agreements in substance with the United States. Since the enactment of FATCA, the IRS has seen an increase in the disclosure of financial accounts and the reporting of income in these accounts by taxpayers.

The Treasury Department and the IRS have continued to work with stakeholders to further refine and reduce burdens of FATCA, including for example, the publication of proposed regulations that would revise existing FATCA guidance to reduce burden (e.g., by eliminating or deferring certain withholding requirements and providing more flexibility regarding certain due diligence requirements). The Treasury Department and the IRS have received positive feedback from stakeholders on these proposals.

The draft report contains a recommendation that the Secretary of Treasury should lead efforts, in coordination with the Secretary of State and Acting Commissioner of Social Securities, to establish a formal means to collaboratively address ongoing issues—including issues accessing financial services and employment and obtaining Social Security numbers—that U.S. persons living abroad encounter from implementation of Foreign Account Tax Compliance Act reporting requirements. (Recommendation 5). While the Treasury Department is not the appropriate agency to lead coordination efforts involving foreign employment issues and issues regarding access to foreign financial services and obtaining Social Security numbers, the Treasury Department is aware of the difficulties that some U.S. citizens residing abroad have raised about the potential effects of FATCA. The Treasury Department will work collaboratively with the State Department and the Social Security Administration to answer questions that Americans abroad have regarding their tax obligations and, where appropriate, to direct U.S. citizens to resources that will help them understand the procedures applied by the Social Security Administration to apply for a Social Security number. As GAO knows, FATCA does not prohibit, restrict or encourage foreign companies or foreign financial institutions to deny employment or services to U.S. persons; however, the Treasury Department will continue to work with the State Department and the Social Security Administration to address these important issues.

Thank you once again for the opportunity to review the draft report. We look forward to continuing to work with you and your office in the future.

Sincerely,

Douglas Poms
International Tax Counsel

# APPENDIX VIII: COMMENTS FROM THE DEPARTMENT OF STATE

United States Department of State
*Comptroller*
Washington, DC  20520
FEB 0 1 2019

Thomas Melito
Managing Director
International Affairs and Trade
Government Accountability Office
441 G Street, N.W.
Washington, D.C. 20548-0001

Dear Mr. Melito:

We appreciate the opportunity to review your draft report, "FOREIGN ASSET REPORTING: Actions Needed to Enhance Compliance Efforts, Eliminate Overlapping Requirements, and Mitigate Burdens on U.S. Persons Abroad", GAO Job Code 102212.

The enclosed Department of State comments are provided for incorporation with this letter as an appendix to the final report.

Sincerely,

Jeffrey C. Mounts (Acting)

Enclosure:
    As stated

cc:    GAO – James R. McTigue, Jr.
       CA/OCS – Michelle Bernier-Toth
       OIG - Norman Brown

**Department of State Comments on GAO Draft Report**

**FOREIGN ASSET REPORTING: Actions Needed to Enhance Compliance Efforts, Eliminate Overlapping Requirements, and Mitigate Burdens on U.S. Persons Abroad (GAO-19-180, GAO Code 102212)**

Thank you for the opportunity to comment on the GAO draft report, *"Foreign Asset Reporting: Action Needed to Enhance Compliance Efforts, Eliminate Overlapping Requirements, and Mitigate Burdens on U.S. Persons Abroad".*

The Department of State, Bureau of Consular Affairs, strives to ensure consular and diplomatic protection to U.S. nationals and U.S. interests abroad. In support of the Department of State USAID Joint Strategic Goal (1) Protect America's Security at Home and Abroad and Goal (4) Ensure Effectiveness and Accountability to the U.S. Taxpayer, the Bureau of Consular Affairs partners with the U.S. Department of the Treasury, the Internal Revenue Service, and the Social Security Administration through our federal benefits and federal obligations programs at U.S. embassies and consulates abroad.

**Recommendations 6: The Secretary of State, in coordination with the Secretary of the Treasury and Acting Commissioner of Social Security, should establish a formal means to collaboratively address ongoing issues- including issues accessing financial services and employment and obtaining Social Security numbers – that U.S. persons living abroad encounter from implementation of Foreign Account Tax Compliance Act reporting requirements.**

Comment: The Department of State concurs with GAO recommendation 6 and welcomes the opportunity to work with the Department of Treasury and SSA to find new channels to improve SSN and ITIN services to U.S. citizens and beneficiaries abroad and reduce barriers to Social Security Number and ITIN adjudication and processing.

# APPENDIX IX: COMMENTS FROM THE SOCIAL SECURITY ADMINISTRATION

SOCIAL SECURITY
Office of the Commissioner

January 14, 2019

Mr. James R. McTigue, Jr.
Director, Tax Issues
Strategic Issues Team
United States Government Accountability Office
441 G Street, NW
Washington, DC 20548

Dear Mr. McTigue,

Thank you for the opportunity to review the draft report, "Foreign Asset Reporting: Actions Needed to Enhance Compliance Efforts, Eliminate Overlapping Requirements, and Mitigate Burdens on U.S. Persons Abroad" (GAO-19-180). Please see our enclosed comments.

Sincerely,

*Stephanie Hall*

Stephanie Hall
Acting Deputy Chief of Staff

**SSA COMMENTS ON THE OFFICE OF THE GOVERNMENT ACCOUNTABILITY OFFICE (GAO) DRAFT REPORT, "FOREIGN ASSET REPORTING: ACTIONS NEEDED TO ENHANCE COMPLIANCE EFFORTS, ELIMINATE OVERLAPPING REQUIREMENTS, AND MITIGATE BURDENS ON U.S. PERSONS ABROAD" (GAO-19-180)**

The original and primary purpose for assigning a Social Security number (SSN) is to allow an employer to uniquely identify and accurately report an individual's earnings covered under the Social Security program and enable us to determine eligibility to program benefits. Our policies for assigning SSNs and issuing Social Security cards are the same for citizens living in the United States or living abroad. We recognize, however, that individuals living abroad may encounter longer wait times to obtain SSNs due to unique challenges related to their countries of residence. We continuously look for opportunities to streamline and improve our SSN issuance process and will work with the Departments of State (State) and the Treasury (Treasury) to ensure individuals eligible for SSNs receive Social Security cards in a timely manner.

Our response to the recommendation is below. We also provided technical comments at the staff level for GAO's consideration.

**SSA's Recommendation 1 -- GAO's Recommendation 7**

In coordination with State and Treasury, establish a formal means to collaboratively address ongoing issues—including issues accessing financial services and employment and obtaining Social Security numbers—that U.S. persons living abroad encounter from implementation of FATCA reporting requirements.

**Response**

We agree.

In: Key Government Reports.                    ISBN: 978-1-53616-001-7
Editor: Ernest Clark                    © 2019 Nova Science Publishers, Inc.

*Chapter 2*

# TAX REFUND PRODUCTS: PRODUCT MIX HAS EVOLVED AND IRS SHOULD IMPROVE DATA QUALITY*

## *Subcommittee on Financial Institutions*

### ABBREVIATIONS

| | |
|---|---|
| ACTC | Additional Child Tax Credit |
| CFPB | Consumer Financial Protection Bureau |
| EITC | Earned Income Tax Credit |
| ERO | Electronic return originators |
| FDIC | Federal Deposit Insurance Corporation |
| Federal Reserve | Board of Governors of the Federal Reserve System |
| FTC | Federal Trade Commission |
| IRS | Internal Revenue Service |

---

* This is an edited, reformatted and augmented version of United States Government
  Accountability Office; Report to Congressional Requesters, Publication No. GAO-19-269,
  dated April 2019.

| OCC | Office of the Comptroller of the Currency |
| Path Act | Protecting Americans from Tax Hikes Act of 2015 |
| SSP | settlement services provider |
| TILA | Truth in Lending Act |

## WHY GAO DID THIS STUDY

American taxpayers spent at least half a billion dollars in 2017 on financial products—issued by banks, through paid tax return preparers—to help them file taxes and get advances or loans against tax refunds.

GAO was asked to review tax-time financial products. Among other things, GAO (1) described market trends and examined IRS data, (2) described characteristics of product users and factors that influence product use, and (3) described product disclosure practices.

GAO reviewed fee and product usage data; conducted a multivariate regression analysis to determine user characteristics; and analyzed disclosures of selected providers that are national chains and those of their bank partners. GAO conducted nongeneralizeable undercover visits of nine randomly selected tax preparers in the Washington, D.C. area to understand how they communicate fees and terms to taxpayers. Preparers were selected to ensure a mixture of regulatory jurisdictions, among other factors. GAO reviewed laws, regulations, and guidance on the products, and interviewed IRS and other government officials and a nongeneralizeable selection of product and service providers, tax preparation companies, consumer groups, and academics.

## WHAT GAO RECOMMENDS

GAO is making two recommendations to IRS to make the collection of product use data more accurate and make data limitations known to users of the data. IRS concurred with both recommendations.

# WHAT GAO FOUND

Trends in the market for tax-time financial products since 2012 include

- the decline of refund anticipation loans (short-term loans subject to finance charges and fees),
- the rise in use of refund transfers (temporary bank accounts in which to receive funds), and
- the introduction of refund advances (loans with no fees or finance charges).

More recent product developments include increased online access to products for self-filers, higher refund advance amounts, the introduction of new products, and for tax year 2019, the reintroduction of fee-based loans.

However, GAO identified some limitations in Internal Revenue Service (IRS) data on product use, including over- or under-counting of certain types of products. IRS has not communicated these data issues to users and has not updated guidance to tax preparers on how to report new product use. As a result, data users (including federal agencies and policymakers) have inaccurate information to inform their findings and decision-making.

Lower-income and some minority taxpayers were more likely to use tax-time financial products, according to GAO analysis of 2017 data from IRS, the Bureau of the Census, and the Federal Deposit Insurance Corporation. Specifically, taxpayers who made less than $40,000 were significantly more likely to use the products than those who made more. African-American households were 36 percent more likely to use the products than white households. Product users tend to have immediate cash needs, according to studies GAO reviewed. For these users, tax-time financial products generally provide easier access to cash and more cash at a lower cost than alternatives such as payday, pawnshop, or car title loans.

GAO's undercover visits with nine tax preparers, its review of selected provider websites, and review of documents obtained from selected banks and tax preparers found disclosures generally followed requirements for disclosing fees. However, disclosure practices by some paid tax preparers may pose challenges for consumers. For example:

- Preparers in GAO's review generally indicated that they present taxpayers with almost all of the documents with fee information after their tax returns have been prepared and the preparers determined the taxpayers qualified for a tax-time financial product. The timing of these disclosures would pose a challenge for taxpayers looking to compare prices for different providers.
- During six of nine undercover visits, GAO investigators explicitly requested literature on product fees but were not provided such information.
- Refund transfer fee information on websites GAO reviewed sometimes was presented only after the tax preparation process started, was in small print, or could be found only after navigating several pages. As a result, taxpayers may face challenges comparing prices.

April 5, 2019

The Honorable Elizabeth Warren
Ranking Member
Subcommittee on Financial Institutions and Consumer Protection
Committee on Banking, Housing, and Urban Affairs
United States Senate

The Honorable Tammy Duckworth
United States Senate

More than 20 million American taxpayers spent at least an estimated half a billion dollars in 2017 on financial products that are based on their anticipated tax refund, according to the National Consumer Law Center. Tax-time financial products, typically offered by banks and made available by providers of tax preparation services, include refund advances and refund anticipation loans (credit products) and refund transfers (deposit product). In fiscal year 2017, the Internal Revenue Service (IRS) processed more than 150 million individual federal income tax returns, and issued almost 120 million refunds totaling almost $383 billion, according to IRS.

You asked us to review trends in the market for tax-time financial products and the transparency of fees charged for these products. This chapter (1) describes trends in the market for tax-time financial products and product fees and examines the reliability of IRS data on these trends, (2) describes characteristics of those who use tax-time financial products and factors that influence their decision to obtain the products, and (3) describes regulatory oversight of industry participants and the disclosure of information on product fees and terms.

To address these objectives, we reviewed relevant federal laws, regulations, and guidance documents from the relevant financial regulators—Consumer Financial Protection Bureau (CFPB), Federal Deposit Insurance Corporation (FDIC), Board of Governors of the Federal Reserve System (Federal Reserve), and the Office of the Comptroller of the Currency (OCC)—the Federal Trade Commission (FTC), and IRS. We interviewed officials from the financial regulators, FTC, and IRS. We also interviewed representatives of various industry participants: five tax preparation providers selected because they are national chains, five banks and settlement service providers selected because they work with the major tax preparation providers, and four consumer advocacy groups and two academic researchers selected to provide a range of perspectives.

To examine trends in the use of tax-time financial products and fees, we analyzed available IRS data from 2008 to 2018 compiled from filed tax returns to determine the types and use of these products. We determined these data have some limitations, as discussed later in the report, but were adequate to suggest general trends when supplemented with other information. To supplement these data, we conducted a literature search and reviewed the websites, promotional materials, and other industry literature and public filings of four providers of online tax preparation services, three tax preparers with physical locations, and four banks to help identify trends in product offerings. The tax preparation firms were selected because they are national tax preparation chains, and the four banks because they partnered with the national tax preparation chains. The information collected from providers is not generalizeable to the population of tax preparers and banks offering these products. To examine trends in product fees, because of limited publicly available industry data we collected fee-related information on product fees, ancillary product fees, tax preparation fees, and aggregate fee data. We collected this information from selected preparers' and banks' websites, advertising materials, and public filings. The fee information is not generalizeable to the population of product and related fees.

To identify characteristics of product users, we used a sample of data on demographic and economic variables from the Bureau of the Census and FDIC from 2011, 2013, 2015, and 2017 to conduct a multivariate regression analysis to determine the relationship between individual characteristics and the decision to obtain a product. We statistically controlled for various income, education, tax-filing, and demographic factors. We used a sample of data from IRS from the 2014, 2015, and 2016 tax years to identify other taxpayer characteristics associated with product use. We determined these data to be sufficiently reliable for the purposes of our analysis by reviewing documentation on and conducting testing of the data for errors. We supplemented this information with a review of literature from government and industry reports on the financial needs of taxpayers, particularly those who obtain these products.

To describe the regulatory oversight of industry participants and the disclosure of information to consumers on tax-time financial products, we reviewed relevant laws and regulations. We reviewed reports and guidance documents from IRS, CFPB, FDIC, Federal Reserve, OCC, and FTC on disclosure of financial product fees and terms. To identify existing issues, we interviewed representatives of industry participants and four consumer advocacy groups selected to provide a range of perspectives.

To review how product terms and fees are disclosed, in February 2018 GAO undercover investigators visited nine randomly selected tax preparers in Washington, D.C., Maryland, and Virginia to inquire about tax-time financial products. We selected locations based on product use and proximity to lower-income households in each location and to ensure a mixture of state laws governing products and service providers. The undercover visits provide illustrative information that is not generalizeable to the disclosure practices of all tax preparers. We also conducted a content analysis of websites of eight tax preparers and five bank providers that offer the products and reviewed consumer-facing disclosures and product agreements from these firms. We selected the tax preparation firms because they are national tax preparation chains, and the five banks because they partnered with these firms. The results of the website content analysis are not generalizeable to the content of all tax preparation firms' websites. Appendix I provides more detail on our scope and methodology.

We conducted this performance audit from July 2017 to April 2019 in accordance with generally accepted government auditing standards. Those standards require that we plan and perform the audit to obtain sufficient, appropriate evidence to provide a reasonable basis for our findings and conclusions based on our audit objectives. We believe that the evidence obtained provides a reasonable basis for our findings and conclusions based on our audit objectives. We conducted our related investigative work in accordance with standards prescribed by the Council of the Inspectors General on Integrity and Efficiency.

## BACKGROUND

### Tax-Time Financial Products

Table 1 provides an overview of tax-time financial products based on information gathered during our review.

**Table 1. Types and Features of Tax-Time Financial Products**

| Product type | Refund advances | Refund anticipation loans | Refund transfers |
|---|---|---|---|
| Availability | • Begins when the Internal Revenue Service (IRS) accepts electronic returns, generally in January, and typically ends on February 28a | • Begins when IRS accepts electronic returns, generally in January, and activity typically ends in March. | • Made available when tax return is filed, generally between January and October |
| Product terms | • Short-term loans<br>• Several loan amounts available from bank provider, taxpayer must qualify (approval and loan amounts based on expected refund)<br>• Secured by expected refund (refund is collateral)<br>• No fees | • Short-term, fee-based loans<br>• Loan amount is up to the refund amount minus tax preparation fees, finance charges, and additional loan and preparation fees<br>• Secured by expected refund (refund is collateral)<br>• Taxpayers responsible for a one-time fee and possibly other charges | • Fee-based temporary bank account set up to receive tax refunds by direct deposit<br>• Taxpayers responsible for one time flat fee |
| Method of payment | • Taxpayer pays no fees; tax preparer generally pays fees to the bank provider | • Fees deducted directly from the loan disbursement | • Fee deducted directly from refund proceeds |
| Timing for receiving funds | • Funds disbursed within 24 hours | • 1-2 days upon loan approval | • Tax refunds deposited to temporary bank account within typical IRS time frames (generally within 21 days from filing)<br>• Taxpayer can receive remaining funds immediately thereafter (depending on method of disbursement) |

Source: GAO analysis of product provider promotional materials. | GAO-19-269.

aRefund advances are generally offered only during the first two months of the tax season. According to two national tax preparation chains, this is because people with cash needs typically file early in the season.

## Participants in the Tax- Time Financial Products Industry

The tax-time financial products industry consists of four main groups of participants: banks, paid providers of tax preparation services, settlement service providers, and software developers.

- Providers of tax preparation services include paid tax return preparers or electronic return originators (ERO).[1] Not all tax preparers are EROs, but because IRS generally requires returns to be filed electronically for tax preparers filing more than 10 returns, tax preparers generally work with or for an ERO that also may be a tax preparer. Paid preparers and EROs offer their services in-person, on the Internet, or through software sold to taxpayers. They generally offer different refund disbursement options to taxpayers and may partner with banks to offer tax-time financial products.

- Software developers provide software needed to file tax returns electronically and offer tax-time financial products through their software to taxpayers. The largest tax preparation companies have their own software that allows them to prepare returns as well as offer tax-time financial products. Applications for the products generally can be completed through the same software used to file the return.

- Banks provide tax-time financial products. They also may approve and process product applications and perform settlement services (discussed below).

- Settlement service providers serve as intermediaries in transactions to deliver tax-time products. They work with banks to accept and process applications for tax products; allocate payments due to paid preparers, other providers, banks, and taxpayers; and provide

---

[1] A tax return preparer is any person who prepares for compensation, or who employs one or more persons to prepare for compensation, all or a substantial portion of any return of tax or any claim for refund of tax under the Internal Revenue Code. 26 U.S.C. § 7701(a)(36). An ERO, which is an authorized IRS e-file provider, originates the electronic submission of the return to IRS. EROs also may act as paid preparers.

distribution instructions to banks. Some banks have affiliates that perform settlement services, and some banks perform these functions themselves.

Figure 1 illustrates the roles of these groups, using the example of a refund transfer transaction.

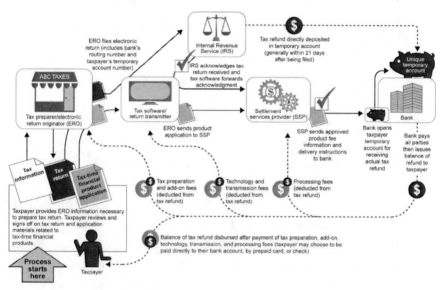

Source: GAO analysis of product provider materials. | GAO-19-269.

Figure 1. Overview of Participant Roles in Providing Refund Transfer Products.

# REGULATORS

## Federal Banking Regulators

The purpose of federal banking supervision is to help ensure that banks throughout the financial system operate in a safe and sound manner and comply with banking laws and regulations in the provision of financial services. At the federal level, banks are supervised by one of the following three prudential regulators and CFPB:

- The Federal Reserve supervises state-chartered banks that opt to be members of the Federal Reserve System, bank holding companies and savings and loan holding companies (and the nondepository institution subsidiaries of those organizations), and nonbank financial companies designated for Federal Reserve supervision by the Financial Stability Oversight Council.

- FDIC supervises all FDIC-insured state-chartered banks that are not members of the Federal Reserve System as well as state savings associations and insures the deposits of all banks and thrifts approved for federal deposit insurance.

- OCC supervises federally chartered national banks, federal savings associations (federal thrifts), and federally chartered branches and agencies of foreign banks.

- CFPB has rulemaking authority to implement provisions of federal consumer financial law and enforces various federal laws and regulations governing consumer financial protection. CFPB also examines banks with more than $10 billion in assets and their affiliates and certain nonbanks for compliance with federal consumer financial laws, accepts consumer complaints on topics such as debt collection and other consumer financial products or services, and educates consumers about their rights under federal consumer financial laws.

FDIC, the Federal Reserve, and OCC are required to conduct a full-scope, on-site risk-management examination of each of their supervised banks at least once during each 12-month period. The regulators may extend the examination interval to 18 months, generally for banks and thrifts that have less than $3 billion in total assets and that meet certain conditions (for example, if they have satisfactory ratings, are well capitalized, and are not subject to a formal enforcement action).[2]

---

[2] 12 U.S.C. § 1820(d)(4); Expanded Examination Cycle for Certain Small Insured Depository Institutions and U.S. Branches and Agencies of Foreign Banks, 83 Fed. Reg. 67033 (Dec. 28, 2018).

The prudential regulators generally conduct consumer compliance examinations every 12–36 months and Community Reinvestment Act examinations every 12–72 months. The specific timing depends on a bank's size and its previous consumer compliance and Community Reinvestment Act rating. But the Dodd-Frank Wall Street Reform and Consumer Protection Act transferred consumer protection oversight and other authorities over certain consumer financial protection laws from multiple federal regulators to CFPB. Additionally, for the transferred laws such as Truth in Lending Act (TILA) and Equal Credit Opportunity Act, CFPB has examination and primary enforcement authority for banks with assets of more than $10 billion and any affiliates of such institutions.[3]

The three prudential regulators also are responsible for supervising for compliance with federal consumer financial laws for insured depository institutions with total assets of $10 billion or less. For example, they examine depository institutions for compliance with consumer financial laws including the Fair Housing Act, the Service members Civil Relief Act, and Section 5 of the Federal Trade Commission Act.

## FTC

FTC can enforce Section 5 of the Federal Trade Commission Act, which prohibits unfair or deceptive acts or practices affecting commerce, and TILA, which seeks to promote the informed use of consumer credit. TILA requires disclosures about the terms and cost of credit and standardizes the manner in which costs associated with borrowing are calculated and disclosed.

FTC can enforce a number of additional statutes against certain entities; they include portions of the Gramm-Leach-Bliley Act, which requires financial institutions, including those providing tax-time financial products,

---

[3] Not all consumer protection statutes were transferred. Some remain within the authority of the prudential regulators, regardless of the bank's asset size. The non-transferred laws include the Fair Housing Act, the Servicemembers Civil Relief Act, and Section 5 of the Federal Trade Commission Act.

to protect consumer data; the Telemarketing and Consumer Fraud and Abuse Prevention Act, which prohibits telemarketers from making misrepresentations in the sale of goods or services, which could include tax-time financial products; and the Military Lending Act, which provides important protections for servicemembers and their dependents seeking and obtaining certain types of consumer credit, including refund anticipation loans.

## IRS

The Office of Professional Responsibility within IRS is responsible for ensuring all tax practitioners (defined as certified public accountants, attorneys, enrolled agents, enrolled actuaries, appraisers, and enrolled retirement plan agents) and other individuals authorized to practice before IRS adhere to regulations relating to Circular 230, which governs practice before IRS.[4]

According to IRS, IRS is neither involved in offering, nor responsible for, tax-time financial products. Nonetheless, IRS stated that it addresses these types of products on its website because it is important for taxpayers to understand the terms of the loan products, which constitute an agreement between them and the third-party lender. Although IRS is not statutorily required to collect data on tax-time products, according to IRS officials, the agency retains information on use of the products. Specifically, IRS compiles information from tax returns that indicates whether the taxpayer also applied for a financial product. IRS also issues guidance to EROs on reporting these data through its *Handbook for Authorized IRS e-File Providers of Individual Income Tax Returns (Pub. 1345)*. IRS makes the usage data publicly available on its website, and provides it on a biweekly basis to industry participants that are members of an IRS working group on security issues. In addition to researchers and consumer advocacy groups,

---

[4] Department of the Treasury, *Regulations Governing Practice before the Internal Revenue Service*, Circular No. 230 (Washington, D.C.: June 2014).

federal entities also use these data, including the National Taxpayer Advocate, who leads IRS's Taxpayer Advocate Service—an independent office in IRS whose objectives include mitigating systemic problems that affect large groups of taxpayers. As industry data on product use are generally limited, agencies and researchers rely on IRS for this information.

## Tax Credits and Protecting Americans from Tax Hikes Act of 2015

Refundable tax credits include the Earned Income Tax Credit (EITC) and the Additional Child Tax Credit (ACTC). The credits are termed refundable because, in addition to offsetting tax liability, any excess credit over the tax liability is refunded to the taxpayer.[5] EITC provides tax benefits to eligible workers earning relatively low wages. For tax year 2018, the maximum EITC amount available was $6,431 for taxpayers filing jointly with three or more qualifying children, and $519 for individuals without children. In 2017, EITC provided more than $65 billion to about 27 million taxpayers. ACTC is the refundable portion of the Child Tax Credit and provides tax relief to low-income families with children.

The Protecting Americans from Tax Hikes Act of 2015 (PATH Act) made several changes to the tax law.[6] One of its provisions stipulates that funds owed taxpayers claiming EITC or ACTC refunds for a tax year cannot be released before February 15 to allow IRS time to review these returns for potential fraudulent activity. This change became effective on January 1, 2017. For the 2018 tax filing season (January through April 2018), refunds for taxpayers who claimed these tax credits were not available in bank accounts or prepaid cards until February 27, 2018.

---

[5] See GAO, *Refundable Tax Credits: Comprehensive Compliance Strategy and Expanded Use of Data Could Strengthen IRS's Efforts to Address Noncompliance*, GAO-16-475 (Washington, D.C.: May 27, 2016) for more information.

[6] The PATH Act was signed into law on December 18, 2015. The provision of this law that restricts when a tax return can be issued was not effective until the 2017 tax filing season for the 2016 tax year.

# IRS DATA ON USE OF TAX-TIME FINANCIAL PRODUCTS HAVE SOME LIMITATIONS, BUT WHEN COMBINED WITH OTHER AVAILABLE DATA SUGGEST PRODUCT OFFERINGS HAVE EVOLVED

IRS data on tax-time financial products for 2016–2018 do not accurately reflect product use and IRS has not updated reporting guidance to tax preparers. IRS data for 2008–2016 and information from industry participants and a consumer advocacy group's reports suggest that trends in the market for tax-time financial products include the decline of refund anticipation loans and that refund transfers became the most used product. Industry data also indicate that product fees for refund transfers increased in 2018; multiple other fees can be associated with tax-time products. New tax-time products and product features continue to be introduced.

## IRS Data for 2016–2018 Do Not Accurately Reflect Product Use and IRS Has Not Updated Reporting Guidance to Tax Preparers

Data collected by IRS are the primary source of information on the use of tax-time financial products and are used by federal entities, policymakers, regulators, researchers, and consumer groups. However, we identified some limitations in the IRS data related to use of refund anticipation loans, refund advances, and refund transfers

### *Two Products Not Differentiated in 2016 and 2017 IRS Data*

First, 2016 and 2017 IRS data may have underreported use of refund advances and overreported refund anticipation loans. IRS officials told us that in 2016 and 2017, IRS made only three indicators available for tax preparers to report tax-time financial products: no bank product, refund anticipation loan, or refund anticipation check (that is, refund transfer). As a result, based on our analysis, it is possible that tax preparers reported refund advances as refund anticipation loans.

According to IRS officials, in 2016, IRS saw a large increase over the prior year in the number of refunds associated with tax-time financial product indicators. The agency performed an internal analysis on these refunds to identify the products being used in the market and found a direct relationship between this increase and new refund advance products. They determined that the original definitions for the indicators did not account for refund advance products.

In 2018, IRS expanded the indicator categories for tax-time financial products to more accurately reflect the products available in the market, including replacing the indicator for refund anticipation loans with two separate indicators for "pre-refund advance products with a fee (RAL)" and "pre-refund advance products with no fees" (most commonly known as refund advances) and adding an open text field to note products not otherwise covered.

Although IRS added another indicator category for refund advances, it has not attached explanatory material to the dataset or otherwise made it known to potential users of the dataset that the 2016 and 2017 data do not distinguish between refund anticipation loans and refund advances. Without explanatory material, users of the data, including the National Taxpayer Advocate and policymakers, could be unaware of the limitations.

## Refund Transfers Also Not Always Reported

Second, since 2016 IRS may have misreported the number of refund transfers. A number of industry experts told us that almost all taxpayers who apply for a refund advance also apply for a refund transfer. However, tax preparers can select only one product indicator when reporting a customer's use of tax-time financial products, according to IRS officials. Consequently, tax preparers can report a refund advance or a refund transfer, but not both. Refund advances were introduced in 2016, so data for the 2016, 2017, and 2018 tax seasons currently are affected. We concluded that IRS data on refund transfer use prior to 2016 are not meaningfully affected because our research shows that from 2012 to 2016, as we discuss later, most product users were using one product, a refund transfer.

IRS officials told us that they had submitted a work request for filing season 2018 to allow tax preparers to select more than one type of product per tax return. The officials said that the request was denied due to competing information technology priorities at IRS.

IRS officials told us that tax preparers instead could use an open text field to indicate more than one product was used. IRS officials told us that the open field originally was created to allow for new product lines that do not fit existing descriptions. However, IRS has not provided additional guidance to tax preparers informing them of the potential alternate use for this field. Similarly, IRS has not informed tax preparers about the 2018 addition of a new indicator for refund advances and it has not updated its Handbook for Authorized IRS E-File Providers of Individual Income Tax Returns (Pub. 1345) on how to accurately code tax-time financial products. Without this additional guidance, tax preparers may continue to inaccurately report tax product information, making it challenging to identify trends and potential concerns with taxpayers' use of these products. Furthermore, IRS has not made this issue known to potential users of the dataset.

A strategic goal from IRS's Strategic Plan (for fiscal years 2018–2022) is to advance data and analytics.[7] Related to data, GAO guidance on assessing the reliability of data states that reliable data can be characterized as being accurate, valid, and complete.[8] In addition, federal internal control standards state that management should internally and externally communicate the necessary quality information to achieve objectives.[9]

---

[7] Internal Revenue Service, Strategic Plan 2018-2022-Publication 3744 (Washington, D.C.: April, 2018)

[8] GAO, *Assessing the Reliability of Computer-Processed Data,* GAO-09-680G (Washington, D.C.: July 1 2009). Reliability means that data are reasonably complete and accurate, meet the intended purposes, and are not subject to inappropriate alteration. Completeness refers to the extent that relevant records are present and the fields in each record are populated appropriately. Accuracy refers to the extent that recorded data reflect the actual underlying information. Consistency, a subcategory of accuracy, refers to the need to obtain and use data that are clear and well defined enough to yield similar results in similar analyses.

[9] GAO, *Standards for Internal Control in the Federal Government*, GAO-14-704G (Washington, D.C.: Sept. 10, 2014).

As a result of the data conflation in 2016 and 2017 for refund advances and refund anticipation loans, ongoing issues with reporting use of refund transfers, and outdated guidance to tax preparers, users of the data (including the National Taxpayer Advocate, policymakers, regulators, researchers, and consumer groups) will have inaccurate information to inform their findings and decision-making.[10]

## Tax-Time Financial Products Have Evolved Since 2012

Despite limitations with IRS data on product use by tax year, our analysis of multiyear trends from these data, supplemented with data collected by the National Consumer Law Center and from Securities and Exchange Commission filings, suggests that use of refund anticipation loans declined, the refund advance was introduced while refund transfers have become the most used tax-time product.

### *Refund Anticipation Loans*

Applications for refund anticipation loans declined sharply from 2010 to 2012, according to IRS data and consumer groups reports. According to a 2010 study, the volume of refund anticipation loans peaked in 2002 with 12.7 million taxpayers.[11] Volume began to decline at a faster rate between 2010 and 2011. According to a report by the National Consumer Law Center and the Consumer Federation of America, banks stopped offering the products in 2012 after the loans came under the scrutiny of federal banking regulators.[12] IRS data continued to show use of refund anticipation loans after 2012 but with banks out of the market for refund anticipation loans, it is unclear what types of financial institutions were offering the loans.

---

[10] While IRS does not use data to monitor tax products, policy makers, regulators, consumer advocates, academics, and other groups use these data to inform policy decisions and monitor changes in the market and how those changes ultimately may affect taxpayers.

[11] Urban Institute, *Characteristics of Users of Refund Anticipation Loans and Refund Anticipation Checks,* (2010); report prepared at the request of the Department of the Treasury.

[12] National Consumer Law Center, *The Party's Over for Quickie Tax Loans: but Traps Remain for Unwary Taxpayers,* (February, 2012); report prepared with contributions from the Consumer Federation of America.

Consumer advocates with whom we spoke agree that nonbank lenders such as payday lenders likely offered the loans; however, we were not able to identify any. The consumer advocates, researchers, and industry participants with whom we spoke also were not able to provide us with any current information about these lenders.

The IRS Taxpayer Advocate Office, the Financial Crimes Enforcement Network, and consumer advocates have long raised concerns about refund anticipation loans.[13] For example, in 2007 the National Taxpayer Advocate expressed concerns about how the loans were offered to consumers and whether consumers adequately understood the product. Consumer advocates questioned the high interest rates the loans could carry, how loan fees reduced EITC benefits taxpayers received, and the ramifications of borrower default. In a 2008 advance notice of proposed rulemaking, IRS and the Department of the Treasury also shared concerns that refund anticipation loans offered tax preparers an incentive to fraudulently inflate refund claims and to market the loans to taxpayers who might not understand the full cost of the product.[14]

Banking regulators raised concerns as well. OCC and FDIC noted consumer protection and safety and soundness risks to banks that offered refund anticipation loans. FDIC encouraged consumers to have tax refunds directly deposited into their own bank accounts and raised concerns about other options that claimed to speed up a refund for a sizable cost, according to FDIC officials. The Office of Thrift Supervision, which had supervisory authority over federal thrifts at the time, ordered a medium-sized thrift to cease making refund anticipation loans in 2010.[15] In part due to concerns

---

[13] See Taxpayer Advocate Service, *2017 Annual Report to Congress* (Washington, D.C.: December 2017). See also Financial Crimes Enforcement Network, *The SAR Activity Review: Trends, Tips and Issues* (Washington, D.C.: August 2004).

[14] *Guidance Regarding Marketing of Refund Anticipation Loans (RALs) and Certain Other Products in Connection with the Preparation of a Tax Return.* 73 Fed. Reg. 1131 (Jan. 7, 2008).

[15] The Office of Thrift Supervision identified issues related to the bank's compliance with advertising regulation and determined the bank had engaged in unfair or deceptive acts or practices in relation to its tax loan program. The Dodd-Frank Wall Street Reform and Consumer Protection Act eliminated the Office of Thrift Supervision and transferred supervisory authorities to OCC for federal savings associations, FDIC for state savings associations, and the Federal Reserve for thrift holding companies and their subsidiaries,

expressed by OCC, national banks stopped offering the loans by 2010 and FDIC-supervised banks stopped offering them by 2012.

An IRS decision also contributed to FDIC enforcement actions on refund anticipation loans. Before 2011, IRS used a tool called the debt indicator that acknowledged whether any of a taxpayer's refund could be used to pay certain outstanding debts.[16] IRS provided the debt indicator to tax preparers at the time the taxpayer's return was filed electronically. Banks used the debt indicator in their underwriting tools to help determine a borrower's likelihood of loan repayment. FDIC determined that without the debt indicator, a bank would have to develop and adopt a more robust underwriting process to make these loans in a safe and sound manner. According to FDIC, IRS's elimination of the debt indicator created a safety and soundness concern because it removed a key data element used for determining a borrower's ability to repay. Losing this information increased the risk of loss for lenders and at that time helped inform FDIC's consent orders with two banks under its supervision to stop offering refund anticipation loans. In 2011 (the first tax season without the debt indicator), the number of returns with a refund anticipation loan indicator reported by IRS decreased to 1.17 million from 6.9 million in the prior year.

IRS data continue to show use of refund anticipation loans after 2012, albeit at a much lower volume. For example, in 2016, IRS data show about 468,500 returns with a refund anticipation loan indicator and in 2017 the number appeared to spike to about 1.7 million.[17] However, as discussed earlier, the data for these two years may be misleading because they likely conflate refund anticipation loans with refund advances. In 2018, IRS created a separate reporting category for refund advances and the 2018 data

---

other than depository institutions. The transfer of powers was completed in July 2011, and the Office of Thrift Supervision officially dissolved in October 2011.

[16] Congress authorizes the Department of the Treasury's Bureau of Fiscal Services to reduce the amount of a tax refund and offset it to pay debts such as delinquent taxes, unpaid child support, or delinquent federally funded student loans.

[17] To determine use for tax-time financial products, we used 2008-2017 IRS data. IRS data are based on the number of accepted returns that include an indicator showing that the taxpayer has applied for a tax product and do not reflect the number of returns that have been approved for the product.

show about 356,000 returns with a refund anticipation loan indicator as of October 2018.

## Refund Transfers

Use of refund transfers—which allow for direct deposit of refund checks through temporary accounts that banks open for taxpayers—far exceeded use of refund anticipation loans and refund advances since 2008, according to IRS data. The number of taxpayers who used a refund transfer more than doubled from 2008 through October 2018 to exceed 21 million. As banks stopped offering refund anticipation loans in 2012, refund transfers (also known as refund anticipation checks) began to increase. Unlike other tax-time financial products generally only available early in the tax season (which generally runs through mid-April), refund transfers are usually available after April.

However, IRS data on refund transfers since 2016 have limitations. Although a refund transfer is not required to get a refund advance, a number of industry experts told us that almost all taxpayers who apply for a refund advance also apply for a refund transfer. But because tax preparers could select only one product indicator when reporting use of tax-time financial products, they could report a refund advance or a refund transfer, but not both. As discussed previously, IRS made changes in 2018 to allow preparers to add information about other product use but has not issued explanatory material about the changes.

## Refund Advances

In 2016, a few banks began offering refund advances to taxpayers. Refund advances are no-fee, nonrecourse loans.[18]

It is difficult to determine usage trends for this product, although available data indicate an increase in use from 2016 to 2017.

---

[18] Nonrecourse loans are not subject to collection action by the bank in the event of a shortage (when the refund is smaller than the anticipated amount).

- First, accurate IRS data on refund advances are not available for 2016 and 2017 because IRS did not provide an option for tax preparers to report refund advance products. As previously discussed, IRS added a separate reporting category for refund advances in 2018. As of October 17, 2018, IRS data show about 1.65 million returns with a refund advance indicator.

- Second, publicly available data from industry and other sources (consumer advocacy and research organizations) are limited. According to data reported by the National Consumer Law Center, major tax preparation companies facilitated the sale of about 365,000 refund advances in 2016. According to industry sources, use increased to about 1.63 million in 2017, when one of the largest tax preparation companies began offering refund advances. Industry data for 2018 were not yet publicly available at the time of this chapter.

- Third, taxpayers often obtain refund advances and refund transfers in tandem. But as discussed previously, IRS reporting indicators did not include an option for reporting use of multiple products until 2018.

Use of refund advances also may have increased in 2017 because tax preparers increased the size of the advances. One lender that offers refund advances to tax preparers told us that the driving factor in demand for refund advances was the available loan amount. The maximum advance amount that tax preparers offered taxpayers in 2016 was $750. In 2017, the maximum increased to $1,300.

Most industry participants and consumer groups told us that they believe that provisions of the PATH Act requiring IRS to delay issuance of EITC or ACTC returns and associated refunds until after February 15 led to an increase in demand for refund advances. They said that the delay puts pressure on taxpayers eligible for EITC or ACTC who depend on getting their refund early in the tax season (a refund advance can help mitigate the impact of this delay). Others stated that an increase in demand due to the PATH Act is possible, but the correlation between the two cannot be determined. One industry provider suggested that increased demand for refund advances also could be the result of marketing by tax preparation companies.

## Limited Public Data Suggest Refund Transfer Fees Generally Increased in 2018

Our analysis of publicly available data about product fees for refund transfers showed that fees increased in 2018. In particular, our analysis of fee data collected by the National Consumer Law Center shows that in 2014–2017 refund transfer fees charged by paid tax preparers remained generally unchanged at between $32.95 and $34.95.[19] According to fee information we were given during our undercover visits, paid tax preparers generally charged their customers $39.95 or $49.95 during the 2018 tax filing season for a refund transfer that sometimes included both federal and state tax refunds. In one case the fee was $65, which included a paper check disbursement. Also in 2018, we found that online providers of tax filing services and software charged online filers who prepared their own returns between $12 and $39.99 for a refund transfer.[20]

According to our analysis, factors that can affect the fee a taxpayer pays for a refund transfer include the following:

- Filing method. Our review of providers' websites shows that taxpayers who filed their own returns online using preparer software

---

[19] From 2014 to 2017, the National Consumer Law Center in partnership with the Consumer Federation of America issued reports on tax-time financial products that included data on the fees charged by major providers for refund transfers. The National Consumer Law Center reports that they obtained this information from the providers' websites, public announcements, and direct communications from the providers.

[20] For fee information—including product fees, fees for ancillary products that taxpayers may have to use related to a tax product, and tax preparation fees—we collected data from multiple sources, including our nine undercover visits. We reviewed information from the websites and product-related literature of eight online tax preparation providers and five banks offering tax-time financial products. Data elements include incentives that banks offer tax preparers related to refund transfers. See appendix I for more information.

paid an average fee of $31.13 in 2018, which was lower than the $39.95 or $49.95 that paid preparers charged their customers.

- Disbursement method. The manner in which the taxpayer chooses to receive a tax refund may affect the fee. For example, our review of industry literature indicates that one bank set the fee at $29.95 if the refund was disbursed to a prepaid card offered by an affiliate vendor or at $39.95 if the refund was directly deposited or disbursed as a check. Another bank gave tax preparers the option to offer a free refund transfer for disbursement onto a prepaid card, $15 for a direct deposit, or $20 for a paper check.

- Incentives offered to tax preparers by banks. Incentives from banks for tax preparers can increase fees for taxpayers. Our review of banks' promotional materials for tax preparers also indicates that some bank providers offer tax preparers different fee structures for a product—that is, the preparers can charge a higher fee to earn a rebate. For example, one bank offered a tax preparer the option to provide a refund transfer to clients for $39 (which includes an $8 incentive paid to the tax preparer) or for $29 (no incentive payment). On their websites, two banks marketed the no-incentive option to tax preparers as a way to be competitive (by offering low-cost options to their customers).

- Using a refund advance. According to a report by the National Consumer Law Center, one bank set a higher fee for a refund transfer if taxpayers also applied for a refund advance. When taxpayers used only a refund transfer, the fee was $29.95 for the federal refund and an additional $9.95 for the state refund, for a total of $39.90. If the taxpayer also applied for a refund advance (a no-fee product), the refund transfer fee was $44.95. Thus, taxpayers paid $5.05 more for a refund transfer if they also received a refund advance.

Our analysis found that, in addition to the product fee, taxpayers may be charged other fees when they use a refund transfer.

- State refund transfer. In some cases, the refund transfer fee covered the deposit of a federal and a state refund. In other cases, the fee only covered the federal refund. In these cases, if the taxpayer received a state refund, the tax preparer charged an additional fee of $10 or $12.
- Disbursement services. According to documentation we reviewed, a tax preparer may charge an additional fee of $25 if taxpayers choose to get their refund as a paper check or $7 for a cash transfer to a third party.
- Prepaid card use. The long-term use of prepaid cards used to disburse a refund may add to the overall cost of getting a tax product. We reviewed cardholder agreements and fee schedules for several prepaid cards commonly used to disburse funds from a tax refund and found they generally carry monthly fees of about $5. The issuer of the prepaid cards also may charge consumers a fee every time they access cash at automated teller machines, deposit more money onto the card, or do not use the card for a certain period of time.
- Software fees. Companies that design tax preparation software may charge a fee or fees associated with the tax product. Taxpayers may pay one or more of these fees when they use a refund transfer to receive their tax refund. The bank deducts these fees from the taxpayer's refund after receiving funds from IRS or the state taxing authority. The fee categories are technology fee (up to $18 in our review), a transmission fee that may be a fixed amount (such as $2) or a variable amount, and a processing fee of $6.

### Comparative Fee Scenarios

To determine how the fees associated with a refund transfer can affect the total tax preparation fees a provider may charge a taxpayer, we reviewed fee data we collected. We then identified the types and totals of fees generally associated with tax products and created four possible scenarios based on this analysis (see Figure 2). We designed two scenarios with online self-filers (taxpayer uses a refund transfer and taxpayer does not use a refund transfer) and two scenarios with paid preparers performing the filing (taxpayer uses a refund transfer and taxpayer does not use a refund transfer).

| | | | Online self-filers | | Paid tax preparer | |
|---|---|---|---|---|---|---|
| | | | No tax product | Refund transfer | No tax product | Refund transfer |
| Fees | Additional | Refund transfer | N/A | $31.13 | N/A | $48.96 |
| | | Transmission | N/A | N/A | N/A | $2.00 |
| | | Technology | N/A | N/A | N/A | $18.00 |
| | | Processing | N/A | N/A | N/A | $6.00 |
| | | Disbursement[a] | N/A | N/A | N/A | $18.00 |
| | | **Subtotal** | **$0.00** | **$31.13** | **$0.00** | **$92.96** |
| | | Paper check (optional)[b] | N/A | N/A | N/A | $25.00 |
| | | **Subtotal** | **$0.00** | **$31.13** | **$0.00** | **$117.96** |
| | Tax preparation | Document handling | N/A | N/A | $20.00 | $20.00 |
| | | Electronic filing | $0.00 | $0.00 | $10.00 | $10.00 |
| | | State | $27.60 | $27.60 | Data unavailable[d] | Data unavailable[d] |
| | | Federal[c] | $30.85 | $30.85 | $192.50[e] | $192.50[e] |
| | | **Subtotal** | **$58.45** | **$58.45** | **$222.50** | **$222.50** |

Source: GAO analysis of industry data. | GAO-19-269.

Note: We collected fee information during our undercover visits. The additional fees in these scenarios are included for illustrative purposes and may not always be charged. A tax preparer may add other fees not included here. Our undercover work did not include online self-filing. Therefore, we were unable to determine if a software provider would charge additional fees after completing the tax return but before transmitting the electronic return to the taxing authority (federal, state, or both).

[a]The disbursement fee is an add-on fee charged by a paid tax preparer. [b]Check cashing fees may apply.

[c]To determine the tax preparation fees, we used the average starting cost for tax preparation we were quoted during our undercover visits. Paid tax preparers generally do not share information on tax preparation fees, because these fees are typically based on a taxpayer's unique tax circumstances. For online self-filers, the software provider generally offers a free option to file a simple federal tax return which is generally limited based on the type of income, deductions or credits used and does not include the cost of filing a state return. For the online self-filing fee in this illustration, we used the average starting cost for all other simple tax preparation services as shown on several online tax preparation websites.

[d]Fees for filing a state return were not discussed during our undercover visits because our fictitious taxpayers had recently moved to the area from a state that does not assess state taxes. In one case we were told the preparation fee included both federal and state filing.

[e]During our undercover visits, tax preparers gave us a range from $93 to $500 and stated that fees were based on the specifics of the return.

Figure 2. Illustrative Example of Refund Transfer Fees Based on Filing Method and Use of Product.

## Tax-Time Financial Products Have Continued to Evolve Since 2016

Recent and emerging developments in the market for tax-time financial products include higher loan amounts and new products, according to our analysis of selected tax preparers' websites and marketing materials, and information we were given during our undercover visits. For example, in 2018 refund advances became available to online filers. They previously were offered only to taxpayers who obtained paid tax preparation services in person (at a "storefront").[21]

The maximum amount for a refund advance has continued to increase. In 2016, the maximum loan amount available to a taxpayer was $750. In 2018, the maximum loan amount available was $3,250 and for 2019, one preparer has offered an advance of up to $3,500. One industry participant told us that the industry in general is in a race to increase borrowing limits to remain competitive and attract more customers.

In 2018, banks offered a new product that combines the features of a refund anticipation loan and a refund advance. The product allows the taxpayer to apply for a refund advance (up to a fixed amount) with no fee or finance charges, the option to apply for an additional loan with a fee (similar to a refund anticipation loan), or a combination of the two products known as a hybrid. For 2018, two banks offered this additional loan (not to exceed $1,000) at an annual percentage rate of 29.9 percent.

For 2019, one bank offered taxpayers the option of a no-fee advance of up to $1,000, or an interest-bearing loan of $2,000, $3,000, or $5,000 based on the expected refund. The interest-bearing loans would carry an annual percentage rate of 26.07 percent in addition to a fee of $30–$75, depending on the loan amount. Also for 2019, one national tax preparation company has offered the option of a no-fee advance of up to $3,500 or a fee-based

---

[21] To identify trends in products offerings in the tax-time financial products industry, we reviewed the websites and available literature for four providers of online tax preparation services, three tax preparers with physical locations, and four banks. We also met with nine product providers such as software developers and providers of settlement services and discussed changes in the market and product offerings. See appendix I for more information.

advance of up to $7,000, which would carry an annual percentage rate of 35.9 percent.

In addition, demand for refund transfers has increased among online self-filers. As more people file their own tax returns by using web-based software, the number of refund transfers used by self-filers may continue to increase.[22] Because few tax preparers offer refund advances to online self-filers, taxpayers are still more likely to get a refund advance from a paid tax preparer.[23]

Finally, issues relating to the applicability of TILA disclosure requirements to refund transfers could affect the market for tax-time products. According to representatives of two consumer advocacy organizations, deferment of tax preparation fees until the refund is received constitutes an extension of credit; therefore, refund transfers should be treated as loan products. Tax preparers and a policy research and education organization with whom we met do not believe that refund transfer fees meet the definition of a loan.

Should regulators decide that a refund transfer constitutes an extension of credit, and would therefore be a credit transaction with a finance charge, refund transfers would become subject to provisions of TILA. These changes could affect taxpayers' access to this product as well as product pricing. According to Securities and Exchange Commission filings of some tax preparers, if refund transfers were successfully characterized as such, the additional requirements and costs could limit their ability to offer these products to clients.

Refund advances were promoted by providers as a fee-free, interest-free credit product, and thus TILA disclosure requirements are generally not considered applicable for them. However, new interest-bearing credit products announced for 2019 may be subject to consumer protection regulations.

---

[22] According to IRS, the percentage of self-prepared e-filers increased 0.5 percent in 2017 from the prior year, and another 3.3 percent in 2018.

[23] According to our analysis of selected online tax preparation providers and interviews with industry participants, at least three online providers offered refund advances in the 2018 tax season.

# LOWER-INCOME AND SOME MINORITY TAXPAYERS WERE MORE LIKELY TO USE TAX-TIME FINANCIAL PRODUCTS FOR VARIOUS REASONS

## Our Analysis Found That Lower-Income, African-American, and Single Taxpayers Were More Likely to Use Tax-Time Financial Products

Using FDIC data, we conducted a multivariate regression analysis to examine the relationship between economic and demographic variables and tax-time financial product use. This approach allowed us to test the significance of the relationships between each variable and the likelihood of using tax-time financial products, while controlling for other factors.[24]

### *Income-Related Characteristics*

Lower-income households were more likely to use tax-time financial products than higher-income households, particularly when they used paid tax preparers to file their taxes, according to our analysis of 2017 FDIC data.[25] More specifically, we estimated that households with incomes between $20,000 and $39,999 were more likely to use tax-time financial products to receive their tax refunds more quickly through paid tax preparers than households with incomes of $60,000 or more.[26]

---

[24] Specifically, we estimated multivariate logistic regression models to assess the statistical significance of the relationships between individual characteristics and the decision to obtain a tax-time financial product. We used logistic regression models because our dependent variable is binary (that is, represents whether or not a household used a product). See appendix II for more information, including limitations.

[25] Federal Deposit Insurance Corporation, *2017 FDIC National Survey of Unbanked and Underbanked Households* (Washington, D.C: October 2018). Our econometric analysis of the survey data controlled for several variables, including household type, children, race and ethnicity, education, age, and homeownership. We observed 798 households that used these products in the 2017 survey year, representing about 2.4 percent of households (plus or minus 0.2 percentage points). That is the benchmark utilization rate against which the results should be interpreted. See appendix I for more information on the analysis design, and see appendix II for more information on this analysis.

[26] According to the Census Bureau, the median household income in 2017 was $61,372.

For example, we estimated that households with incomes between $20,000 and $29,999 were 34 percent more likely to use tax-time financial products than households with incomes of $60,000 or more;[27] and

- households with incomes between $30,000 and $39,999 were 61 percent more likely to use the products than households with income of $60,000 or more.[28]
- Moreover, our analysis of FDIC data suggests that households that received EITC were more likely to use tax-time financial products, compared to households that did not receive EITC.[29]

Our results also suggest that wealth, as measured by homeownership, was associated with the household decision whether to use tax-time financial products. Homeowners were 34 percent less likely to use tax-time financial products than non-homeowners, controlling for other factors.

## Other Characteristics, Including Race, Age, and Household Head

Households of some minority groups were more likely to use tax-time financial products when filing tax returns than white households. For example, using FDIC data, we estimated that African-American households

---

[27] All reported estimates from our econometric analysis of 2017 FDIC data are statistically significant at the 10 percent level or less. See appendix II for confidence intervals associated with estimates from this analysis.

[28] The estimates for households with incomes of $20,000–$29,999 and $30,000–$39,999 are not statistically significantly different from each other. Our analysis of FDIC data is subject to limitations. For example, our analysis used a relatively small number of observations of households that used tax-time financial products and focuses on consumers who accessed tax-time financial products to receive their tax refunds more quickly through paid tax preparers. Consumers also may access the products when self-filing online to cover the cost of the tax preparation. Moreover, our results may not generalize to other time periods. Characteristics associated with use of the products may differ with product type. We were not able to account for community characteristics that may influence the decision to use tax-time financial products through paid tax preparers.

[29] In 2017, households had to have incomes of $53,930 or less to qualify for EITC, depending on tax filing status and number of dependents.

were 36 percent more likely to use tax-time financial products than white households after controlling for other factors. Other research (a 2013 study) found that African Americans were more likely to use refund anticipation loans than white individuals.[30]

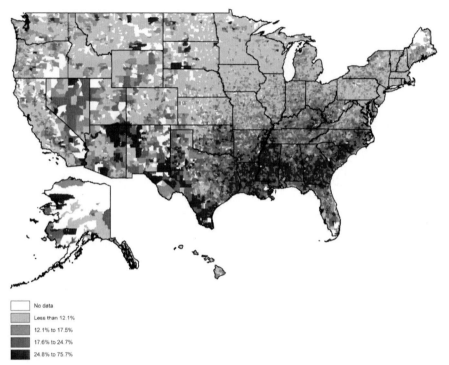

| | |
|---|---|
| | No data |
| | Less than 12.1% |
| | 12.1% to 17.5% |
| | 17.6% to 24.7% |
| | 24.8% to 75.7% |

Source: GAO analysis of IRS Statistics of Income data: MapInfo (map). | GAO-19-269.
Notes: Zip code data are based on population data filed and processed by the Internal Revenue Service during the 2016 tax year. Zip codes with less than 100 tax returns are excluded.

Figure 3. Proportion of Tax Returns with Tax-Time Financial Products in 2016, by Zip Code.

---

[30] Signe Mary McKernan, Caroline Ratcliffe, and Daniel Kuehn, "Prohibitions, Price Caps, and Disclosures: A Look at State Policies and Alternative Financial Product Use," *Journal of Economic Behavior and Organization*, vol. 95 (November 2013).

According to our analysis of 2016 IRS data, which included information about tax-time financial product use and locality, use of tax-time financial products was more concentrated in some areas of the South and the West (see Figure 3).[31]

Our analysis of FDIC data further suggests that other characteristics associated with use of tax-time financial products include age and household type. For example, households headed by younger persons (15–39 years old) were more than twice as likely to use the products as households headed by older persons (60 or older), controlling for other factors.

Households headed by single adults with families were more likely to use tax-time financial products than households headed by married couples.[32] For example, according to our analysis of FDIC data, we estimated that households headed by unmarried females with families were 76 percent more likely to use tax-time financial products than households headed by married couples, controlling for other factors. Using IRS data from 2016, we found that a higher proportion of product users filed as unmarried heads of household, compared to the general tax filing population. Among those who used tax-time financial products, about 39 percent filed as single, 22 percent filed as married, and 37 percent as unmarried heads of household.[33]

---

[31] We analyzed the share of tax returns with tax-time financial products at the zip code level using 2016 IRS Statistics of Income data.

[32] Households headed by single adults with families are single persons with children or dependents.

[33] By comparison, about 46 percent of all taxpayers who filed their taxes electronically filed as single, 35 percent filed as married, and 16 percent filed as unmarried heads of household, according to IRS. The remaining taxpayers filed using other statuses, including widowed. IRS data from 2016 are representative of the population of taxpayers who filed their taxes electronically in tax year 2016. Tax-time financial product use is measured as having used a product or none. In contrast to FDIC data, which only include households that accessed tax-time financial products through paid preparers, IRS data include taxpayers who accessed products through paid tax preparers and by self-filing taxes online. See appendix II for additional information. All percentage estimates from 2016 IRS data have margins of errors of plus or minus 1 percentage point or less.

## Reasons for Using Refund Products Include Obtaining Cash Faster and Not Paying Tax Preparation Fees Up Front

Reasons to use tax-time financial products include more quickly obtaining cash from the expected tax refund, not having to pay tax preparation fees out of pocket, and obtaining cash more cheaply than with alternative short-term funding options, according to our review of federal and industry reports.[34]

### *Quick Access*

Taxpayers generally might have to wait weeks for refunds from IRS:

- Taxpayers who file paper returns can expect to receive their refund about 6–8 weeks after the date on which IRS receives their return, according to IRS guidance.
- Taxpayers who file electronically generally can expect to receive their refunds within 21 days, or faster if they opt to have refunds deposited directly into their bank accounts.
- As previously discussed, IRS must delay payments of refunds on which EITC, ACTC, or both are claimed until at least February 15 of each year. Effectively, the refunds might not be disbursed to bank accounts (or prepaid cards) of tax filers until the end of the month.

In contrast, users of tax-time products can obtain cash very quickly. For example, refund advance recipients generally receive loan funds within 24 hours of applying, and in some instances within the same hour they apply, according to selected tax preparer documents and websites that we reviewed. Refund transfer products also allow those who do not have the option of directly depositing refunds into a temporary account instead of waiting longer to receive a paper check. According to our analysis of IRS data from

---

[34] We reviewed federal government and industry reports on alternative financial products and on the financial needs of individuals with characteristics similar to those of taxpayers who used the products.

2016, tax-time financial product users were more likely than other taxpayers to receive their tax refunds by direct deposit.

---

**Free Filing Services**

The Internal Revenue Service (IRS) offers the following free filing services:
Fillable forms. IRS offers forms that can be completed online and electronically submitted to IRS. The forms are available without age, income, or residency restrictions.

Free file software. IRS, in partnership with the Free File Alliance (members of the tax software industry), provides free online filing options to eligible taxpayers. Twelve leading tax software providers make a version of their products available exclusively at IRS.gov for taxpayers with an adjusted gross income up to $66,000 (in 2018).

Volunteer Income Tax Assistance. The program provides free basic income tax preparation with electronic filing by IRS-certified volunteers to qualified individuals, including to persons who earn $55,000 or less, have disabilities, or have limited proficiency in English.

Tax Counseling for the Elderly. The program provides free tax preparation by IRS-certified volunteers to all taxpayers, particularly those 60 or older. Program volunteers specialize in pension and retirement-related issues unique to seniors.

Source: GAO analysis of IRS information. | GAO-19-269

---

Taxpayers may use tax-time financial products because they need cash quickly. Studies we reviewed found that product recipients tend to have pressing financial obligations. One study's review of available literature from 2010 found that product recipients tend to live paycheck to paycheck or lack sufficient savings to cover prior, current, or future spending.[35] Another study published in 2010 found that recipients use the products to pay for pressing financial obligations, both expected and unexpected, and for their tax preparation. According to the study, many users of tax-time

---

[35] Brett Theodos, Rachel Brash, et al., *Who Needs Credit at Tax Time and Why: A Look at Refund Anticipation Loans and Refund Anticipation Checks* (Washington, D.C.: Urban Institute, November 2010).

products become delinquent on rent, utilities, and other expenses during the winter with the expectation that they will be able to pay obligations after receiving tax refunds.[36] As one study found, the annual tax refund represents the largest single cash infusion received all year by about 40 percent of checking account holders.[37]

## Tax Preparation Fees Not Paid Out of Pocket

Lower-income taxpayers also use tax-time financial products to defer payment of fees related to tax return preparation, according to federal government and industry reports that we reviewed. Tax preparation fees vary greatly based on the tax forms used, including the EITC worksheet. One of the largest national tax preparation chains reported that its average tax preparation fee was between $205 and $240 in 2017.

Consumers may perceive any costs associated with tax-time financial products and tax return preparation as lower than they actually may be because the costs are not paid out of pocket. Fees for the products and tax return preparation are deducted from the refund before it reaches the consumer. In general, studies have found that the transparency of a payment method affected the payer's willingness to spend.[38] One consumer advocacy organization representative posited that paying for tax-time financial products and tax preparation from a refund makes consumers less sensitive to the real cost of tax-time products and preparation services.

Instead of using tax-time financial products to defer payment of tax preparation fees, lower-income taxpayers can access free filing services

---

[36] Urban Institute, *Characteristics of Users of Refund Anticipation Loans and Refund Anticipation Checks*, (Washington, D.C.: 2010).

[37] Diana Farrell, Fiona Greig, and Amar Hamoudi, *Deferred Care: How Tax Refunds Enable Healthcare Spending*, (JPMorgan Chase Institute: January 2018).

[38] Frank van der Horst and Ester Matthijsen, "The Irrationality of Payment Behavior," *DNB Occasional Studies*, vol. 11, no. 4 (2013). According to this report, a more transparent payment method increases the pain of making the payment and decreases the amount the payer is willing to spend.

through several IRS programs (see sidebar). However, these options do not allow taxpayers to use tax-time financial products to access refunds faster.

IRS estimates that about 70 percent of taxpayers are eligible to access its free filing software, and we estimated about 3 percent of taxpayers use this service. According to IRS officials, while IRS does not have a marketing budget to promote the free file programs, the predominant reason so few taxpayers use them is because there are many free tax preparation options on the market, such as tax preparation software.

## Higher Refunds and Tax Preparation Assistance

Taxpayers also may use paid tax preparers because they do not think they can fill out tax returns on their own, believe that preparers will help them receive higher refunds, or both, according to federal government and industry reports we reviewed. For taxpayers who did not use tax-time financial products, we did not find a clear association between paid tax preparation and higher average refunds. On the other hand, for taxpayers who used tax-time financial products, we found that average tax refunds were higher for taxpayers who filed through paid tax preparers than for taxpayers who self-filed online (see Table 2). According to IRS data, nearly all taxpayers who used refund loan products filed their taxes through paid tax preparers, as refund advances were not available online until the 2018 tax filing season. There may be various reasons for the association between higher refunds, paid tax preparation, and product use. Those who use tax-time financial products tend to be eligible for tax credits such as EITC, which can increase the size of tax refunds. Fifty-four percent of EITC claimants used a paid preparer. However, a 2017 study found that the combination of paid tax preparation and tax-time financial product use was associated with relatively high incorrect tax payments (specifically, overpayments of EITC compared to online self-filing and product use or no product use).[39]

---

[39] Maggie R. Jones, *Tax Preparers, Refund Anticipation Products, and EITC Noncompliance* (Washington, D.C.: Center for Administrative Records Research and Applications, U.S. Census Bureau, December 2017).

**Table 2. Average Refund Amounts, by Tax Filing Methods
and Tax-Time Product Usage, 2014–2016**

|  | 2014 | | 2015 | | 2016 | |
|---|---|---|---|---|---|---|
|  | Self-prepared online | Practitioner prepared | Self-prepared online | Practitioner prepared | Self-prepared online | Practitioner prepared |
| No tax-time financial product | $2,103 | $2,028 | $2,029 | $2,108 | $2,548 | $2,168 |
| Tax-time financial product | $3,359 | $3,954 | $3,340 | $4,044 | $3,255 | $4,064 |

Notes: The table presents average refund amounts by tax filing method and tax-time financial product use. Differences in average refund amounts across tax-time financial product use are statistically significant with the exception of self-prepared taxes online in 2016. Differences in average refund amounts across tax filing methods are statistically significant with the exception of tax refunds with no tax-time financial product in 2016. Statistical significance is measured at the 5 percent level, meaning the difference in estimates is significant at the 95 percent confidence level.

Furthermore, our analysis of IRS data found that taxpayers who used tax-time financial products received higher refunds on average than those who did not use tax-time financial products, regardless of tax filing method—although other factors might explain this association. For example, taxpayers who have high refunds have a greater incentive to use the products than taxpayers who have relatively small refunds or owe taxes.

## Tax-Time Financial Products Cheaper Than Alternatives

For lower-income taxpayers, tax-time products generally provide more cash at a lower cost than other small-dollar loan alternatives such as payday loans, auto title loans, and pawnshop loans, according to our review of federal government and industry reports.[40] The amounts of alternative loan

---

[40] Users of tax-time financial product were more likely to use other alternative financial services to obtain short-term infusions of cash, as suggested by our analysis of 2017 FDIC data. We found a significant correlation between households that used tax-time financial products and households that used services, such as nonbank check cashing, nonbank money orders, payday loans, and pawnshops.

products are based on the value of the collateral the consumer provides. Average loan amounts are $150 for pawnshops, about $500 for payday loans, and under $1,000 for automobile title loans, according to industry statistics and CFPB and other studies. In contrast, refund advances were offered for up to $3,250 for the 2018 tax filing season.

Furthermore, the alternative products generally include fees, unlike refund advances. For example, fees for payday loans generally range from $10 to $30 per $100 borrowed. Automobile title lenders generally charge a fixed price per $100 borrowed, with a common fee limit of 25 percent of the loan per month. In contrast, refund advances are offered at no cost to the consumer.

Tax-time financial products also may be easier to access because, unlike alternative loans, they generally can be obtained without regard to credit history. However, tax-time financial products generally are only available during tax season.

Loans provided by nonfinancial companies (often called FINtech firms) are another source of short-term financing. However, FINtech firms generally provide much larger loan amounts than tax-time financial products, and include fees, unlike refund advances.

## PROVIDERS WE REVIEWED GENERALLY DISCLOSED REQUIRED INFORMATION BUT SOME DISCLOSURE PRACTICES MAY HINDER CONSUMER DECISION-MAKING

The federal banking regulators oversee banks that offer tax-time financial products and IRS sets standards of practice for certain service providers (including some tax preparers). While our nongeneralizeable review found that selected banks and tax preparers generally followed existing OCC and IRS disclosure requirements, some tax preparers' disclosure practices may present challenges for consumers trying to compare product options.

# Industry Participants Are Subject to Varying Levels of Oversight

## *Banks and Settlement Service Providers*

FDIC, the Federal Reserve, or OCC are responsible for the safety and soundness supervision of banks within their authority (which offer tax-time financial products) and may have supervisory authority over third-party service providers (which provide settlement services). We identified five banks that partnered with several national tax preparation chains in recent years to offer tax-time financial products (refund transfers and refund advances). Of the five banks, FDIC supervised one medium-sized and one small bank, OCC supervised two medium-sized banks, and Federal Reserve supervised one medium-sized bank.[41]

As previously discussed, FDIC, the Federal Reserve, and OCC are to conduct full-scope, on-site risk-management examinations of each of their supervised banks at least once in each 12–18 month period. FDIC officials told us that its regular safety and soundness examinations may include an examination of the bank's tax-time financial product offerings. OCC officials told us that they examine tax-time financial products in every annual examination of the banks they supervise that offer these products.

Because the five banks each has total assets of less than $10 billion, the three regulators also are responsible for enforcing compliance with federal consumer financial laws (such as TILA and the Electronic Fund Transfer Act) that govern disclosure requirements for certain tax-time financial products. Officials from the regulators told us that they received few complaints about tax-time financial products offered by their supervised banks. We discuss the disclosure requirements and compliance with the requirements in more detail later in this section.

The regulators' consumer compliance examiners also may review a bank's tax-time financial products—if, for example, a bank offers a new

---

[41] For the purpose of this report, small banks are banks with less than $1 billion in assets. Medium-sized banks are those with average assets of at least $1 billion and less than $10 billion. Large banks have $10 billion or more in assets on average.

product or there are a number of consumer complaints about a current product. Examiners employ a risk-focused approach with a focus on consumer harm in selecting products to evaluate for compliance with applicable consumer laws and regulations. Furthermore, compliance examiners may decide, based on the potential for consumer harm and a bank's compliance management system, that there is enough residual risk to scope the product into the examination. FDIC officials said that a bank with a lot of activity in the market for tax-time financial products would have to assure examiners that it had performed appropriate due diligence.

Regulators also can take other oversight actions, ranging from enforcement to raising awareness among consumers. In 2015, CFPB took an enforcement action, along with the Navajo Nation, to ban an owner of four tax preparation franchises from the market and levy civil penalties for understating refund anticipation loan rates and deceiving customers about the status of their tax refunds.[42] Our search of CFPB's complaint database did not identify any consumer complaints on tax-time financial products. CFPB published a blog post in February 2018 that describes the different tax-time financial product options and the process for obtaining them, and cautions consumers to consider all fees, charges, and timing associated with the products.[43]

FTC staff we interviewed told us that supervision authority over many financial services providers has been given to CFPB, but that FTC still has the authority to enforce many financial statutes and rules, including rules administered by CFPB.[44] FTC brought an enforcement action in 2017 against an online tax preparation provider alleging that it failed to secure consumer accounts. FTC officials also told us that, while they received

---

[42] Consumer Financial Protection Bureau, "CFPB and Navajo Nation Take Action to Stop an Illegal Tax-Refund Scheme" (Washington, D.C.: Apr. 14, 2005): see https://www.consumerfinance.gov/about-us/newsroom/cfpb-and-navajo-nation-take-action-to-stop-an-illegal-tax-refund-scheme// Downloaded on December 17, 2018.

[43] Consumer Financial Protection Bureau, "Tax Refund Tips: Understanding Refund Advance Loans and Checks" (Washington, D.C.: Feb. 13, 2018). Accessed online on February 15, 2018, at https://www.consumerfinance.gov/about-us/blog/tax-refund-tips-understanding-refund-advance-loans-and-checks/.

[44] CFPB and FTC have a memorandum of understanding that involves coordinating enforcement actions over consumer financial products and services, which may include tax-time financial products.

numerous complaints on tax-related issues, FTC's complaint database does not separately classify complaints based exclusively on tax-time financial products.[45]

FTC also has issued guidance to educate consumers regarding tax-related scams and other consumer protection issues that arise during tax time, and to businesses, including tax professionals, to help them detect cyber threats. FTC also co-sponsors a series of educational events for consumers and businesses surrounding tax identity theft awareness week.

## Software Developers

Software companies we interviewed stated that they are subject to IRS regulations relating to electronic filing of tax returns. Software developers provide tax software to tax preparers so that they may file tax returns electronically and assist taxpayers in obtaining tax-time financial products. One software company told us that this involves working with IRS to ensure that returns can be electronically submitted, IRS can receive data, and the software is in compliance with IRS's required data schemas.

## Tax Return Preparers

IRS officials said that IRS does not monitor or have direct oversight authority over tax-time financial products, but requires some paid tax preparers to meet standards of practice or other requirements. The extent to which IRS has oversight over paid preparers depends partly on whether the preparer is a tax practitioner or unenrolled preparer.Tax practitioners are subject to regulations (Circular 230) that establish standards of practice.[46] For

---

[45] According to FTC officials, FTC's complaints about tax-related issues overwhelmingly are composed of reports about government imposter scams, namely IRS impersonators who tried to trick consumers into sending the scammers money for taxes they did not owe. In addition, FTC's complaint database received thousands of complaints in 2018 relating to issues with tax preparers.

[46] Circular 230 (Regulations Governing Practice before the Internal Revenue Service) also established penalties for noncompliance.

example, practitioners must return tax records to clients, exercise due diligence in preparing tax returns, and submit records and requested information to IRS in a timely manner. IRS officials told us that they monitor the suitability of these practitioners and their adherence to the rules.

Additionally, certain tax practitioners known as enrolled agents generally are required to pass a three-part examination and complete annual continuing education, while attorneys and certified public accountants are licensed by states but are still subject to Circular 230 standards of practice if they represent taxpayers before IRS.

Alternatively, unenrolled preparers—the remainder of the paid preparer population and the majority of paid preparers—generally are not subject to these requirements. In 2011, IRS issued final regulations to establish a new class of registered tax return preparers to support tax professionals, increase confidence in the tax system, and increase taxpayer compliance. However, the U.S. District Court for the District of Columbia ruled in 2013 and the U.S. Court of Appeals for the District of Columbia Circuit affirmed in 2014 that IRS lacked sufficient authority to regulate all tax preparers.[47] IRS officials also told us that all authorized IRS e-file providers have to follow certain requirements to be able to file tax returns electronically.

### Banks and Tax Preparers in Our Review Generally Followed Guidance for Disclosing Product Fees, but All Related Fees Were Not Always Disclosed Clearly or Early in Process

We found selected authorized IRS e-file providers generally followed the requirements established by IRS on the disclosure of product fees, and banks generally followed the disclosure guidance relating to tax-time

---

[47] Loving v. I.R.S., 917 F. Supp. 2d 67 (D.D.C., 2013) aff'd 742 F.3d 1013 (D.C. Cir., 2014). In 2014, IRS issued a Revenue Procedure that stated until Congress provides the Department of the Treasury and IRS with legislative authority to regulate tax preparers, IRS has established a program to encourage tax return preparers that are not attorneys, certified public accountants, or enrolled agents to improve their knowledge. Rev. Proc. 2014-42 (2014). The U.S. Court of Appeals for the District of Columbia upheld the program in 2018. Am. Inst. of Certified Pub. Accountants v. I.R.S., 746 Fed. Appx. 1 (D.C. Cir., Aug. 14, 2018).

financial products issued by OCC.[48] (We conducted nongeneralizeable reviews of website content, industry documents, and disclosures made during our undercover visits.) Two of the five banks we reviewed are regulated by OCC. One of the two FDIC-supervised bank and the Federal Reserve-supervised bank told us that they voluntarily follow OCC guidance.

More specifically, IRS established the following disclosure requirements for authorized IRS e-file providers, generally known as EROs, that relate to tax-time financial products:

- EROs must obtain taxpayers' written consent before disclosing any tax return information to other parties in relation to an application for a tax product.
- EROs must ensure taxpayers understand that if they use a tax product, the refund will be sent to the bank and not to them.
- If taxpayers choose to use a fee-based loan, EROs must advise that the product is an interest-bearing loan and not an expedited refund.
- EROs must advise taxpayers that the bank may charge them interest, fees, or both, in the case of any shortages on the refund.
- EROs also must disclose all deductions to be made from the expected refund and the net amount of the refund.[49]

In 2015, OCC issued risk-management guidance for national banks that offer tax refund-related products. This guidance advises that banks should specify to customers, as applicable, the total cost of the tax product, separately from the tax preparation cost;

---

[48] OCC guidance is provided in *Tax-Refund Related Products: Risk Management Guidance*, Bulletin 2015-36, IRS requirements are issued in *Handbook for Authorized IRS e-file Providers of Individual Income Tax Returns*, Publication 1345, Rev. 04-18,

[49] United States. Dept. of the Treasury. Internal Revenue Service. *Publication 1345: Handbook for Authorized IRS e-file Providers of Individual Tax Income Tax Returns*, 2019. Web. This guidance applies to firms accepted to participate in IRS e-file, which include EROs, transmitters, and software developers involved in e-file activities. Because our review did not include an assessment of the tax preparation process, we were not able to make observations on IRS requirements related to consent or disclosure of all deductions from the refund.

- that total costs will be deducted from and reduce the refund amount;
- that tax refunds can be sent directly to the taxpayer without the additional costs of a tax product;
- that customers with deposit accounts can receive their refund without incurring fees through direct deposit in about the same time as it would take to receive a tax refund-related product;[50] and
- the ongoing periodic maintenance and transaction fees related to any product intended for long-term use.

In addition, OCC's guidance establishes that banks should clearly disclose all material aspects of the product in writing before the consumer applies or pays any fees for a tax-time financial product.

Also, representatives of the American Coalition for Taxpayer Rights, a group representing the leading tax preparation, tax software, and bank providers, told us that its members signed a joint statement with attorneys general from six states on disclosure practices for refund transfers.[51] The member providers agreed to explain to taxpayers the different options for filing and receiving a tax refund, including no-cost options, and the associated costs and features of each option. The providers also agreed to disclose the optional nature of the products, the timing of the refund, and to present the disclosures in a clear and conspicuous manner understandable by a reasonable consumer.

Our nongeneralizeable review of documents received from selected banks and tax preparers found disclosures generally followed OCC guidance or IRS requirements, respectively. However, our review of these documents and selected tax preparer websites also found—and our undercover visits of

---

[50] Specifically, a refund transfer does not accelerate receipt of a refund for taxpayers with a bank account who can direct IRS to directly deposit the refund. Taxpayers may receive funds within 24 hours of filing a return only when they apply for a loan that is collateralized against the expected refund, such as a refund advance or a fee-based refund anticipation loan when available.

[51] The American Coalition for Taxpayers' Rights is an industry group representing leading banks and tax preparation and tax software companies which together provide the majority of tax-time financial products. This joint statement was signed by some of the leading companies and attorneys general from the states of Colorado, Kansas, Kentucky, Mississippi, Rhode Island and Utah.

selected tax preparers suggested—that the level of transparency on product fees varied and product fees and information were not always clearly disclosed.

- Bank documents were more likely than information provided by paid preparers (in person or online) to include more disclosures about the fees and terms of tax-time financial products. For example, of the 12 bank documents we reviewed, all disclosed that funds would be sent to the bank if the taxpayer used a tax product. Almost all the bank documents disclosed the fees associated with the product and all disclosed that the fees would be deducted from the refund. In contrast, while written disclosure is not required, less than one third of ERO documents disclosed that the taxpayer using a tax-time financial product would receive funds from the bank instead of IRS.

- However, almost all the documents are presented to taxpayers after returns have been prepared and preparers have determined that taxpayers qualified for a product. The timing of when a tax preparer makes these disclosures would pose a challenge for taxpayers looking to compare prices for different providers. That is, they would not learn of the total fees—partly because the paid preparer could not determine the amount of some tax preparation fees until well into the preparation of the tax return.

- A taxpayer trying to determine the cost of using a tax refund to pay for online tax preparation services only would be able to compare the prices of two of the eight online providers we reviewed. The remaining six did not disclose this fee in a prominent way—with some disclosures made in small print or requiring navigation through several pages after the product page—or at all.

- A taxpayer choosing to file taxes using the services of a paid tax preparer in a brick-and mortar-location, and opting to use the refund to pay for tax preparation fees, would be unlikely to be able to compare prices among different providers.[52] For example, during six of our undercover visits, our investigators explicitly requested literature on product fees. However, the preparers stated that they did not have the literature available or only provided us with business cards and other promotional material.

Our analysis shows that providers do not consistently explain products or disclose fees to taxpayers. For example, providers told us, and industry documents show, that a refund transfer is not required to get a refund advance. However, during our site visits, tax preparers tied the use of a refund transfer to a refund advance four out of five times. In two of these cases, the tax preparer included the fee for a refund transfer as part of processing an advance product, while in another two cases the tax preparer said that a refund transfer was required with the advance. Also, during our site visits, three of the nine tax preparers did not disclose the cost of a refund transfer.

Appendix III provides more information on our analysis of bank and tax preparer disclosure practices.

According to industry participants, only taxpayers expecting a refund can qualify for a tax product; consequently, the tax preparer generally cannot determine whether the taxpayer qualifies until after the tax return is completed. Once this is determined, the tax preparer must request the taxpayer's consent to offer a tax product.[53] EROs with whom we met told us they may disclose fee information at various points throughout the process of tax preparation, and do so verbally or through their in-store computer

---

[52] During our undercover visits, three of nine tax preparers did not disclose the fee for using the refund to pay for tax preparation fees. Six preparers disclosed it in a manner that was not clear or accurate: In three of the six cases, the preparer included products the taxpayer did not request. In the other three cases, the preparer stated tax preparation fees would be paid from the refund without explaining this was an optional service.

[53] An ERO must obtain taxpayers' consent to disclose their tax information to a financial institution in connection with an application for a tax-time financial product.

interface. Bank disclosures are provided to the taxpayer before the product application has been submitted.[54]

Some researchers and representatives from consumer advocacy organizations with whom we met were concerned about the timing of disclosures of tax-time financial product fees. Consumer advocates said disclosures given to taxpayers were inadequate, unhelpful, or timed in such a way as to prevent meaningful comparison shopping. Specifically, one consumer advocacy organization said that taxpayers they serve do not understand the fees associated with filing through preparers. Representatives from another consumer advocacy organization said that taxpayers do not know the total cost for tax-related financial products and services until they already have taken steps to file their returns. In its 2017 Report to Congress, the National Taxpayer Advocate recommended that IRS require all e-file participants offering tax-refund financial products to provide a standard "truth-in-lending" statement to help taxpayers better understand the terms of the refund anticipation loan product.[55] IRS did not adopt the National Taxpayer Advocate's recommendation but agreed that e-file providers should be transparent about the costs associated with the loan products offered to taxpayers as part of the return preparation process.

As previously discussed, courts have determined that IRS does not have sufficient authority to regulate individuals who are solely tax preparers and not licensed by IRS—in effect, the majority of the paid preparer population.[56] Previously, we asked Congress to consider legislation granting IRS the authority to regulate paid tax preparers, if it agreed that significant

---

[54] Because refund advances do not carry finance charges and refund transfer fees have not been legally defined as finance charges, TILA disclosure requirements do not apply to these products.

[55] National Taxpayer Advocate, *Annual Report to Congress*, 2017. (Washington, D.C.: December 2017).

[56] Any tax professional who is compensated for preparing a federal tax return must obtain an IRS Preparer Tax Identification Number (PTIN). While PTIN holders are authorized to prepare federal tax returns, only enrolled agents are licensed by the IRS. Enrolled agents are subject to a suitability check and must pass a three-part Special Enrollment Examination, which is a comprehensive exam that requires them to demonstrate proficiency in federal tax planning, individual and business tax return preparation, and representation. They must complete 72 hours of continuing education every 3 years.

paid preparer errors existed.[57] As of March 2019, this Congressional action we have recommended remains open. The lack of consistency about the timing of fee disclosures for tax-time financial products may add to the rationale for Congress to consider regulating preparers. Such statutory authority could allow IRS to require that tax preparers make tax-time financial product disclosures or ensure meaningful transparency in the sale of the products.

## CONCLUSION

For lower-income taxpayers with pressing financial obligations, tax-time financial products can offer an alternative to higher-cost short-term products such as payday loans. Taxpayers can purchase tax-time financial products from many tax preparers; however, according to our review of selected tax preparers and banks, the price and associated fees of these products can vary. And disclosure practices by some paid tax preparers may pose challenges for consumers looking to compare prices for different providers.

IRS is an essential source for data on tax-time financial products, but to date IRS has offered limited options to tax preparers for accurately reporting usage of all available tax-time products. Furthermore, IRS has not informed tax preparers about changes made in reporting options and has not informed users of IRS's product data about known issues with the data. Consequently, data on product usage are not reliable. Improving the quality of data collected on these products would help ensure that federal agencies, policymakers, regulators, consumer advocacy groups, and researchers have quality information to report on tax policy and consumer protection issues and inform their decision-making.

---

[57] See GAO, *Paid Tax Return Preparers: In a Limited Study, Preparers Made Significant Errors,* GAO-14-467T (Washington, D.C.: Apr. 8, 2014)

## RECOMMENDATIONS FOR EXECUTIVE ACTION

We are making a total of two recommendations to IRS.

The Commissioner of Internal Revenue Service should communicate data issues regarding the refund anticipation loan indicators for tax years 2016 and 2017 and the refund transfer indicators since tax year 2016—for example, by attaching explanatory material to the dataset. (Recommendation 1)

The Commissioner of Internal Revenue Service should improve the quality of tax-time financial product data collected; for example, by allowing authorized e-file providers to indicate more than one type of tax-time financial product for each return or by informing tax preparers of the addition of new product definitions and instructions on how to accurately code the products. (Recommendation 2)

## AGENCY COMMENTS AND OUR EVALUATION

We provided a draft of this chapter to IRS, FDIC, Federal Reserve, OCC, CFPB, and FTC for review and comment. IRS provided written comments, which are reproduced in appendix IV and discussed below. FDIC, Federal Reserve, OCC, CFPB, and FTC provided technical comments, which we incorporated as appropriate.

In its comments, IRS concurred with both recommendations, and described how it planned to address them. In response to our first recommendation, IRS stated that it plans to provide the appropriate notations with the datasets. In response to our second recommendation, IRS stated that it plans to pursue programming changes and clarify instructions for tax return preparers to promote accurate coding of refund-related products. We believe that these actions, if implemented, would address our recommendations and improve the quality of data IRS reports on these products.

As agreed with your offices, unless you publicly announce the contents of this chapter earlier, we plan no further distribution until 30 days from the report date. At that time, we will send copies to the appropriate congressional committees and IRS, FDIC, Federal Reserve, OCC, and FTC.

Michael Clements
Director, Financial Markets and Community Investment

# APPENDIX I: OBJECTIVES, SCOPE, AND METHODOLOGY

This chapter (1) describes trends in the market for tax-time financial products and product fees and examines the reliability of IRS data on these trends, (2) describes characteristics of those who use tax-time financial products and factors that influence the decision to obtain the products, and (3) describes regulatory oversight of industry participants and the disclosure of information on product fees and terms.

To examine trends in the use of tax-time financial products, we used 2008–2018 Internal Revenue Service (IRS) data compiled from tax filings to determine the types and use of these products.[58] We assessed the reliability of these data by interviewing IRS officials about the controls and quality assurance practices they used to compile these data. We determined the data alone did not provide a reliable count of refund transfers, refund anticipation loans, or refund advances in 2016, 2017, and 2018, but were adequate to suggest general trends when supplemented with other information. To supplement the IRS data, we collected information from reports issued by the National Consumer Law Center, reviewed Securities and Exchange Commission filings for two selected tax preparers, and interviewed representatives from National Consumer Law Center and both tax preparers on the offerings of tax-time financial products. We selected

---

[58] IRS data on product use are based on the number of returns that include an indicator showing that the taxpayer applied for a tax-time financial product, and do not reflect product applications that have been approved.

these preparers because they are major providers of tax preparation services and tax products.

To identify and review trends in product offerings, we reviewed the websites, promotional materials, and other industry literature including Securities and Exchange Commission filings of a nongeneralizeable selection of four providers of online tax preparation services, three tax preparers with physical locations that also offer services online, and four banks. We also discussed changes in the market and product offerings with nine of the industry providers with whom we met. We accessed provider websites before and during the 2018 tax season. The tax preparation firms were selected because they are national tax preparation chains, and the five banks were selected because they partnered with the national tax preparation chains and major developers of tax preparation software. In addition, we reviewed studies related to these products published by GAO, federal agencies, four consumer advocacy and research groups, and two academic researchers. We used these studies primarily to corroborate findings from our data analysis. We focused on studies from 2010 and later; however, we also reviewed an older report to gain a greater understanding of how the market for tax-time financial products evolved. We identified these studies through expert recommendations and citations in studies.

To examine trends in fees for tax-time financial products, we collected fee-related information from several different sources (because of limited publicly available industry data). All of the information cannot be used to generalize our findings to the retail tax preparation industry.

- Product fees. For 2018, we collected information on product fees from six paid tax preparers and four banks. For tax years 2014 to 2017, we used product fee information as reported by the National Consumer Law Center. For 2018, we also reviewed fee data from six providers of online tax preparation software, two that provide services in person and online, and four that only provide services online. We selected these providers after conducting internet searches and reviewing reports by consumer advocates and federal agencies. Data elements included fees for refund transfers and refund advances. For 2018, data elements also included the dollar amount for the incentives banks offered tax preparers for each refund transfer sold.

- Ancillary product fees. We collected information on ancillary product fees from four tax preparers, four banks, and three software developers for tax years 2017 and 2018. Data elements included fees for disbursement methods such as prepaid cards and paper checks and other charges related to the use of a tax-time financial product such as technology and transmission fees.
- Tax preparation fees. We collected information on tax preparation fees from eight tax preparers with physical locations and eight online providers of tax preparation services for 2018. Data elements included fees for federal and state filing.
- Aggregate fees. We collected aggregate tax-time financial product, ancillary product, and tax preparation fee information from studies issued by consumer protection advocates.

We collected the above information from websites, advertising materials, and public filings with the Securities and Exchange Commission of tax preparers, banks, and software developers.

To identify some of the demographic and economic characteristics of product users, we used data from the Bureau of the Census and the Federal Deposit Insurance Corporation (FDIC) from 2011, 2013, 2015, and 2017 to conduct a multivariate regression analysis to determine the influence of individual characteristics on the decision to obtain a product. We statistically controlled for various income, education, and demographic factors. While the FDIC data contain a rich set of demographic and economic variables, they include limited data on characteristics specifically related to tax filing. To identify specific tax-filing characteristics associated with product use, we also used a probability sample of data from IRS from the 2014, 2015, and 2016 tax years to calculate the percentages of taxpayers who used tax-time financial products according to various tax-filing characteristics, including tax filing status and tax filing method. We also used the sample data to calculate the percentage of taxpayers who used free filing services, including free file software, programs, and fillable forms. We reviewed documentation on and conducted testing of the data we used and determined they were sufficiently reliable for reporting economic, demographic, and tax-filing characteristics associated with product use. For more detailed information on our analysis of characteristics associated with tax-time financial product use, see appendix II.

To better understand user characteristics associated with the decision to obtain a tax-time financial product identified by our analysis, we reviewed relevant federal and industry reports on the financial needs of individuals with characteristics similar to taxpayers who obtained these products. We focused on reports from 2010 and later. We also reviewed our prior studies and studies from the Consumer Financial Protection Bureau (CFPB) on alternative credit products and compared their features and fees to those of tax-time financial products. In addition, we interviewed representatives from consumer groups, four Low-Income Taxpayer Clinics, and IRS's Taxpayer Advocate Service to obtain their perspectives on characteristics associated with tax-time financial product users.

To describe the regulatory oversight of industry participants associated with tax-time financial products, we reviewed relevant federal laws and regulations, and reports and guidance documents from IRS and federal regulators, including the CFPB, FDIC, the Board of Governors of the Federal Reserve System, Office of the Comptroller of the Currency (OCC), and Federal Trade Commission. We inquired about consumer complaint data related to tax-time financial products at the federal regulators and interviewed officials from the federal agencies and representatives from five tax preparation providers, five banks and bank affiliates such as settlement service providers, four consumer advocacy organizations, three software developers, two researchers, one provider of alternative financial services, and one industry group to gain their perspectives on the benefits and risks of the tax-time financial products and how any related concerns were being addressed. The tax preparation firms were selected because they are national tax preparation chains, and the five banks and three software developers were selected because they partnered with the national tax preparation chains. The four consumer advocacy organizations, two researchers, alternative financial service provider, and industry group were selected for their experience and to provide a range of perspectives.

To review how product terms and fees are disclosed by tax preparers, in February 2018 GAO investigators acting in an undercover capacity visited a nongeneralizeable sample of nine randomly selected tax preparers in Washington, D.C., Maryland, and Virginia to inquire about tax-time financial products. We selected the two states and Washington, D.C. to ensure a mixture of state and local laws governing the products and providers. From the two states and Washington, D.C., we selected one metropolitan statistical area based on the concentration of product users and the proximity to lower-income households. We randomly selected three individual tax preparers in each of the three metropolitan statistical areas to visit, based on proximity to taxpayers in lower-income households and to ensure a mixture of urban and rural communities and company sizes. We visited offices of large tax preparation chains and single-office tax preparation businesses. Results cannot be used to generalize our findings to the retail tax preparation industry. Our investigators posed as taxpayers seeking tax preparation services who wanted to pay for the tax preparation fees with the expected refund or obtain an advance based on their anticipated tax refund. They requested available documents associated with tax preparation, refund advance and refund transfer products, and different disbursement options and fees. Because GAO investigators did not experience the tax preparation or the product application process, we were not able to assess the timing of any disclosures typically made after the tax return preparation process would begin. In addition, we received some consumer-facing disclosures and product agreements that were typically provided during the product application process from two tax preparers and two banks.

We also conducted a content analysis of websites of eight selected tax preparers that offer tax-time financial products. The tax preparers were selected as national providers of tax preparation services with an online presence, and the results are not generalizeable to the retail tax preparation industry. Three of the providers offer tax preparation services online and through physical retail locations and five of the providers offer their services online only. We reviewed these websites to understand the extent to which they disclose fees to the taxpayer for tax preparation services, tax-time financial products, disbursement, and additional products or services, and to review the ease with which these disclosures are accessible.

In addition to consumer-facing disclosures we received from providers with whom we met, we searched online for additional disclosures provided by the tax preparers and banks in our review and reviewed seven disclosures from two national tax preparation chains and 12 disclosures from five banks offering tax-time financial products. We then compared the disclosures against IRS and OCC requirements for disclosure for product terms and conditions. IRS established certain disclosure requirements for authorized IRS e-file providers.[59] OCC instructs banks it supervises to make certain disclosures to product consumers.[60] More specifically, we analyzed tax products and fee disclosures obtained from our undercover visits of selected tax preparers, online reviews, and directly from tax preparers and banks to determine the type and timing of disclosures made in these instances and whether they were consistent with IRS disclosure requirements and followed OCC guidance.

We conducted this performance audit from July 2017 to April 2019 in accordance with generally accepted government auditing standards. Those standards require that we plan and perform the audit to obtain sufficient, appropriate evidence to provide a reasonable basis for our findings and

---

[59] The e-file providers must obtain taxpayers' consent before disclosing any personal tax information to other parties in relation to a product application; ensure taxpayers understand that if using a tax product, refund will be sent to the bank and not to them; if a taxpayer chooses to use a fee-based loan, advise that product is an interest-bearing loan and not an expedited refund; advise taxpayers that the bank may charge them interest or fees (or both) in case of any shortages on the refund; and disclose all deductions to be made from the expected refund and net refund amount. IRS requirements are issued in *Handbook for Authorized IRS e-file Providers of Individual Income Tax Returns*, Publication 1345, Rev. 04-2018.

[60] Banks are to specify to customers that the total cost of the tax-time financial product is separate from the tax preparation cost; the total costs will be deducted from and reduce the refund amount; tax refunds can be sent directly to the taxpayer without the additional costs of a tax product; customers with deposit accounts can receive their refund without incurring fees through direct deposit in about the same time that it would take to receive a tax refund-related product; and that there are costs and terms related to long-term use of product. OCC guidance is provided in *Tax-Refund Related Products: Risk Management Guidance*, Bulletin 2015-36,

conclusions based on our audit objectives. We believe that the evidence obtained provides a reasonable basis for our findings and conclusions based on our audit objectives. We conducted our related investigative work in accordance with standards prescribed by the Council of the Inspectors General on Integrity and Efficiency.

# APPENDIX II: ANALYSIS OF CHARACTERISTICS ASSOCIATEDWITH TAX-TIME FINANCIAL PRODUCT USE

This technical appendix outlines the development, estimation, results, and limitations of the econometric model and other data analysis we described in the report. We undertook this analysis to better understand the characteristics associated with the decision to obtain a tax-time financial product.

## Data

### *Federal Deposit Insurance Corporation*

To assess the characteristics associated with tax-time financial product use, we used data from the Federal Deposit Insurance Corporation's (FDIC) National Survey of Unbanked and Underbanked Households for 2011, 2013, 2015, and 2017, which is a supplement of the Current Population Survey. We used the following variables on households and heads of households to examine how various demographic and economic characteristics are related to the use of tax-time financial products:

- Household income.
- Household type.
- Homeownership status.
- Race and ethnicity of the head of household.

- Educational attainment of the head of household.
- Age of the head of household.
- Head of household has children.
- Household used refund anticipation loan or a tax preparation service to receive a tax refund faster than the Internal Revenue Service (IRS) would provide it in the past 12 months. This is a dummy variable, which equals 1 if the household used products and 0 otherwise.
  - o A refund anticipation loan is a tax-time financial product. Based on our interviews and other research reports, refund anticipation loans and other tax-time financial products (including refund anticipation checks) may be used by consumers to get their tax return faster than IRS could provide it. We refer to this variable as "used tax-time financial product" for simplicity in the report, and we explain the relevant caveats and limitations below.
  - o This variable is the basis for the sample used for this analysis.

See Table 3 for the estimated distributions of these variables for all households, as well as households that used tax-time financial products in 2017.

We also examined the relationship between the use of tax-time financial products and being unbanked, as well as the association between using tax-time financial products and alternative financial services (those offered outside the banking system). We used additional data from FDIC's National Survey of Unbanked and Underbanked Households on the following variables:

- Household used other alternative financial services in the past 12 months, including nonbank check cashing, nonbank money orders, payday loans, and pawn shops.
- Household used prepaid card(s) in the past 12 months.
- Household was unbanked in the past 12 months.

## Table 3. Characteristics of Households and Heads of Households, 2017

| Household characteristics | | Estimated percentage of population | Estimated percentage of population that used tax-time financial products |
|---|---|---|---|
| Income | Less than $10,000 | 6.6 | 7.7 |
| $10,000 to $19,999 | | 10.3 | 12.3 |
| $20,000 to $29,999 | | 10.6 | 12.9 |
| $30,000 to $39,999 | | 11.5 | 16.9 |
| $40,000 to $49,999 | | 8.2 | 8.4 |
| $50,000 to $59,000 | | 8.1 | 8.4 |
| More than $60,000 | | 44.6 | 33.5 |
| Household type | Married couple | 47.4 | 36.2 |
| Unmarried male-headed family | 5.1 | 6.7 | |
| Unmarried female-headed family | 11.8 | 22.9 | |
| Single male | 16.9 | 17.7 | |
| Single female | 18.8 | 16.5 | |
| Homeownership | Homeowner | 63.9 | 44.4 |
| Non-homeowner | 36.1 | 55.6 | |
| **Head of household characteristics** | | | |
| Race/ethnicity | White, non-Hispanic | 66.7 | 55.6 |
| African American, non-Hispanic | 12.7 | 20.6 | |
| Asian, non-Hispanic | 4.9 | 5.8 | |
| American Indian/Alaska Native, non Hispanic | 0.8 | 1.0 | |
| Hispanic, any race | 13.5 | 15.6 | |
| Mixed race/other, non-Hispanic | 1.5 | 1.5 | |
| Education | Less than college education | 35.2 | 37.9 |
| Some college education or more | 64.8 | 62.1 | |
| Age | 15–29 years | 12.8 | 23.2 |
| | 30–39 years | 17.0 | 25.6 |
| | 40–49 years | 16.9 | 18.3 |
| | 50–59 years | 18.9 | 15.6 |
| | 60 years and older | 34.3 | 17.3 |
| Children | Has own children | 26.7 | 37.5 |
| | Has no own children | 73.3 | 62.5 |
| Sample size | 33,561 | | |
| Estimated population size | 123 million | | |

Source: GAO analysis of Federal Deposit Insurance Corporation data. | GAO-19-269.

Notes: We used data from the 2017 Federal Deposit Insurance Corporation's National Survey of Unbanked and Underbanked Households. The sample size is 33,561, representing an estimated population of about 123 million. Of the households sampled, 798 used tax-time financial products, representing an estimated population of about 3 million, and 32,372 did not use the products, representing an estimated population of about 118 million. We estimated that 2.4 percent of households used the products, plus or minus 0.2 percentage points. The first column is the estimated percentage of households and heads of households in the sample, conditional on being part of various demographic subgroups. These statistics are weighted using household-level weights. All estimates in the first column have relative standard errors of about 12.5 percent or less. The second column is the estimated percentage of households and heads of households who used tax-time financial products in the past 12 months, conditional on being part of various demographic subgroups. These statistics are also weighted using household-level weights. Estimates in the second column generally have relative standard errors of about 20 percent or less, with the exception of American Indian/Alaskan Natives and mixed race/other non-Hispanics due to relatively small sample sizes, but estimates for these subgroups are statistically significant.

See Table 4 for estimated distributions of household responses to questions related to unbanked status and usage of other alternative financial services for all households, as well as households that used tax-time financial products in 2017.

## *IRS*

To further identify tax-filing characteristics associated with tax-time financial product use and trends, we also used data from a probability sample of 2 percent of all electronically filed tax returns from IRS for tax years 2014, 2015, and 2016. In 2016, the sample size was 2,952,418, representing a population of 147,625,598 tax returns. According to IRS, the sample is representative of all electronically filed tax returns for the relevant tax years. In this sample, IRS provided data on the following variables:

- Tax filing method, including online (self-filed using tax software) or through a paid practitioner (including tax preparers with physical storefronts).
- Taxpayer used free filing services from IRS, including the Free File program and free fillable forms.
- Tax filing status, including single, married, and head of household.
- Disbursement options for tax refunds (direct deposit or paper check) or tax balance due.
- Tax refund amount.

**Table 4. Household Responses to Questions Related to Unbanked Status and Alternative Financial Services Usage, 2017**

| | | Estimated percentage of population | Estimated percentage of population that used tax-time financial products |
|---|---|---|---|
| Used nonbank check cashing in past 12 months | Used | 6.2 | 15.5 |
| | Did not use | 92.2 | 84.4 |
| | Did not know/refused to answer | 1.6 | 0.0 |
| Used nonbank money order in past 12 months | Used | 14.0 | 32.7 |
| | Did not use | 84.2 | 67.3 |
| | Did not know/refused to answer | 1.7 | 0.0 |
| Used payday loan in past 12 months | Used | 1.8 | 7.9 |
| | Did not use | 96.6 | 92.0 |
| | Did not know/refused to answer | 1.7 | 0.1 |
| Used pawn shop in past 12 months | Used | 1.5 | 6.7 |
| | Did not use | 96.9 | 93.3 |
| | Did not know/refused to answer | 1.6 | 0.0 |
| Used prepaid card in past 12 months | Used | 9.5 | 21.4 |
| | Did not use | 88.9 | 78.4 |
| | Did not know/refused to answer | 1.6 | 0.2 |
| Unbanked in past 12 months | Unbanked | 3.9 | 5.4 |
| | Banked | 89.4 | 85.2 |
| | Did not know/refused to answer | 0.4 | 0.1 |

Source: GAO analysis of Federal Deposit Insurance Corporation data. | GAO-19-269.

Notes: We used data from the 2017 Federal Deposit Insurance Corporation's National Survey of Unbanked and Underbanked Households. The sample size is 33,561, representing an estimated population of about 123 million. Of the households sampled, 798 used tax-time financial products, representing an estimated population of about 3 million and 32,372 did not use the products, representing an estimated population of about 118 million. We estimated that 2.4 percent of households used the products, plus or minus 0.2 percentage points. Sample size is slightly different for unbanked status (N = 31,653) due to nonresponse, and unbanked means no one in the household had a checking or savings account in the past 12 months. As a result, the percentages for this variable do not add to 1. The first column is the estimated percentage of households in the full sample that used alternative financial services, prepaid cards, or were unbanked in the past 12 months. All estimates in the first column have relative standard errors of about 10 percent or less. The second column is the estimated percentage of households that used tax-time financial products in the past 12 months and used alternative financial services, prepaid cards, or were unbanked in the past 12 months. All statistics are weighted using household-level weights. Estimates in the second column generally have relative standard errors of 20 percent or less with some exceptions. Estimates of those who did not know or refused to answer about nonbank check cashing, payday loan, pawn shop, and prepaid card use and unbanked status are not statistically significantly different from zero.

- Tax year.
- Tax-time financial product use, including refund anticipation loans, refund anticipation checks, or no tax-time financial products. In tax year 2016, we estimated that about 18 percent of taxpayers used a tax-time financial product, plus or minus less than 1 percentage point.

We also used IRS data from the Statistics of Income division for tax year 2016 to assess the geographical concentration of product use at the zip-code level. Zip code data from the IRS Statistics of Income division are based on population data that was filed and process by IRS in tax year 2016. Due to some data suppression from IRS for privacy purposes, zip codes with less than 100 tax returns are excluded from the data. As a result, in 2016 the total returns represented in the IRS zip code data are 145,302,140 and the number of tax returns with a tax-time financial product was 21,654,760, meaning about 15 percent of tax filing units in these data used a tax-time financial product.

## Methodology

### *Regression Analysis Using FDIC Data*

Using FDIC data, we conducted a multivariate regression analysis to examine the relationship between each explanatory variable and tax-time financial product use. Specifically, we estimated multivariate logistic regression models. Regression models allow us to test significant relationships between economic and demographic variables and the likelihood of using tax-time financial products, while controlling for other factors.

We used logistic regression models because our dependent variable is binary. The dependent variable represents whether a household used tax-time financial products. We collapsed "no" and "did not know/refused" into a single category for our regression analysis, so that the dependent variable is equal to 1 if the household used tax-time financial products and 0 otherwise.

Logistic regressions allow the relationships between various characteristics and tax-time financial product usage to be described as odds ratios. Odds ratios that are statistically significant and greater than 1.00 indicate that households or heads of households with those characteristics are more likely to use tax-time financial products. Odds ratios that are less than 1.00 indicate that households or heads of households with those characteristics are less likely to use tax-time financial products. For categorical variables, this increase or decrease in the likelihood of product use is in comparison to an omitted category, or reference group. For example, the odds ratio for households headed by African Americans is statistically significant and 1.36. This implies that the odds of tax-time financial product use for households headed by African Americans are 1.36 times the odds of use for households headed by whites, holding other factors constant. Put another way, households headed by African Americans are about 36 percent more likely to use tax-time financial products than households headed by white individuals, if other conditions remain constant. This result and others are discussed further in the results section below. We also present 95 percent confidence intervals, which helps clarify the statistical significance of the odds ratios.

Our baseline estimates were derived from logistic regressions that accounted for the survey features of the FDIC data. Our main regression results used data from the 2017 survey year. We also estimated logistic regressions using data from the 2015, 2013, and 2011 survey years, using the same variables when possible. Our baseline specification includes explanatory variables for race and ethnicity, education, age, household type, income, and homeownership. We used groups of indicator variables or categorical variables to control for all characteristics.

In other specifications, we included controls for children, unbanked status, use of alternative financial services other than tax-time financial products, state indicators, and region indicators to check the robustness of our results.

We also assessed the sensitivity of our analyses by restricting the analysis to households that only answered "yes" or "no" to tax-time financial product use. We excluded answers of "did not know/refused," so that the dependent variable is equal to 1 if the household used tax-time financial products and 0 if the household did not use tax-time financial products.

In a more limited analysis, we merged data from the 2017 FDIC data, which is the June 2017 supplement of the Current Population Survey, with the 2017 Annual Social and Economic Supplement, which is the March 2017 supplement of the Current Population Survey. We performed the additional analysis because the March 2017 supplement has data on tax-filing characteristics, including tax credits used by households. Given the structure of the Current Population Survey, some households were surveyed in both the March and June 2017 supplements, and those households comprise the sample used in this part of the analysis. We identified those represented in both supplements using household and person identifiers, as well as data on sex, race and ethnicity, and age. Using this merged sample, we estimated logistic regressions that both did and did not account for the survey features of the data. We included the same explanatory variables as our baseline estimates, along with indicators for use of the Earned Income Tax Credit, Additional Child Tax Credit, and Child Tax Credit.

### *Analysis of IRS Data*

Using the 2 percent sample of IRS data, we estimated the percentages of tax filers with varying tax-filing characteristics by year and average refund amounts by year. All estimates are weighted at the tax filing unit level. Using the IRS's zip code data from the Statistics of Income division for 2016, we calculated the number of total tax filing units and tax filing units who used tax-time financial product at the zip code level.

## Caveats and Limitations

### *Regression Analysis Using FDIC Data*

Our results have limitations and should be interpreted with caution. For example, our analysis identifies correlations between characteristics and tax-time financial product use and not causal relationships. Moreover, there may be variables that are correlated with tax-time financial product use that are not included in our models. For example, we are not able to account for community characteristics that may influence the decision to use the products due to data limitations. We used statistical tests for multicollinearity (high intercorrelations among two or more independent variables) and goodness of fit to check the validity of the model to the extent possible, given the use of complex survey data.

Our analysis of the characteristics associated with the use of tax-time financial products uses a relatively small number of observations. For example, we observe 798 households that used these products in the 2017 survey year, representing about 2.4 percent of households (plus or minus 0.2 percentage points), and that is the benchmark utilization rate against which the results should be interpreted. Moreover, IRS data indicate that more than 20 million tax filers used tax-time financial products in 2016, representing about 20 percent of tax filers who filed their taxes electronically. These data sets use different units of analysis, and there can be multiple tax filers in one household, especially for those who use Earned Income Tax Credit. However, comparing the two suggests that the survey data may not include all users of tax-time financial products. Given the question used to measure the dependent variable, our analysis focuses on those who use tax-time financial products to get their tax refund more quickly. While a key reason people use tax-time financial products is to meet cash needs, there may be other reasons people use the products, including covering the cost of tax preparation.

Our results may not generalize to other time periods. There have been a number of changes in the market for tax-time financial products in recent years. Our results may not generalize to all products currently available in the market. However, our results from 2017 are generally similar with the

2015, 2013, and 2011 survey years, despite a number of changes to the tax-time financial product market during these years. Our findings suggest that similar types of households have utilized tax-time financial products regardless of industry and market changes, particularly if households used paid preparers and tax-time financial products to expedite their tax refunds.

Our analysis focuses on households that used tax-time financial products and accessed them through paid preparers. However, taxpayers also may have accessed specific types of tax-time financial products when they used online software to file their own taxes. For example, individuals who file their own taxes online may use the products to cover the cost of the software that helps them prepare their taxes. The characteristics of people who use products for these reasons may be different than what we found in our analysis.

### Analysis of IRS Data

The IRS data are representative of tax returns filed electronically and not of tax returns filed by other means, including by paper. The results may not generalize to years for which we do not have data.

The indicators in the data for specific types of tax-time financial products, including the indicators for refund anticipation loans and refund anticipation checks have some significant limitations. In tax years 2014–2016, IRS only allowed tax-time financial products to be coded as refund anticipation loans or refund anticipation checks (that is, there was no code to indicate that two or more products were used together).

However, there were some major changes in the industry during this period, particularly with regards to refund anticipation loans, that suggest that these indicators do not measure the same types of products over time. Given the limitations of the definitions of specific tax-time financial products, most of our analysis focuses on the universe of tax-time financial products in the IRS data and not on differences by specific types of products.

# Results

## *Regression Analysis Using FDIC Data*

### Table 5. Factors Associated with Tax-Time Financial Product Use, 2017

| Explanatory variables | Odds ratios | 95% confidence interval lowerbound | 95% confidence interval, upper bound |
|---|---|---|---|
| **Income** (omitted - income $60,000 or more) | | | |
| Income less than $10,000 | 1.02 | 0.68 | 1.52 |
| | (0.21) | | |
| Income between $10,000 and $19,999 | 1.32 | 0.94 | 1.86 |
| | (0.23) | | |
| Income between $20,000 and $29,999 | 1.34* | 1.00 | 1.81 |
| | (0.20) | | |
| Income between $30,000 and $39,999 | 1.61*** | 1.24 | 2.09 |
| | (0.22) | | |
| Income between $40,000 and $49,999 | 1.19 | 0.87 | 1.62 |
| (0.19) | | | |
| Income between $50,000 and $59,999 | 1.22 | 0.86 | 1.74 |
| | (0.22) | | |
| **Household type** (omitted -married) | | | |
| Unmarried male head of household with family | 1.25 | 0.88 | 1.79 |
| | (0.23) | | |
| Unmarried female head of household with family | 1.76*** | 1.36 | 2.30 |
| | (0.24) | | |
| Single male | 1.11 | 0.83 | 1.47 |
| | (0.16) | | |
| Single female | 1.12 | 0.82 | 1.54 |
| | (0.18) | | |
| **Homeownership** (omitted – non homeowner) | | | |
| Head of household is homeowner | 0.66*** | 0.52 | 0.82 |
| | (0.08) | | |
| **Children** (omitted - no children) | | | |
| Head of household has children present | 1.13 | 0.88 | 1.44 |
| | (0.14) | | |
| Race and ethnicity (omitted -white, non-Hispanic head of household) | | | |

| Explanatory variables | Odds ratios | 95% confidence interval lowerbound | 95% confidence interval, upper bound |
|---|---|---|---|
| African American, non-Hispanic head of household | 1.36** | 1.07 | 1.73 |
| | (0.17) | | |
| American Indian/Alaskan Native, non-Hispanic head of household | 1.17 | 0.52 | 2.64 |
| | (0.49) | | |
| Asian, non-Hispanic head of household | 1.18 | 0.74 | 1.88 |
| | (0.28) | | |
| Hispanic, any race of head of household | 0.93 | 0.73 | 1.20 |
| | (0.12) | | |
| Mixed race/other non-Hispanic head of household | 0.84 | 0.39 | 1.82 |
| | (0.33) | | |
| **Education** (omitted - no college education) | | | |
| Head of household has some college education or more | 0.96 | 0.81 | 1.13 |
| | (0.08) | | |
| **Age** (omitted - 60 years or older) | | | |
| Age of head of household between 15 and 29 | 2.55*** | 1.87 | 3.48 |
| | (0.41) | | |
| | Odds ratios | 95% confidence interval lowerbound | 95% confidence interval, upper bound |
| Age of head of household between 30 and 39 | 2.36*** | 1.72 | 3.23 |
| | (0.38) | | |
| Age of head of household between 40 and 49 | 1.89*** | 1.36 | 2.64 |
| | (0.32) | | |
| Age of head of household between 50 and 59 | 1.62*** | 1.21 | 2.17 |
| | (0.24) | | |
| **Number of observations** | **33,561** | | |

Legend: *** = $p < 0.01$; ** = $p < 0.05$; and* = $p < 0.1$.

Source: GAO analysis of Federal Deposit Insurance Corporation data. | GAO-19-269.

Notes: We used from data from the 2017 Federal Deposit Insurance Corporation's National Survey of Unbanked and Underbanked Households. Odds ratios are estimated from a multivariate logistic regression that accounted for the survey features of the data. Standard errors are calculated using successive difference replication based on the household weight and replicate weights are in parentheses. The baseline household characteristics (omitted categories) are households with incomes over $60,000, married couples, non-homeowners, white and non-Hispanic heads of households, heads of household with no college education, heads of household over 60 years old, and heads of household with no children.

Our analysis suggests a number of economic and demographic characteristics are associated with tax-time financial product use, particularly when purchased through a tax preparer to expedite the tax refund, after controlling for other factors. In 2017, relatively lower-income households were more likely to use the products than higher-income households.

Households headed by single women with families were more likely to use tax-time financial products than households headed by married couples. Furthermore, householders who owned their homes were less likely to use tax-time financial products. African American households were more likely to use the products compared to white households. Finally, relatively younger households were more likely to use the products than older ones. The results of the main specification of our logistic regression are presented in Table 5.

Our results for other specifications using 2017 data were generally similar. For example, adding an additional control for unbanked status did not substantively change the results. In alternative specifications that included an indicator for use of other alternative financial services, we found a significant and positive correlation between using tax-time financial products and other alternative financial services, including nonbank check cashing, nonbank money orders, payday loans, and pawn shops. Moreover, including state and region indicators did not substantively affect the results. Using the sample restricted to just "yes" and "no" responses also did not substantively change the results.

Our results for other years were generally similar, with some exceptions. For example, in other survey years prior to 2017, we found that in addition to African American households, Native American households also were more likely to use tax-time financial products than white households. Moreover, education and children were significant correlates in prior survey years.

### Analysis of IRS Data

We found that nearly 1 in 5 taxpayers who filed their taxes electronically used tax-time financial products each year from 2014 to 2016, while less than 3 percent of filers used free filing services available through IRS during the same period.

We also found that in 2016, tax-time financial product use was associated with receiving tax refunds through direct deposit, which is a faster way to receive a tax refund than paper check. Users of tax-time financial products also were more likely to file as heads of household (tax filing status) than taxpayers who did not use tax-time financial products. Moreover, taxpayers who used the products received higher tax refunds on average than taxpayers who did not use the products, especially when they used paid tax preparers to file their taxes.

Finally, analyzing the zip code of the filers, we found that use of tax-time financial product was concentrated in some areas of the South and the West.

# APPENDIX III: DISCLOSURE OF PRODUCT AND RELATED FEES AND TERMS

## Disclosure of Product Fees and Terms

### *Undercover Visits*

Our limited nongeneralizeable review of documents received from selected banks and tax preparers found disclosures generally followed Office of the Comptroller of the Currency (OCC) guidance or Internal Revenue Service (IRS) requirements for fees disclosure, respectively. However, we noted from our undercover visits of selected tax preparers that the extent and clarity of the disclosures offered to customers varied. Furthermore, in our review of selected tax preparers' websites, we found that fees and information about products were not always clearly disclosed.

All nine tax preparers we visited offered the option to pay for the tax preparation fees with the tax refund by using a refund transfer, but they did not always clearly communicate how these options work.[61] For example,

---

[61] Because the investigators did not experience the tax preparation or the product application process, we were not able to assess the timing of any disclosures typically made after the tax return preparation process would begin.

three preparers did not disclose the refund transfer fee, and in a few instances, the refund transfer was provided alongside a refund advance and we were not given the option to pay for the tax preparation fees out of pocket. In other cases, the refund transfer fee was disclosed, but the product was not always identified as optional (that is, not required for tax preparation).

During six of our undercover visits, our investigators explicitly requested literature on product fees. However, the preparers either stated they did not have the literature available or only provided us with business cards and promotional material. The other three times we did not ask for, and were not offered literature on product fees, features, or terms.

In two of our visits, the tax preparers offered our investigators a refund advance after we expressed an interest in getting the refund quickly. In another two visits, we were offered unsolicited refund advances. When offering the product, these four tax preparers bundled the refund advance with a refund transfer (an optional product). By adding a refund transfer, the tax preparer effectively added a fee-based product to the refund advance, a product that otherwise is free to the taxpayer. During one of the visits, we were offered a refund advance only after we specifically asked for it.

### *Website Content Analysis*

We reviewed the websites of eight selected providers of tax preparation services. We found that while these providers generally disclosed product fees, these disclosures were not made in a consistent manner. For example, all eight of the websites we reviewed offered taxpayers the option to use the expected refund to pay for tax preparation fees. Most of the time, the fee associated with this option was not clearly disclosed on the website. Only two of the eight providers clearly disclosed this fee on the products page; the other six did not disclose the fee in a prominent way or at all. In addition, all five providers that offered refund advances fully disclosed fee information for this product.

Three of the eight online tax preparation service providers had physical locations in addition to their online presence. Of these three, only one disclosed on its website the refund transfer fee for taxpayers who filed a return in-person at one of their offices. For the second preparer with a physical presence, the refund transfer fee quoted for the online service was significantly lower than the fee we were quoted for in-person services at an office. The third preparer with a physical and online presence did not disclose the refund transfer fee for either the in-person service or online filing.

## Document Review

We received and reviewed seven disclosure documents originated by two national tax preparation companies both of which are electronic return originators (ERO) and 12 bank documents from five banks in the industry. We compared the disclosure documents against IRS requirements for disclosure of fees for tax products and we compared the bank documents to OCC guidance related to disclosure of product, disbursement, and additional fees.[62] Both sets of documents in our nongeneralizeable review generally disclosed the product fees in accordance with IRS requirements or OCC guidance as appropriate. Bank forms, including disclosures, are presented to taxpayers once they have decided to apply for a tax product. This practice is consistent with OCC's guidance, which states that the details of a product should be provided to consumers before they apply for it. However, our analysis found that almost all of these documents are presented to taxpayers after returns have been prepared and tax preparers have determined the taxpayers were qualified for a tax-time financial product. The timing of when a tax preparer make these disclosures would make it challenging for a taxpayer to compare product prices from different providers or make more informed purchasing decisions.

Moreover, all the ERO documents we reviewed with information on refund advances disclosed that the taxpayer would be receiving a loan and not a refund. However, of the six ERO disclosure documents that disclosed

---

[62] The tax preparers' documents we reviewed included product disclosures and information provided to the taxpayer during the tax preparation process. The bank documents included product applications and disclosures.

fees, four disclosed additional fees that might be associated with tax refund products, such as disbursement fees.

Of the 12 bank documents we reviewed, all disclosed that funds would be sent to the bank if taxpayers used a tax product. Almost all the documents disclosed the fees associated with the tax product and that the fees would be deducted from the refund. And four of five documents related to a loan product disclosed that the taxpayer would be receiving a loan and not a tax refund. The majority of the documents also disclosed that the taxpayer may receive the refund directly from the taxing authority without incurring additional costs and within the same time frame without using a tax product.

All the tax preparer documents and the banks' disclosure documents were brief and written in plain language. However, almost all the bank application documents were longer than four pages and included technical and industry language.


## Disclosure of Disbursement Fees, Including on Prepaid Cards

Based on our document reviews of selected tax preparers and banks and as suggested by our undercover visits of nine selected tax preparers, the disclosure of fees for disbursing funds was inconsistent, particularly around prepaid cards. Prepaid cards are often used to disburse funds from a tax-time product. Based on our analysis of providers' promotional content, in some cases a tax preparer will offer prepaid cards as the only disbursement option. The cards generally carry additional fees for longterm use (such as monthly, withdrawal, reload, and inactivity fees). Prepaid cards usually are reloadable and can be used to pay bills and make retail purchases. IRS does not have guidelines for disclosing fees for the long-term use of prepaid card. However, OCC requires that banks disclose if a tax product may be used on a long-term basis and disclose fees associated with extended use of the product.

During our visits, seven of the nine tax preparers provided the option to have the tax refund deposited on a prepaid card.[63] However, only two of the seven preparers noted any potential fee information associated with the short or long-term use of prepaid cards. These two preparers said that there was no additional charge to have the taxpayer's refund deposited on a prepaid card, and the other five did not explain whether any fees would be charged for this transaction.

Five of the seven preparers that offered a prepaid card explained that the card could be used for transactions other than receiving the tax refund. However, only two of the five disclosed any fee information associated with long-term use of the card. Another two of the five preparers referred our undercover agents to the issuer of the card for additional information. The remaining preparer did not disclose that additional fees would apply to long-term use of the card.

Four of the eight tax preparation websites we reviewed disclosed partial information about fees related to the disbursement of funds to the taxpayer. Three of the eight websites only disclosed disbursement fee information related to use of prepaid cards. We found fee information in one of the eight websites only after doing a word search. Fees associated with the long-term use of prepaid card fees were not disclosed by three of the six preparers that offered this disbursement option. Two websites disclosed partial fee information and only one disclosed all the fees and terms associated with the long-term use of a prepaid card. Six of these websites advised the taxpayer to see the terms and conditions of the card, four included a link to the terms and conditions of the card, and two did not include a link.

Bank documents generally disclosed the fees associated with different disbursement methods such as paper checks and prepaid cards; however, fees related to the long-term use of prepaid cards were not always disclosed. Almost half of the documents we reviewed that include the use of a prepaid card did not acknowledge that fees were associated with the long-term use

---

[63] In fall 2016, CFPB issued a final rule on prepaid accounts that includes requirements for disclosing fees related to prepaid accounts. The rule was amended in 2017 and 2018 and is expected to have an effective date of April 1, 2019.

of prepaid cards, while others included only partial information or a general statement that "fees may apply."

# APPENDIX IV: COMMENTS FROM THE INTERNAL REVENUE SERVICE

DEPUTY COMMISSIONER

**DEPARTMENT OF THE TREASURY**
INTERNAL REVENUE SERVICE
WASHINGTON, D.C. 20224

March 22, 2019

Mr. Michael Clements
Director, Financial Markets
  and Community Investment
U.S. Government Accountability Office
441 G Street, N.W.
Washington, DC 20548

Dear Mr. Clements:

I have reviewed the draft report entitled *TAX REFUND PRODUCTS: Product Mix Has Evolved and IRS Should Improve Data Quality* (GAO-19-269) and appreciate the opportunity to provide comments. Financial products associated with potential income tax refunds are marketplace offerings provided by the income tax return preparation industry to its customers. The IRS neither administers nor promotes the sale or use of these products. We recognize that variations have occurred in recent years affecting the nature and number of refund-related products and how they are promoted to the public.

As noted in the report, we have expanded the data captured on returns to more accurately reflect the products offered in today's market. We also continue to pursue programming changes that will further improve our ability to identify the use of multiple refund-related products on a single return. Better-defined descriptors of the refund-related products used by taxpayers will be useful for users of that data; however, the presence or absence of that data does not impact our ability to process tax returns or issue refunds. Consequently, due to programming resources being finite and subject to competing priorities, completion of this work is dependent on prioritization and funding.

We agree with your recommendations to communicate the limitations associated with the Refund Anticipation Loan indicators for tax years 2016 and 2017. Additionally, we will update Publication 1345, Handbook for Authorized IRS e-file Providers of Individual Income Tax Returns, to clarify guidance on how the use of refund-related products should be coded on returns.

Sincerely,

Kirsten B. Wielobob
Deputy Commissioner for
Services and Enforcement

**Recommendations for Executive Action**

**RECOMMENDATION 1**
The Commissioner of Internal Revenue Service should communicate data issues regarding the Refund Anticipation Loan (RAL) indicators for tax year 2016 and 2017 and the refund transfer indicators since tax year 2016 – for example, by attaching explanatory material to the dataset.

**COMMENT**
We agree with this recommendation and will provide the appropriate notations with the datasets.

**RECOMMENDATION 2**
The Commissioner of Internal Revenue Service should improve the quality of tax-time financial product data collected; for example, by allowing authorized e-file providers to indicate more than one type of tax-time financial product for each return or by informing tax preparers of the addition of new product definitions and instructions on how to accurately code the products.

**COMMENT**
We agree with this recommendation. Programming changes will be pursued and instructions for tax return preparers will be clarified to promote accurate coding of refund-related products.

# GOVERNMENT OPERATIONS

In: Key Government Reports.                     ISBN: 978-1-53616-001-7
Editor: Ernest Clark                         © 2019 Nova Science Publishers, Inc.

*Chapter 3*

# 2020 CENSUS: FURTHER ACTIONS NEEDED TO REDUCE KEY RISKS TO A SUCCESSFUL ENUMERATION[*]

*Robert Goldenkoff and Nick Marinos*

## WHY GAO DID THIS STUDY

The Bureau, a component of the Department of Commerce (Commerce), is responsible for conducting a complete and accurate decennial census of the U.S. population. The decennial census is mandated by the Constitution and provides vital data for the nation. A complete count of the nation's population is an enormous undertaking as the Bureau seeks to control the cost of the census, implement operational innovations, and use new and modified IT systems. In recent years, GAO has identified challenges that raise serious concerns about the Bureau's ability to conduct a cost-effective

---

[*] This is an edited, reformatted and augmented version of United States Government Accountability Office; Testimony before the Subcommittee on Commerce, Justice, Science, and Related Agencies, Committee on Appropriations, House of Representatives, Publication No. GAO-19-431T, dated April 30, 2019.

count. For these reasons, GAO added the 2020 Census to its High-Risk list in February 2017.

GAO was asked to testify about the reasons the 2020 Census remains on the High-Risk List and the steps the Bureau needs to take to mitigate risks to a successful census. To do so, GAO summarized its prior work regarding the Bureau's planning efforts for the 2020 Census. GAO also included preliminary observations from its ongoing work examining the IT systems readiness and cybersecurity for the 2020 Census. This information is related to, among other things, the Bureau's progress in developing and testing key systems and the status of cybersecurity risks.

## WHAT GAO RECOMMENDS

GAO is making two recommendations to the Bureau to (1) better ensure that cybersecurity weaknesses are addressed within prescribed time frames, and (2) improve its process for addressing cybersecurity weaknesses identified by DHS.

## WHAT GAO FOUND

The 2020 Decennial Census is on GAO's list of high-risk programs primarily because the Census Bureau (Bureau) (1) is using innovations that are not expected to be fully tested, (2) continues to face challenges in implementing information technology (IT) systems, and (3) faces significant cybersecurity risks to its systems and data. Although the Bureau has taken initial steps to address risk, additional actions are needed as these risks could adversely impact the cost, quality, schedule, and security of the enumeration.

- Innovations: The Bureau is planning several innovations for the 2020 Census, including allowing the public to respond using the internet. These innovations show promise for controlling costs, but they also introduce new risks, in part, because they have not been used extensively, if at all, in earlier enumerations. As a result, testing is essential to ensure that key IT systems and operations will function as planned. However, citing budgetary uncertainties, the Bureau scaled back operational tests in 2017 and 2018, missing an opportunity to fully demonstrate that the innovations and IT systems will function as intended during the 2020 Census. To manage risk to the census, the Bureau has developed hundreds of mitigation and contingency plans. To maximize readiness for the 2020 Census, it will also be important for the Bureau to prioritize among its mitigation and contingency strategies those that will deliver the most cost-effective outcomes for the census.

- Implementing IT systems: The Bureau plans to rely heavily on IT for the 2020 Census, including a total of 52 new and legacy IT systems and the infrastructure supporting them. To help improve its implementation of IT, in October 2018, the Bureau revised its systems development and testing schedule to reflect, among other things, lessons learned during its 2018 operational test. However, GAO's ongoing work has determined that the Bureau is at risk of not meeting near-term IT system development and testing schedule milestones for two upcoming 2020 Census operational deliveries, including address canvassing (i.e., verification of the location of selected housing units). These schedule management challenges may compress the time available for the remaining system development and testing, and increase the risk that systems will not function as intended. It will be important that the Bureau effectively manages IT implementation risk to ensure that it meets near-term milestones for system development and testing, and that it is ready for the major operations of the 2020 Census.

- Cybersecurity: The Bureau has established a risk management framework that requires it to conduct a full security assessment for each system expected to be used for the 2020 Census and, if deficiencies are identified, to determine the corrective actions needed to remediate those deficiencies. As of March 2019, the

Bureau had over 500 corrective actions from its security assessments that needed to be addressed, including nearly 250 that were considered "high-risk" or "very high-risk." However, of these 250 corrective actions, the Bureau identified 115 as being delayed. Further, 70 of the 115 were delayed by 60 or more days. According to the Bureau, these corrective actions were delayed due to technical challenges or resource constraints. Resolving identified vulnerabilities within the Bureau's established time frames can help reduce the risk that unauthorized individuals may exploit weaknesses to gain access to sensitive information and systems. To its credit, the Bureau is also working with the Department of Homeland Security (DHS) to support its 2020 Census cybersecurity efforts. For example, DHS is helping the Bureau ensure a scalable and secure network connection for the 2020 Census respondents and to strengthen its response to potential cyber threats. During the last 2 years, as a result of these activities, the Bureau has received 17 recommendations from DHS to improve its cybersecurity posture. However, the Bureau lacks a formal process for tracking and completing corrective actions for these recommendations which would help to ensure that DHS's efforts result in improvements to the Bureau's cybersecurity posture.

In addition to addressing risks which could affect innovations and the security of the enumeration, the Bureau has the opportunity to improve its cost estimating process for the 2020 Census, and ultimately the reliability of the estimate itself, by reflecting best practices. In October 2017, the 2020 Census life-cycle cost estimate was updated and is now projected to be $15.6 billion, a more than $3 billion (27 percent) increase over its earlier estimate. GAO reported in August 2018 that although the Bureau had taken steps to improve its cost estimation process for 2020, it needed to implement a system to track and report variances between actual and estimated cost elements. According to Bureau officials, they plan to release an updated version of the 2020 Census life-cycle estimate in the spring of 2019. To ensure that future updates to the life-cycle cost estimate reflect best practices, it will be important for the Bureau to implement GAO's recommendation related to the cost estimate.

Over the past decade, GAO has made 97 recommendations specific to the 2020 Census to help address these risks and other concerns. Commerce has generally agreed with these recommendations and has taken action to address many of them. However, as of April 2019, 24 of the recommendations had not been fully implemented. Of the 24 open recommendations, 11 were directed at improving the implementation of the innovations for the 2020 Census. To ensure a cost-effective enumeration, it will be important for the Bureau to address these recommendations.

Chairman Serrano, Ranking Member Aderholt, and Members of the Subcommittee:

We are pleased to be here today to discuss the U.S. Census Bureau's (Bureau) progress in preparing for the 2020 Decennial Census. Conducting the decennial census of the U.S. population is mandated by the Constitution and provides vital data for the nation. The information that the census collects is used to apportion the seats of the House of Representatives; redraw congressional districts; allocate billions of dollars each year in federal financial assistance; and provide a social, demographic, and economic profile of the nation's people to guide policy decisions at each level of government. Further, businesses use census data to market new services and products and to tailor existing ones to demographic changes.

A complete count of the nation's population is an enormous undertaking. The Bureau, a component of the Department of Commerce (Commerce), is seeking to control the cost of the 2020 Census while it implements several innovations and manages the processes of acquiring and developing information technology (IT) systems. In recent years, we have identified challenges that raise serious concerns about the Bureau's ability to conduct a cost-effective count of the nation, including issues with the agency's research, testing, planning, scheduling, cost estimation, systems development, and cybersecurity risk management practices.

Over the past decade, we have made 97 recommendations specific to the 2020 Census to help address these and other concerns. Commerce has generally agreed with our recommendations and has made progress in implementing them. However, 24 of the recommendations had not been fully implemented as of April 2019, although the Bureau had taken initial steps to address many of them, and one recommendation has been closed but not implemented.

We also added the 2020 Decennial Census to our high-risk list in February 2017, and it remains on our high-risk list today.[1] As preparations for the next census continue to ramp up, fully implementing our recommendations to address the risks jeopardizing the 2020 Census is more critical than ever.

At your request, our testimony today will describe (1) why the 2020 Decennial Census remains a high-risk area and (2) the steps that Commerce and the Bureau need to take going forward to mitigate the risks jeopardizing a secure and cost-effective census.

The information in this statement is based primarily on our prior work regarding the Bureau's planning efforts for 2020.[2]

For that body of work, we reviewed, among other things, relevant Bureau documentation, including the 2020 Census Operational Plan; recent decisions on preparations for the 2020 Census; and outcomes of key IT milestone reviews.

In the summer of 2018 we visited the Bureau's 2018 End-to-End test site in Providence County, Rhode Island to observe door-to-door field enumeration during the non-response follow-up, an operation where enumerators personally visit to count the household. We also discussed the

---

[1] GAO, *High-Risk Series: Substantial Efforts Needed to Achieve Greater Progress on High-Risk Areas,* GAO-19-157SP (Washington, D.C.: Mar. 6, 2019) and *High-Risk Series: Progress on Many High-Risk Areas, While Substantial Efforts Needed on Others,* GAO-17-317 (Washington, D.C.: Feb. 15, 2017). GAO maintains a high-risk program to focus attention on government operations that it identifies as high-risk due to their greater vulnerabilities to fraud, waste, abuse, and mismanagement or the need for transformation to address economy, efficiency, or effectiveness challenges.

[2] For example, GAO, *2020 Census: Additional Steps Needed to Finalize Readiness for Peak Field Operations,* GAO-19-140 (Washington, D.C.: Dec. 10, 2018); *2020 Census: Continued Management Attention Needed to Address Challenges and Risks with Developing, Testing, and Securing IT Systems,* GAO-18-655 (Washington, D.C.: Aug. 30, 2018); *2020 Census: Bureau Has Made Progress with Its Scheduling, but Further Improvement Will Help Inform Management Decisions,* GAO-18-589 (Washington, D.C.: July 26, 2018); and, *2020 Census: Actions Needed to Address Challenges to Enumerating Hard-to-Count Groups,* GAO-18-599 (Washington, D.C.: July 26, 2018).

status of our recommendations with Commerce and Bureau staff. Other details on the scope and methodology for our prior work are provided in each published report on which this testimony is based.

In addition, we included information in this statement from our ongoing work on the readiness of the Bureau's IT systems for the 2020 Census. Specifically, we collected and reviewed documentation on the status and plans for system development and testing, and for addressing cybersecurity risk, for the 2020 Census. This includes the Bureau's integration and implementation plan, memorandums documenting outcomes of security assessments, and reports prepared by the Department of Homeland Security (DHS) for the Bureau on cybersecurity risks. We also interviewed relevant agency officials.

We provided a copy of the applicable new information that we are reporting in this testimony to the Bureau and DHS for comment on April 12, 2019.The Bureau provided technical comments, which we addressed as appropriate.

We conducted the work on which this statement is based in accordance with generally accepted government auditing standards. Those standards require that we plan and perform the audit to obtain sufficient, appropriate evidence to provide a reasonable basis for our findings and conclusions based on our audit objectives. We believe that the evidence obtained provides a reasonable basis for our findings and conclusions based on our audit objectives.

## BACKGROUND

As shown in Table 1 the cost of counting the nation's population has been escalating with each decade. The 2010 Census was the most expensive in U.S. history at about $12.3 billion, and was about 31 percent more costly than the $9.4 billion 2000 Census (in 2020 dollars).[3]

---

[3] According to the Bureau, these figures rely on fiscal year 2020 constant dollar factors derived from the Chained Price Index from "Gross Domestic Product and Deflators Used in the

According to the Bureau, the total cost of the 2020 Census in October 2015 was estimated at $12.3 billion and in October 2017 that cost estimate grew to approximately $15.6 billion, approximately a $3 billion increase.[4]

### Table 1. The Cost of Previous Decennial Censuses and the Estimated Cost of the 2020 Census

| Benchmark | | Cost | Explanation |
|---|---|---|---|
| 2000 | Census | $9.4 billion | Final cost of the 2000 Census |
| 2010 | Census | $12.3 billion | Final cost of the 2010 Census |
| 2020 | Census estimated cost in October 2015 | $12.3 billion | Initial cost estimate of the 2020 Census |
| 2020 | Census estimated cost in October 2017 | $15.6 billion | Revised cost estimate of the 2020 Census |
| 2020 | Census cost estimate less a portion of contingency funds | $14.1 billion | Cost estimate the Bureau is managing operations to for the 2020 Census |

Source: GAO analysis of Census Bureau data. | GAO-19-431T.

Additionally, Bureau officials told us that while the estimated cost of the census had increased to $15.6 billion, it was nevertheless managing the 2020 Census to a lower cost of $14.1 billion. Bureau officials explained that the $14.1 billion includes all program costs and contingency funds to cover risks and general estimating uncertainty.

The remaining $1.5 billion estimated cost is additional contingency for "unknown unknowns"—that is, low probability events that could cause massive disruptions—and several what-if scenarios such as an increase in the wage rate or additional supervisors needed to manage field operations.[5]

---

Historical Tables: 1940–2020" table from the Fiscal Year 2016 Budget of the United States Government.

[4] The historical life-cycle cost figures for prior decennials as well as the initial estimate for 2020 provided by Commerce in October 2017 differ slightly from those reported by the Bureau previously. According to Commerce documents, the more recently reported figures are "inflated to the current 2020 Census time frame (fiscal years 2012 to 2023)," rather than to 2020 constant dollars as the earlier figures had been. Specifically, since October 2017, Commerce and the Bureau have reported the October 2015 estimate for the 2020 Census as $12.3 billion; this is slightly different than the $12.5 billion the Bureau had initially reported.

[5] The $15.6 billion cost estimate for the 2020 Census includes a total of $2.6 billion in contingency funds.

Moreover, as shown in Figure 1, the average cost for counting a housing unit increased from about $16 in 1970 to around $92 in 2010 (in 2020 constant dollars). At the same time, the return of census questionnaires by mail (the primary mode of data collection) declined over this period from 78 percent in 1970 to 63 percent in 2010. Declining mail response rates has led to higher costs because the Bureau sends temporary workers to each non-responding household to obtain census data.

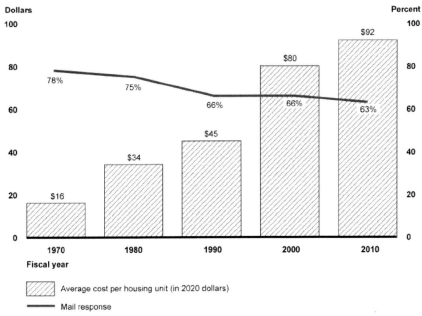

Source: GAO analysis of Census Bureau data. | GAO-19-431T.

Figure 1. The Average Cost of Counting Each Housing Unit (in 2020 Dollars) Has Escalated Each Decade, While the Percentage of Mail Response Rates Has Declined.

Achieving a complete and accurate census has become an increasingly daunting task, in part, because the population is growing larger, more diverse, and more reluctant to participate in the enumeration. In many ways, the Bureau has had to invest substantially more resources each decade to conduct the enumeration.

In addition to these external societal challenges that make achieving a complete count a daunting task, the Bureau also faces a number of internal management challenges that affect its capacity and readiness to conduct a cost-effective enumeration. Some of these issues—such as acquiring and developing IT systems and preparing reliable cost estimates—are long-standing in nature.

At the same time, as the Bureau looks toward 2020, it also faces newly emerging and evolving uncertainties. For example, on March 26, 2018, the Secretary of Commerce announced his decision to add a question to the decennial census on citizenship status. On January 15, 2019, the U.S. District Court for the Southern District of New York ruled on one of a number of legal challenges to the Secretary's decision. That ruling is being appealed, thus, leaving the use of the question uncertain.

The U.S. Supreme Court is scheduled to begin hearing arguments in April 2019 regarding the addition of the citizenship question to the census form. In our prior work we have noted the risks associated with late changes of any nature to the design of the census if the Bureau is unable to fully test those changes under operational conditions.[6]

The Bureau also faced budgetary uncertainties that, according to the Bureau, led to the curtailment of testing in 2017 and 2018. However, the Consolidated Appropriations Act, 2018 appropriated for the Periodic Censuses and Programs account $2.544 billion, which more than doubles the Bureau's request in the President's Fiscal Year 2018 Budget of $1.251 billion.[7] According to the explanatory statement accompanying the act, the appropriation, which is available through fiscal year 2020, is provided to ensure the Bureau has the necessary resources to immediately address any issues discovered during operational testing, and to provide a smoother transition between fiscal year 2018 and fiscal year 2019.[8]

---

[6] GAO, *2010 Census: Little Time Remains to Address Operational Challenges,* GAO-09-408T (Washington, D.C.: Mar. 5, 2009).

[7] Consolidated Appropriations Act, 2018, Pub. L. No. 115-141, Division B, Title I (Mar. 23, 2018).

[8] Joint explanatory statement of conference, 164 Cong. Rec. H2045, H2084 (daily ed. Mar. 22, 2018) (statement of Chairman Frelinghuysen), specifically referenced in section 4 of the Consolidated Appropriations Act, 2018, Pub. L. No. 115-141, § 4 (Mar. 23, 2018).

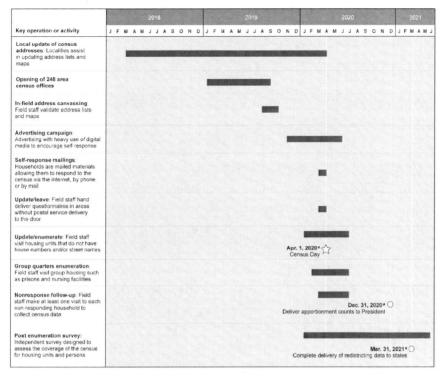

| Key operation or activity | 2018 | 2019 | 2020 | 2021 |
|---|---|---|---|---|
| | J F M A M J J A S O N D | J F M A M J J A S O N D | J F M A M J J A S O N D | J F M A M J |
| Local update of census addresses: Localities assist in updating address lists and maps | | | | |
| Opening of 248 area census offices | | | | |
| In-field address canvassing: Field staff validate address lists and maps | | | | |
| Advertising campaign: Advertising with heavy use of digital media to encourage self-response | | | | |
| Self-response mailings: Households are mailed materials allowing them to respond to the census via the internet, by phone or by mail | | | | |
| Update/leave: Field staff hand deliver questionnaires in areas without postal service delivery to the door | | | | |
| Update/enumerate: Field staff visit housing units that do not have house numbers and/or street names | | | Apr. 1, 2020ᵃ Census Day | |
| Group quarters enumeration: Field staff visit group housing such as prisons and nursing facilities | | | | |
| Nonresponse follow-up: Field staff make at least one visit to each non-responding household to collect census data | | | Dec. 31, 2020ᵃ Deliver apportionment counts to President | |
| Post enumeration survey: Independent survey designed to assess the coverage of the census for housing units and persons | | | | Mar. 31, 2021ᵃ Complete delivery of redistricting data to states |

Source: GAO summary of Census Bureau data. | GAO-19-431T.
ᵃIndicates dates that are mandated by law.

Figure 2. Timeline of Selected Decennial Events.

The availability of those resources enabled the Bureau to continue preparations for the 2020 Census during the 35 days when appropriations lapsed for the Bureau. Moreover, the Consolidated Appropriations Act, 2019 appropriated for the Periodic Censuses and Programs account $3.551 billion.[9] According to Bureau officials, this level of funding for fiscal year 2019 is sufficient to carry out 2020 Census activities as planned.

Importantly, the census is conducted against a backdrop of immutable deadlines. In order to meet legally mandated reporting requirements, census activities need to take place at specific times and in the proper sequence.

---

[9] Consolidated Appropriations Act, 2019, Pub. L. No. 116-6, Division C, Title I (Feb. 15, 2019).

Thus, it is absolutely critical for the Bureau to stay on schedule. Figure 2 shows some dates for selected decennial events.

## The Bureau Has Begun Opening Offices and Hiring Temporary Staff

The Bureau has begun to open its area census offices (ACO) for the 2020 Census. It has signed leases for all 248 ACOs, of which 39 of the offices will be open for the address canvassing operation set to begin in August 2019 where staff verifies the location of selected housing units. The remaining 209 offices will begin opening this fall. In 2010 the Bureau opened 494 census offices. The Bureau has been able to reduce its infrastructure because it is relying on automation to assign work and to record payroll. Therefore there is less paper—field assignments, maps, and daily payroll forms—to manually process.

For the 2020 Census, the Bureau is refining its recruiting and hiring goals, but tentatively plans to recruit approximately 2.24 million applicants and hire nearly 500,000 temporary field staff from that applicant pool for two key operations: address canvassing, and nonresponse follow-up, where they visit households that do not return census forms to collect data in person. In 2010 the Bureau recruited 3.8 million applicants and hired 628,000 temporary workers to conduct the address canvassing and nonresponse follow-up field operations. According to Bureau officials, it has reduced the number of temporary staff it needs to hire because automation has made field operations more efficient and there is less paper.

As of April 15, 2019, for its early operations efforts which includes hiring listers for address canvassing, the Bureau has processed approximately 264,000 applicants which represent 128.4 percent of its 205,000 recruiting goal. The Bureau is also in the process of hiring approximately 1,500 partnership specialists needed by June 2019 to help increase awareness and participation in the 2020 Census in minority communities and hard-to-reach populations. As of April 17, 2019, the

Bureau has hired 467 partnership specialists, and another 329 applicants are waiting to have their background checks completed.

Moreover, Bureau officials also stated that the current economic environment (i.e., the low unemployment rate compared to the economic environment of the 2010 Census) has not yet impacted their ability to recruit staff. The Bureau will continue to monitor the impact of low unemployment on its ability to recruit and hire at the local and regional levels.

## The Bureau Plans to Rely Heavily on IT for the 2020 Census

For the 2020 Census, the Bureau is significantly changing how it intends to conduct the census, in part by re-engineering key census-taking methods and infrastructure, and making use of new IT applications and systems. For example, the Bureau plans to offer an option for households to respond to the survey via the internet and enable field-based enumerators[10] to use applications on mobile devices to collect survey data from households. To do this, the Bureau plans to utilize 52 new and legacy IT systems, and the infrastructure supporting them, to conduct the 2020 Census.

A majority of these 52 systems have been tested during operational tests in 2017 and 2018. For example, the Bureau conducted its 2018 End-to-End test, which included 44 of the 52 systems and was intended to test all key systems and operations in a census-like environment to ensure readiness for the 2020 Census.

Nevertheless, additional IT development and testing work needs to take place before the 2020 Census. Specifically, officials from the Bureau's Decennial Directorate said they expect that the systems will need to undergo further development and testing due to, among other things, the need to add functionality that was not part of the End-to-End test, scale system performance to support the number of respondents expected during the 2020

---

[10] Enumerators are Census Bureau employees who travel from door-to-door throughout the country to try to obtain census data from individuals who do not respond through other means, including the internet, on paper, or by phone.

Census, and address system defects identified during the 2018 End-to-End test.

To prepare the systems and technology for the 2020 Census, the Bureau is also relying on significant contractor support. For example, it is relying on contractors to develop a number of systems and components of the IT infrastructure, including the IT platform that is intended to be used to collect data from households responding via the internet and telephone, and for non-response follow-up activities. Contractors are also deploying the IT and telecommunications hardware in the field offices and providing device-as-a-service capabilities by procuring the mobile devices and cellular service to be used for non-response follow-up[11].

In addition to the development of technology, the Bureau is relying on a technical integration contractor to integrate all of the key systems and infrastructure. The contractor's work is expected to include, among other things, evaluating the systems and infrastructure and acquiring the infrastructure (e.g., cloud or data center) to meet the Bureau's scalability and performance needs; integrating all of the systems; and assisting with technical, performance and scalability, and operational testing activities.

## 2020 Census Identified by GAO as a High-Risk Area

In February 2017, we added the 2020 Decennial Census as a high-risk area needing attention from Congress and the executive branch.[12] This was due to significant risks related to, among other things, innovations never before used in prior enumerations,[13] the acquisition and development of IT systems, and expected escalating costs.

---

[11] In non-response follow-up, if a household does not respond to the census by a certain date, the Bureau will send out employees to visit the home. The Bureau's plan is for these enumerators to use a census application, on a mobile device provided by the Bureau, to capture the information given to them by the in-person interviews.

[12] GAO-17-317.

[13] The Bureau has fundamentally re-examined its approach for conducting the 2020 Census to help reduce costs. To do this, the agency plans to use innovations in four broad areas (described later in this statement): re-engineering field operations, using administrative records, verifying addresses in-office, and developing an Internet self-response option.

Among other things, we reported that the commitment of top leadership was needed to ensure the Bureau's management, culture, and business practices align with a cost-effective enumeration. We also stressed that the Bureau needed to rigorously test census-taking activities; ensure that scheduling adheres to best practices; improve its ability to manage, develop, and secure its IT systems; and have better oversight and control over its cost estimation process.

Our experience has shown that the key elements needed to make progress toward being removed from the High-Risk List are top-level attention by the administration and agency leaders grounded in the five criteria for removal, as well as any needed congressional action. The five criteria for removal that we identified in November 2000 are as follows:[14]

- Leadership Commitment. The agency has demonstrated strong commitment and top leadership support.
- Capacity. The agency has the capacity (i.e., people and resources) to resolve the risk(s).
- Action Plan. A corrective action plan exists that defines the root causes and solutions, and that provides for substantially completing corrective measures, including steps necessary to implement solutions we recommended.
- Monitoring. A program has been instituted to monitor and independently validate the effectiveness and sustainability of corrective measures.
- Demonstrated Progress. The agency has demonstrated progress in implementing corrective measures and in resolving the high-risk area.

These five criteria form a road map for efforts to improve, and ultimately address, high-risk issues. Addressing some of the criteria leads to progress, while satisfying all of the criteria is central to removal from the list.

---

[14] GAO, *Determining Performance and Accountability Challenges and High Risks,* GAO-01-159SP (Washington, D.C.: Nov. 1, 2000).

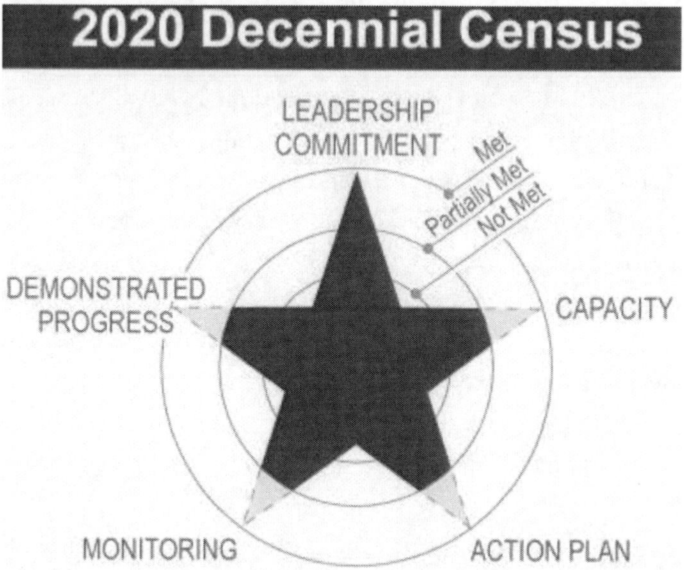

Source: GAO analysis. | GAO-19-431T.

Note: Each point of the star represents one of the five criteria for removal from the High-Risk List and each ring represents one of the three designations: not met, partially met, or met. An unshaded point at the innermost ring means that the criterion has not been met, a partially shaded point at the middle ring means that the criterion has been partially met, and a fully shaded point at the outermost ring means that the criterion has been met.

Figure 3. Status of High-Risk Area for the 2020 Decennial Census, as of March 2019.

As we reported in the March 2019 high-risk report,[15] the Bureau's efforts to address the risks and challenges for the 2020 Census had fully met one of the five criteria for removal from the High-Risk List—leadership commitment—and partially met the other four, as shown in Figure 3. Additional details about the status of the Bureau's efforts to address this high-risk area are discussed later in this statement.

---

[15] GAO-19-157SP.

# THE 2020 CENSUS REMAINS HIGH RISK DUE TO CHALLENGES FACING THE ENUMERATION

The 2020 Census is on our list of high-risk programs because, among other things, (1) innovations never before used in prior enumerations are not expected to be fully tested, (2) the Bureau continues to face challenges in implementing IT systems, (3) the Bureau faces significant cybersecurity risks to its systems and data, and (4) the Bureau's cost estimate for the 2020 Census was unreliable.[16] If not sufficiently addressed, these risks could adversely impact the cost and quality of the enumeration. Moreover, the risks are compounded by other factors that contribute to the challenge of conducting a successful census, such as the nation's increasingly diverse population and concerns over personal privacy.

## Key Risk #1: The Bureau Has Redesigned the Census with the Intent to Control Costs, but Has Scaled Back Critical Tests

The basic design of the enumeration—mail out and mail back of the census questionnaire with in-person follow-up for non-respondents—has been in use since 1970. However, a lesson learned from the 2010 Census and earlier enumerations is that this traditional design is no longer capable of cost-effectively counting the population.

In response to its own assessments, our recommendations, and studies by other organizations, the Bureau has fundamentally re-examined its approach for conducting the 2020 Census. Specifically, its plan for 2020 includes four broad innovation areas: re-engineering field operations, using administrative records, verifying addresses in-office, and developing an internet self-response option (see Table 2).

If they function as planned, the Bureau initially estimated that these innovations could result in savings of over $5 billion (in 2020 constant

---

[16] GAO-17-317.

dollars) when compared to its estimates of the cost for conducting the census with traditional methods. However, in June 2016, we reported that the Bureau's initial life-cycle cost estimate developed in October 2015 was not reliable and did not adequately account for risk.[17] As discussed earlier in this statement, the Bureau has updated its estimate from $12.3 billion and now estimates a life-cycle cost of $15.6 billion, which would result in a smaller potential savings from the innovative design than the Bureau originally estimated. According to the Bureau, the goal of the cost estimate increase was to ensure quality was fully addressed.

**Table 2. The Census Bureau (Bureau) Is Introducing Four Innovation Areas for the 2020 Census**

| Innovation area | Description |
|---|---|
| Re-engineered field operations | The Bureau intends to automate data collection methods, including its case management system. |
| Administrative records | In certain instances, the Bureau plans to reduce enumerator collection of data by using administrative records (information already provided to federal and state governments as they administer other programs such as, Medicare and Medicaid records). |
| Verifying addresses in-office | To ensure the accuracy of its address list, the Bureau intends to use "in-office" procedures and on-screen imagery to verify addresses and reduce street-by-street field canvassing. |
| Internet self-response option | The Bureau plans to offer households the option of responding to the survey through the internet. The Bureau has not previously offered such an option on a large scale. |

Source: GAO analysis of Census Bureau data. | GAO-19-431T.

While the planned innovations could help control costs, they also introduce new risks, in part, because they include new procedures and technology that have not been used extensively in earlier decennials, if at all. Our prior work has shown the importance of the Bureau conducting a robust testing program, including the 2018 End-to-End test.[18] Rigorous testing is a critical risk mitigation strategy because it provides information

---

[17] GAO, *2020 Census: Census Bureau Needs to Improve Its Life-Cycle Cost Estimating Process*, GAO-16-628 (Washington, D.C.: June 30, 2016).

[18] GAO, *2020 Census: Bureau Needs to Better Leverage Information to Achieve Goals of Reengineered Address Canvassing*, GAO-17-622 (Washington, D.C.: July 20, 2017).

on the feasibility and performance of individual census-taking activities, their potential for achieving desired results, and the extent to which they are able to function together under full operational conditions. To address some of these challenges we have made numerous recommendations aimed at improving reengineered field operations, using administrative records, verifying the accuracy of the address list, and securing census responses via the internet.

The Bureau has held a series of operational tests since 2012, but according to the Bureau, it scaled back its most recent field tests because of funding uncertainties. For example, the Bureau canceled the field components of the 2017 Census Test including non-response follow-up, a key census operation.[19] In November 2016, we reported that the cancelation of the 2017 Census Test was a lost opportunity to test, refine, and integrate operations and systems, and that it put more pressure on the 2018 End-to-End test to demonstrate that enumeration activities will function under census-like conditions as needed for 2020.

However, in May 2017, the Bureau scaled back the operational scope of the 2018 End-to-End test and, of the three planned test sites, only the Rhode Island site would fully implement the 2018 End-to-End test. The Washington and West Virginia sites would test just one field operation. In addition, due to budgetary concerns, the Bureau decided to remove three coverage measurement operations (and the technology that supports them) from the scope of the test.[20] However, removal of the coverage measurement operations did not affect testing of the delivery of apportionment or redistricting data.

Without sufficient testing, operational problems can go undiscovered and the opportunity to improve operations will be lost, in part because the 2018 End-to-End test was the last opportunity to demonstrate census technology and procedures across a range of geographic locations, housing

---

[19] In non-response follow-up, if a household does not respond to the census by a certain date, the Bureau will conduct an in-person visit by an enumerator to collect census data using a mobile device provided by the Bureau.

[20] Coverage measurement evaluates the quality of the census data by estimating the census coverage based on a post-enumeration survey.

types, and demographic groups under decennial-like conditions prior to the 2020 Census. To manage risk to the census, the Bureau has developed hundreds of mitigation and contingency plans. To maximize readiness for the 2020 Census, it will also be important for the Bureau to prioritize among its mitigation and contingency strategies those that will deliver the most cost-effective outcomes for the census.

We reported on the 2018 End-to-End test in December 2018 and noted that the Bureau had made progress addressing prior test implementation issues but still faced challenges.[21] As the Bureau studies the results of its testing to inform the 2020 Census, it will be important that it addresses key program management issues that arose during implementation of the test. Namely, by not aligning the skills, responsibilities, and information flows for the first-line supervisors during field data collection, the Bureau limited its role in support of enumerators within the re-engineered field operation. The Bureau also lacked mid-operation training or guidance, which, if implemented in a targeted, localized manner, could have further helped enumerators navigate procedural modifications and any commonly encountered problems when enumerating. It will be important for the Bureau to prioritize its mitigation strategies for these implementation issues so that it can maximize readiness for the 2020 Census.

## Key Risk #2: The Bureau Faces Challenges in Implementing IT Systems

We have previously reported that the Bureau faces challenges in managing and overseeing IT programs, systems, and contractors supporting the 2020 Census.[22] Specifically, we have noted challenges in the Bureau's efforts to manage, among other things, the schedules and contracts for its systems. As a result of these challenges, the Bureau is at risk of being unable

---

[21] GAO-19-140.
[22] GAO-18-655.

to fully implement the systems necessary to support the 2020 Census and conduct a cost-effective enumeration.

## The Bureau Has Made Initial Progress against Its Revised Development and Testing Schedule, but Risks Missing Near-Term Milestones

To help improve its implementation of IT for the 2020 Census, the Bureau recently revised its systems development and testing schedule. Specifically, in October 2018, the Bureau organized the development and testing schedule for its 52 systems into 16 operational deliveries.[23] Each of the 16 operational deliveries has milestone dates for, among other things, development, performance and scalability testing, and system deployment. According to Bureau officials in the Decennial Directorate, the schedule was revised, in part, due to schedule management challenges experienced, and lessons learned, while completing development and testing during the 2018 End-to-End test.

The Bureau has made initial progress in executing work against its revised schedule. For example, the Bureau completed development for the systems in the first operational delivery—for 2020 Census early operations preparations—in July 2018, and deployed these systems into production in October 2018.

---

[23] The 52 systems being used in the 2020 Census are to be deployed multiple times in a series of operational deliveries (which include operations such as address canvassing or self-response). That is, a system may be deployed for one operation in the 2020 Census (such as address canvassing), and be deployed again for a subsequent operation in the test (such as self-response). As such, additional development and testing may occur each time a system is deployed.

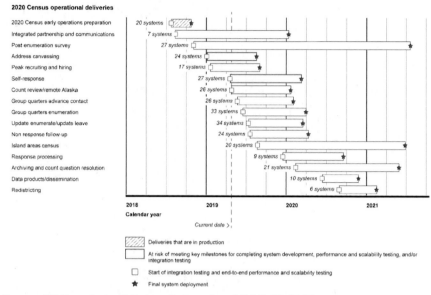

Source: GAO analysis of Census Bureau data. | GAO-19-431T.

Note: The 52 systems being used in the 2020 Census are to be deployed multiple times in a series of operational deliveries (which include operations such as address canvassing or self-response). That is, a system may be deployed for one operation in the 2020 Census (such as address canvassing), and be deployed again for a subsequent operation in the test (such as self-response). As such, additional development and testing may occur each time a system is deployed.

Figure 4. Status of 16 Operational Deliveries for the 2020 Census, as of April 2019.

However, our current work has determined that the Bureau is at risk of not meeting several near-term systems testing milestones. As of April 2019, six systems[24] that are expected to be used in a total of two operational deliveries are at risk of not meeting milestone dates which would signal that the systems have completed development and are ready for testing. These six systems are needed for, among other things, field assignment management and worker performance tracking during address canvassing, data collection for operations, business and support automation, and

---

[24] As of April 2019, the six systems were Enterprise Census and Survey Enabling Platform– Operational Control System; Enterprise Census and Survey Enabling platform– Field Operation Control System; Control and Response Data System; Decennial Response Processing System; Census Questionnaire Assistance; and Automated Tracking and Control.

customer support during self-response. According to Bureau documentation, these systems were at risk due, in part, to the lack of finalized system requirements and specifications. Figure 4 presents an overview of the status for all 16 operational deliveries, as of April 2019.

## *The Bureau Faces Additional Risks Due to Compressed IT Development and Testing Time Frames*

The at-risk systems previously discussed add uncertainty to a highly compressed time frame over the next 4 months. Importantly, between April and August 2019, the Bureau is expected to begin integration testing for the systems in seven operational deliveries, including internet self-response and non-response follow-up. Officials from the Bureau's integration contractor noted concern that the current schedule leaves little room for any delays in completing the remaining development and testing activities.

In addition to managing the compressed testing time frames, the Bureau also has to quickly finalize plans related to its IT infrastructure. For example, in March 2019, the Bureau's technical integration contractor stated that it needed the Bureau to obtain approval from federal partners for its Trusted Internet Connection or finalize alternative plans in order to complete performance and scalability testing in a timely manner.[25] As of mid-April 2019, the Bureau stated that it was still awaiting final approval. Given that these plans may impact systems being tested this summer or deployed into production for the address canvassing operation in August 2019, it is important that the Bureau quickly addresses this matter.

Our past reporting noted that the Bureau faced significant challenges in managing its schedule for system development and testing that occurred in 2017 and 2018.[26] We reported that while the Bureau had continued to make progress in developing and testing IT systems for the 2020 Census, it had experienced delays in developing systems to support the 2018 End-to-End

---

[25] External network traffic (traffic that is routed through agency's external connections) must be routed through a Trusted Internet Connection. External connections include those connections between an agency's information system or network and the globally-addressable internet or a remote information system or network and networks located on foreign territory.

[26] GAO-18-655.

test. These delays compressed the time available for system and integration testing and for security assessments. In addition, several systems experienced problems during the test. We noted then, and reaffirm now, that continued schedule management challenges may compress the time available for the remaining system and integration testing and increase the risk that systems may not function or be as secure as intended.

The Bureau has acknowledged that it faces risks to the implementation of its systems and technology. As of March 2019, the Bureau had identified about 330 active risks for the 2020 Census program, through its risk management process, including 20 high risks that may have substantial technical and schedule impacts if realized. Taken together, these risks represent a cross-section of issues, such as the effects of late changes to technical requirements, the need to ensure adequate time for system development and performance and scalability testing, contracting issues, privacy risks, and skilled staffing shortages. Going forward, it will be important that the Bureau effectively manages these risks to better ensure that it meets near-term milestones for system development and testing, and is ready for the major operations of the 2020 Census.

## Key Risk #3: The Bureau Faces Significant Cybersecurity Risks to Its Systems and Data

The risks to IT systems supporting the federal government and its functions, including conducting the 2020 Census, are increasing as security threats continue to evolve and become more sophisticated.

These risks include insider threats from witting or unwitting employees, escalating and emerging threats from around the globe, and the emergence of new and more destructive attacks. Underscoring the importance of this issue, we have designated information security as a government-wide high-risk area since 1997 and, in our most recent biennial report to Congress, ensuring the cybersecurity of the nation was one of nine high-risk areas that we reported needing especially focused executive and congressional attention.[27]

Our prior and ongoing work has identified significant challenges that the Bureau faces in securing systems and data for the 2020 Census.[28] Specifically, the Bureau has faced challenges related to completing security assessments, addressing security weaknesses, resolving cybersecurity recommendations from DHS, and addressing numerous other cybersecurity concerns (such as phishing).[29]

### *The Bureau Has Made Progress in Completing Security Assessment, but Critical Work Remains*

Federal law specifies requirements for protecting federal information and information systems, such as those systems to be used in the 2020 Census. Specifically, the Federal Information Security Management Act of 2002 and the Federal Information Security Modernization Act of 2014 (FISMA) require executive branch agencies to develop, document, and implement an agency-wide program to provide security for the information and information systems that support operations and assets of the agency.[30]

In accordance with FISMA, National Institute of Standards and Technology (NIST) guidance, and Office of Management and Budget (OMB) guidance, the Bureau's Office of the Chief Information Officer (CIO) established a risk management framework. This framework requires system developers to ensure that each of the Bureau's systems undergoes a full security assessment, and that system developers remediate critical deficiencies.

According to the Bureau's risk management framework, the systems expected to be used to conduct the 2020 Census will need to have complete

---

[27] GAO-19-157SP.

[28] GAO-18-655.

[29] Phishing is a digital form of social engineering that uses authentic-looking, but fake emails to request information from users or direct them to a fake website that requests information.

[30] The Federal Information Security Modernization Act of 2014, Pub. L. No. 113-283, 128 Stat. 3073 (Dec. 18, 2014) largely superseded the Federal Information Security Management Act of 2002, enacted as Title III, E-Government Act of 2002, Pub. L. No. 107-347, 116 Stat. 2899, 2946 (Dec. 17, 2002).

security documentation (such as system security plans) and an approved authorization to operate prior to their use. Currently, according to the Bureau's Office of the CIO:

- Fourteen of the 52 systems have authorization to operate, and will not need to be reauthorized before they are used in the 2020 Census[31]
- Thirty-two of the 52 systems have authorization to operate, and may need to be reauthorized before they are used in the 2020 Census
- Six of the 52 systems do not have authorization to operate, and will need to be authorized before they are used in the 2020 Census.

Figure 5 summarizes the authorization to operate status for the systems being used in the 2020 Census, as reported by the Bureau in April 2019.

As we have previously reported, while large-scale technological changes (such as internet self-response) increase the likelihood of efficiency and effectiveness gains, they also introduce many cybersecurity challenges. The 2020 Census also involves collecting personally identifiable information (PII) on over a hundred million households across the country, which further increases the need to properly secure these systems.

Thus, it will be important that the Bureau provides adequate time to perform these security assessments, completes them in a timely manner, and ensures that risks are at an acceptable level before the systems are deployed. We have ongoing work examining how the Bureau plans to address both internal and external cyber threats, including its efforts to complete system security assessments and resolve identified weaknesses.

---

[31] According to the Bureau's risk management framework, once a system obtains an authorization, it is transitioned to the continuous monitoring process where the authorizing official can provide ongoing authorization for system operation as long as the risk level remains acceptable. Further, according to the framework, authorized systems do not need a formal reauthorization unless the system's authorizing official determines that the risk posture of the system needs to change. This could occur, for example, if the system undergoes significant new development.

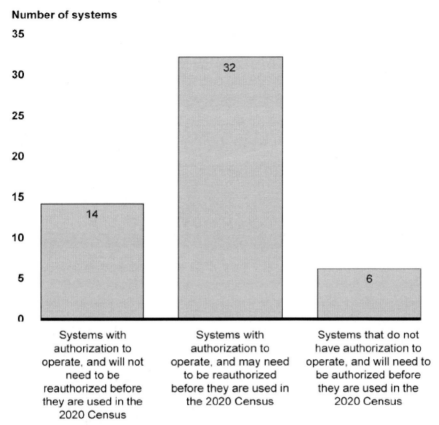

Source: GAO analysis of Census Bureau data. | GAO-19-431T.

Figure 5. Authorization to Operate Status for the 52 Systems Being Used by the Census Bureau in the 2020 Census as of April 2019.

## The Bureau Has Identified a Significant Number of Corrective Actions to Address Security Weaknesses, but Has Not Always Been Timely in Completing Them

FISMA requires that agency-wide information security programs include a process for planning, implementing, evaluating, and documenting remedial actions (i.e., corrective actions) to address any deficiencies in the information security policies, procedures, and practices of the agency.

Agencies must establish procedures to reasonably ensure that all information security control weaknesses, regardless of how or by whom they are identified, are addressed through the agency's remediation processes.

For each identified control weakness, the agency is required to develop and implement a plan of actions and milestones (POA&M) based on findings from security control assessments, security impact analyses, continuous monitoring of activities, audit reports, and other sources. Additionally, the Bureau's framework requires that security assessment findings that need to be remediated are to be tracked as POA&Ms. These POA&Ms are expected to provide a description of the vulnerabilities identified during the security assessment that resulted from a control weakness.

As of March 2019, the Bureau had over 500 open POA&Ms to remediate for issues identified during security assessment activities, including ongoing continuous monitoring. Of these open POA&Ms, 247 (or about 48 percent) were considered "high-risk" or "very high-risk."

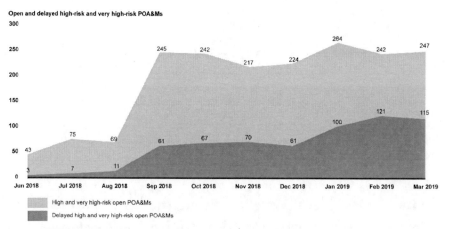

Source: GAO analysis of Census Bureau data. | GAO-19-431T.

Figure 6. Open and Delayed High-Risk and Very High-Risk Plans of Action and Milestones (POA&Ms) for Census Bureau Systems, June 2018 – March 2019.

While the Bureau established POA&Ms for addressing these identified security control weaknesses, it did not always complete remedial actions in accordance with its established deadlines. For example, of the 247 open "high-risk" or "very high-risk" POA&Ms we reviewed through March 2019, the Bureau identified 115 as being delayed. Further, 70 of the 115 had missed their scheduled completion dates by 60 or more days. In addition, the number of open "high-risk" or "very high-risk" POA&Ms that the Bureau identified as delayed has substantially increased since June 2018, as shown in Figure 6.

According to the Bureau, these POA&Ms were identified as delayed due to technical challenges or resource constraints to remediate and close them. However, without resolving identified vulnerabilities in a timely manner, the Bureau faces an increased risk, as continuing opportunities exist for unauthorized individuals to exploit these weaknesses and gain access to sensitive information and systems.

## The Bureau Has Begun Implementing DHS's Cybersecurity Recommendations, but Has Not Established a Formal Process to Address Them

The Bureau is working with federal and industry partners, including the Department of Homeland Security, to support the 2020 Census cybersecurity efforts. Specifically, the Bureau is working with DHS to ensure a scalable and secure network connection for the 2020 Census respondents (e.g., virtual Trusted Internet Connection with the cloud), improve its cybersecurity posture (e.g., improve risk management processes and procedures), and to strengthen its response to potential cyber threats (e.g., federal cyber incident coordination).

Federal law describes practices for strengthening cybersecurity by documenting or tracking corrective actions. As previously mentioned, FISMA requires executive branch agencies to establish a process for planning, implementing, evaluating, and documenting remedial actions to address any deficiencies in their information security policies, procedures, and practices. GAO's internal control standards also state that agencies should establish effective internal control monitoring that includes a process to promptly resolve the findings of audits and other reviews.[32] Specifically,

---

[32] GAO, *Standards for Internal Control in the Federal Government*, GAO-14-704G (Washington, D.C.: Sept. 10, 2014).

agencies should document and complete corrective actions to remediate identified deficiencies on a timely basis. This would include correcting identified deficiencies or demonstrating that the findings and recommendations do not warrant agency action.

Since January 2017, DHS has been providing cybersecurity assistance (including issuing recommendations) to the Bureau in preparation for the 2020 Census, and the Bureau has reported making progress in addressing those recommendations. Specifically, DHS has been providing cybersecurity assistance to the Bureau in five areas:

- management coordination and executive support, including a CyberStat Review;[33]
- cybersecurity threat intelligence and information sharing enhancement through, among other things, a DHS cyber threat briefing to the Bureau's leadership;
- network and infrastructure security and resilience, including National Cybersecurity Protection System (also called EINSTEIN) support;[34]
- incident response and management readiness through a Federal Incident Response Evaluation assessment;[35] and
- risk management and vulnerability assessments on specific targets provided by the Bureau.

In the last 2 years, as a result of these activities, DHS has provided 17 recommendations for the Bureau to strengthen its cybersecurity efforts.

---

[33] According to OMB, CyberStat Reviews are face-to-face, evidence-based meetings intended to ensure agencies are accountable for their cybersecurity posture. OMB, DHS, and Commerce participated in the Fiscal Year 2017 CyberStat Review related to the Bureau.

[34] The National Cybersecurity Protection System, operationally known as the EINSTEIN program, is an integrated system-of-systems that is intended to deliver a range of capabilities, including intrusion detection, intrusion prevention, analytics, and information sharing. This program was developed to be one of the tools to aid federal agencies in mitigating information security threats.

[35] As part of the CyberStat Review, DHS conducted a Federal Incident Response Evaluation assessment in October 2017. The purpose of the assessment was, in part, to review the Bureau's incident management practices and provide recommendations that, if addressed, would strengthen the Bureau's cybersecurity efforts.

Among other things, the recommendations pertained to strengthening incident management capabilities, penetration testing[36] and web application assessments of select systems, and phishing assessments to gain access to sensitive PII. Due to the sensitive nature of the recommendations, we are not identifying the specific recommendations or specific findings associated with them in this statement.

**Table 3. GAO Assessment of the Status of 17 Recommendations to the Census Bureau by the Department of Homeland Security, as of February 2019**

| Status | Number of recommendations |
|---|---|
| Completed actions | 3 |
| Further improvements needed for actions the Census Bureau considered complete | 1 |
| Actions In progress | 13 |

Source: GAO analysis of Census Bureau data. | GAO-19-431T.

As of February 2019, the Bureau had fully completed actions to address three recommendations, needed to further improve on actions taken for one recommendation it indicated had been completed, and needed to complete actions in progress for the remaining 13 recommendations (as summarized in Table 3).

However, the Bureau had not established a formal process for documenting, tracking, and completing corrective actions for all the recommendations provided by DHS. To the Bureau's credit, it had incorporated the corrective actions associated with the three completed recommendations into its formal process used for tracking POA&Ms, which includes identifying remediation activities, resources required, milestones, and completion dates. The Bureau did not incorporate the remaining 14

---

[36] The National Institute of Standards and Technology defined penetration testing as security testing in which the evaluators mimic real-world attacks in an attempt to identify ways to circumvent the security features of an application, system, or network. Penetration testing often involves issuing real attacks on real systems and data, using the same tools and techniques used by actual attackers.

recommendations into the POA&M process. Instead, in November 2018, the Bureau created an informal document to track the 17 DHS recommendations, but this document does not consistently include details such as the resources required, expected completion date, or whether the recommendations do not warrant agency action.

Until the Bureau implements a formal process for tracking and implementing appropriate corrective actions to remediate identified cybersecurity weaknesses from DHS, and addresses the identified deficiencies, it faces an increased likelihood that these weaknesses will go uncorrected and may be exploited to cause harm to agency's 2020 Census IT systems and gain access to sensitive respondent data. Implementing a formal process would also help to ensure that DHS's efforts result in improvements to the Bureau's cybersecurity posture.

## *The Bureau Faces Several Other Cybersecurity Challenges in Implementing the 2020 Census*

The Bureau faces other significant cybersecurity challenges in addition to those previously discussed. More specifically, we previously reported[37] that the extensive use of IT systems to support the 2020 Census redesign may help increase efficiency, but that this redesign introduces critical cybersecurity challenges. These challenges include those related to the following:

- Phishing. We have previously reported that advanced persistent threats may be targeted against social media web sites used by the federal government. In addition, attackers may use social media to collect information and launch attacks against federal information systems through social engineering, such as phishing.[38] Phishing is

---

[37] GAO, *Information Technology: Better Management of Interdependencies between Programs Supporting 2020 Census Is Needed,* GAO-16-623 (Washington, D.C.: Aug. 9, 2016) and *Information Technology: Uncertainty Remains about the Bureau's Readiness for a Key Decennial Census Test,* GAO-17-221T (Washington, D.C.: Nov. 16, 2016).

[38] GAO, *Social Media: Federal Agencies Need Policies and Procedures for Managing and Protecting Information They Access and Disseminate,* GAO-11-605 (Washington, D.C.: June 28, 2011).

a digital form of social engineering that uses authentic-looking, but fake, emails, websites, or instant messages to get users to download malware, open malicious attachments, or open links that direct them to a website that requests information or executes malicious code. Phishing attacks could target respondents, as well as Bureau employees and contractors. The 2020 Census will be the first one in which respondents will be heavily encouraged to respond via the internet. This will likely increase the risk that cyber criminals will use phishing in an attempt to steal personal information.

- Disinformation from social media. We previously reported that one of the Bureau's key innovations for the 2020 Census is the large-scale implementation of an internet self-response option. The Bureau is encouraging the public to use the internet self-response option through expanded use of social media. However, the public perception of the Bureau's ability to adequately safeguard the privacy and confidentiality of the 2020 Census internet self-responses could be influenced by disinformation spread through social media. According to the Bureau, if a substantial segment of the public is not convinced that the Bureau can safeguard public response data against data breaches and unauthorized use, then response rates may be lower than projected, leading to an increase in cases for follow-up and subsequent cost increases.

- Ensuring that individuals gain only limited and appropriate access to 2020 Census data. The Bureau plans to enable a public-facing website and Bureau-issued mobile devices to collect PII (e.g., name, address, and date of birth) from the nation's entire population— estimated to be over 300 million. In addition, the Bureau is planning to obtain and store administrative records containing PII from other government agencies to help augment information that enumerators did not collect.

- The number of reported security incidents involving PII at federal agencies has increased dramatically in recent years. Because of these challenges, we have recommended, among other things, that federal agencies improve their response to information security incidents and data breaches involving PII, and consistently develop and implement privacy policies and procedures. Accordingly, it will be important for the Bureau to ensure that only respondents and Bureau officials are able to gain access to this information, and enumerators and other employees only have access to the information needed to perform their jobs.

- Ensuring adequate control in a cloud environment. The Bureau has decided to use cloud solutions as a key component of the 2020 Census IT infrastructure. We have previously reported that cloud computing has both positive and negative information security implications and, thus, federal agencies should develop service-level agreements with cloud providers. These agreements should specify, among other things, the security performance requirements — including data reliability, preservation, privacy, and access rights — that the service provider is to meet.[39] Without these safeguards, computer systems and networks, as well as the critical operations and key infrastructures they support, may be lost; information—including sensitive personal information—may be compromised; and the agency's operations could be disrupted.

- Ensuring contingency and incident response plans are in place to encompass all of the IT systems to be used to support the 2020 Census. Because of the brief time frame for collecting data during the 2020 Census, it is especially important that systems are available for respondents to ensure a high response rate. Contingency planning and incident response help ensure that, if normal operations are interrupted, network managers will be able to detect, mitigate, and recover from a service disruption while preserving access to vital information. Implementing important security controls, including policies, procedures, and techniques for contingency planning and incident response, helps to ensure the confidentiality, integrity, and availability of information and systems, even during disruptions of service. Without contingency

---

[39] GAO, *Information Security: Agencies Need to Improve Cyber Incident Response Practices,* GAO-14-354 (Washington, D.C.: Apr. 30, 2014).

and incident response plans, system availability might be impacted and result in a lower response rate.

The Bureau's CIO has acknowledged these cybersecurity challenges and is working to address them, according to Bureau documentation. In addition, we have ongoing work looking at many of these challenges, including the Bureau's plans to protect PII, use a cloud-based infrastructure, and recover from security incidents and other disasters.

## Key Risk #4: The Bureau Will Need to Control Any Further Cost Growth and Develop Cost Estimates That Reflect Best Practices

Since 2015, the Bureau has made progress in improving its ability to develop a reliable cost estimate. We have reported on the reliability of the $12.3 billion life-cycle cost estimate released in October 2015 and the $15.6 billion revised cost estimate released in October 2017.[40] In 2016 we reported that the October 2015 version of the Bureau's life-cycle cost estimate for the 2020 Census was not reliable. Specifically, we found that the 2020 Census life-cycle cost estimate partially met two of the characteristics of a reliable cost estimate (comprehensive and accurate) and minimally met the other two (well-documented and credible). We recommended that the Bureau take specific steps to ensure its cost estimate meets the characteristics of a high-quality estimate. The Bureau agreed and has taken action to improve the reliability of the cost estimate.

In August 2018 we reported that while improvements had been made, the Bureau's October 2017 cost estimate for the 2020 Census did not fully reflect all the characteristics of a reliable estimate. (See Figure 7).

---

[40] GAO-16-628 and GAO, *2020 Census: Census Bureau Improved the Quality of Its Cost Estimation but Additional Steps Are Needed to Ensure Reliability*, GAO-18-635 (Washington, D.C.: Aug. 17, 2018).

In order for a cost estimate to be deemed reliable as described in GAO's Cost Estimating and Assessment Guide[41] and thus, to effectively inform 2020 Census annual budgetary figures, the cost estimate must meet or substantially meet the following four characteristics:

- Well-Documented. Cost estimates are considered valid if they are well-documented to the point they can be easily repeated or updated and can be traced to original sources through auditing, according to best practices.
- Accurate. Accurate estimates are unbiased and contain few mathematical mistakes.
- Credible. Credible cost estimates must clearly identify limitations due to uncertainty or bias surrounding the data or assumptions, according to best practices.
- Comprehensive. To be comprehensive an estimate should have enough detail to ensure that cost elements are neither omitted nor double-counted, and all cost-influencing assumptions are detailed in the estimate's documentation, among other things, according to best practices.

The 2017 cost estimate only partially met the characteristic of being well-documented. In general, some documentation was missing, inconsistent, or difficult to understand. Specifically, we found that source data did not always support the information described in the basis of estimate document or could not be found in the files provided for two of the Bureau's largest field operations: Address Canvassing and Non-Response Follow-Up. We also found that some of the cost elements did not trace clearly to supporting spreadsheets and assumption documents.

---

[41] GAO, *GAO Cost Estimating and Assessment Guide: Best Practices for Developing and Managing Capital Program Costs (Supersedes GAO-U7-1134SP),* GAO-09-3SP (Washington, D.C.: Mar. 2, 2009).

| Characteristic | 2015 Assessment | 2017 Assessment |
|---|---|---|
| Well-Documented | ◗ Minimally met | ◑ Partially met |
| Accurate | ◑ Partially met | ◕ Substantially met |
| Credible | ◗ Minimally met | ◕ Substantially met |
| Comprehensive | ◑ Partially met | ● Met |

● Met    ◕ Substantially met    ◑ Partially met    ◗ Minimally met    ○ Not met

Source: GAO analysis of Census Bureau data. | GAO-19-431T.

Figure 7. Overview of the Census Bureau's 2015 and 2017 Cost Estimates Compared to Characteristics of a Reliable Cost Estimate.

Failure to document an estimate in enough detail makes it more difficult to replicate calculations, or to detect possible errors in the estimate; reduces transparency of the estimation process; and can undermine the ability to use the information to improve future cost estimates or even to reconcile the estimate with another independent cost estimate. The Bureau told us it would continue to make improvements to ensure the estimate is well-documented.

## Increased Costs Are Driven by an Assumed Decrease in Self-Response Rates and Increases in Contingency Funds and IT Cost Categories

The 2017 life-cycle cost estimate includes significantly higher costs than those included in the 2015 estimate. The largest increases occurred in the Response, Managerial Contingency, and Census/Survey Engineering categories. For example, increased costs of $1.3 billion in the response category (costs related to collecting, maintaining, and processing survey response data) were in part due to reduced assumptions for self-response rates, leading to increases in the amount of data collected in the field, which is more costly to the Bureau.

Contingency allocations increased overall from $1.35 billion in 2015 to $2.6 billion in 2017, as the Bureau gained a greater understanding of risks facing the 2020 Census. Increases of $838 million in the Census/Survey Engineering category were due mainly to the cost of an IT contract for integrating decennial survey systems that was not included in the 2015 cost estimate. Bureau officials attribute a decrease of $551 million in estimated costs for Program Management to changes in the categorization of costs associated with risks.

Specifically, in the 2017 version of the estimate, estimated costs related to program risks were allocated to their corresponding work breakdown structure (WBS) element. Figure 8 shows the change in cost by WBS category for 2015 and 2017.

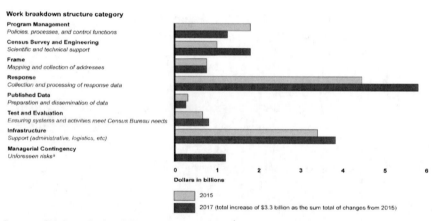

Source: GAO analysis of Census Bureau data. | GAO-19-431T.

[a]The 2015 cost estimate also included managerial contingency amounts totaling $829 million; however, these were not presented as a separate work breakdown structure category.

Figure 8. Change in 2020 Census Cost Estimate by Work Breakdown Structure Category, 2015 vs. 2017.

More generally, factors that contributed to cost fluctuations between the 2015 and 2017 cost estimates include:

- Changes in assumptions. Among other changes, a decrease in the assumed rate for self-response from 63.5 percent in 2015 to 60.5 percent in 2017 increased the cost of collecting responses from nonresponding housing units.
- Improved ability to anticipate and quantify risk. In general, contingency allocations designed to address the effects of potential risks increased overall from $1.3 billion in 2015 to $2.6 billion in 2017.
- An overall increase in IT costs. IT cost increases, totaling $1.59 billion, represented almost 50 percent of the total cost increase from 2015 to 2017.
- More defined contract requirements. Bureau documents described an overall improvement in the Bureau's ability to define and specify contract requirements. This resulted in updated estimates for several contracts, including for the Census Questionnaire Assistance contract.[42]

However, while the Bureau has been able to better quantify risk; in August 2018 we also reported that the Secretary of Commerce included a contingency amount of about $1.2 billion in the 2017 cost estimate to account for what the Bureau refers to as "unknown unknowns." According to Bureau documentation these include such risks as natural disasters or cyber attacks. The Bureau provides a description of how the risk contingency for "unknown unknowns" is calculated; however, this description does not clearly link calculated amounts to the risks themselves. Thus, only $14.4 billion of the Bureau's $15.6 billion cost estimate has justification. According to Bureau officials, the cost estimate remains at

---

[42] This contract has two primary functions: to provide (1) questionnaire assistance by telephone and email for respondents by answering questions about the census in general and regarding specific items on the census form, and (2) an option for respondents to complete a census interview over the telephone.

$15.6 billion, but they are managing the 2020 Census at a lower level of funding—$14.1 billion and, at this time, do not plan to request funding for the $1.2 billion contingency fund for unknown unknowns or $369 million in funding for selected discrete program risks for what-if scenarios such as an increase in the wage rate or additional supervisors needed to manage field operations. Instead of requesting funding for these contingencies upfront the Bureau plans to work with OMB and Commerce to request additional funds, if the need arises.

According to Bureau officials they anticipate that the remaining $1.1 billion in contingency funding included in the $14.1 billion will be sufficient to carry out the 2020 Census. In June 2016 we recommended the Bureau improve control over how risk and uncertainty are accounted for. This prior recommendation remains valid given the life-cycle cost estimate still includes the $1.2 billion unjustified contingency fund for "unknown unknowns."

Moreover, given the cost growth between 2015 and 2017 it will be important for the Bureau to monitor cost in real-time, as well as, document, explain and review variances between planned and actual cost. In August 2018 we reported that the Bureau had not been tracking variances between estimated life-cycle costs and actual expenses. Tools to track variance enable management to measure progress against planned outcomes and will help inform the 2030 Census cost estimate. Bureau officials stated that they already have systems in place that can be adapted for tracking estimated and actual costs. We will continue to monitor the status of the tracking system.

According to Bureau officials it plans to release an updated version of the 2020 Census life-cycle estimate in the spring of 2019. To ensure that future updates to the life-cycle cost estimate reflect best practices, it will be important for the Bureau to implement our recommendation related to the cost estimate.

# CONTINUED MANAGEMENT ATTENTION NEEDED TO KEEP PREPARATIONS ON TRACK AND HELP ENSURE A COST-EFFECTIVE ENUMERATION

## 2020 Challenges Are Symptomatic of Deeper Long-Term Organizational Issues

The difficulties facing the Bureau's preparation for the decennial census in such areas as planning and testing; managing and overseeing IT programs, systems, and contractors supporting the enumeration; developing reliable cost estimates; prioritizing decisions; managing schedules; and other challenges, are symptomatic of deeper organizational issues.

Following the 2010 Census, a key lesson learned for 2020 that we identified was ensuring that the Bureau's organizational culture and structure, as well as its approach to strategic planning, human capital management, internal collaboration, knowledge sharing, capital decision-making, risk and change management, and other internal functions are aligned toward delivering more cost-effective outcomes.[43]

The Bureau has made improvements over the last decade, and continued progress will depend in part on sustaining efforts to strengthen risk management activities, enhancing systems testing, bringing in experienced personnel to key positions, implementing our recommendations, and meeting regularly with officials from its parent agency, Commerce.

Going forward, we have reported that the key elements needed to make progress in high-risk areas are top-level attention by the administration and agency officials to (1) leadership commitment, (2) ensuring capacity, (3) developing a corrective action plan, (4) regular monitoring, and (5) demonstrated progress. Although important steps have been taken in at least some of these areas, overall, far more work is needed.[44] We discuss three of five areas below.

---

[43] GAO, *2010 Census: Preliminary Lessons Learned Highlight the Need for Fundamental Reforms,* GAO-11-496T (Washington, D.C.: Apr. 6, 2011).
[44] GAO-17-317.

The Secretary of Commerce has successfully demonstrated leadership commitment. For example, the Bureau and Commerce have strengthened this area with executive-level oversight of the 2020 Census by holding regular meetings on the status of IT systems and other risk areas. In addition, in 2017 Commerce designated a team to assist senior Bureau management with cost estimation challenges. Moreover, on January 2, 2019, a new Director of the Census Bureau took office, a position that had been vacant since June 2017.

With regard to capacity, the Bureau has improved the cost estimation process of the decennial when it established guidance including:

- roles and responsibilities for oversight and approval of cost estimation processes,
- procedures requiring a detailed description of the steps taken to produce a high-quality cost estimate, and
- a process for updating the cost estimate and associated documents over the life of a project.

However, the Bureau continues to experience skills gaps in the government program management office overseeing the $886 million contract for integrating the IT systems needed to conduct the 2020 Census. Specifically, as of February 2019, 15 of 44 positions in this office were vacant.

For the monitoring element, we found to track performance of decennial census operations, the Bureau relied on reports to track progress against pre-set goals for a test conducted in 2018. According to the Bureau, these same reports will be used in 2020 to track progress. However, the Bureau's schedule for developing IT systems during the 2018 End-to-End test experienced delays that compressed the time available for system testing, integration testing, and security assessments. These schedule delays contributed to systems experiencing problems after deployment, as well as cybersecurity challenges. In the months ahead, we will continue to monitor the Bureau's progress in addressing each of the five elements essential for reducing the risk to a cost-effective enumeration.

## Further Actions Needed on Our Recommendations

Over the past several years we have issued numerous reports that underscored the fact that, if the Bureau was to successfully meet its cost savings goal for the 2020 Census, the agency needed to take significant actions to improve its research, testing, planning, scheduling, cost estimation, system development, and IT security practices. As of April 2019, we have made 97 recommendations related to the 2020 Census. The Bureau has implemented 72 of these recommendations, 24 remain open, and one recommendation was closed as not implemented.

Of the 24 open recommendations, 11 were directed at improving the implementation of the innovations for the 2020 Census. Commerce generally agreed with our recommendations and is taking steps to implement them. Moreover, in April 2018 we designated 15 recommendations as "priority." Priority recommendations are those recommendations that we believe warrant priority attention from heads of key departments and agencies. Eight of these 15 priority recommendations have been closed as implemented over the past year.[45]

On July 19, 2018, in response to our April 2018 letter calling his attention to our priority recommendations, the Commerce Secretary concurred that there was still much work to be done, and that the number of our priority recommendations concerning the 2020 Census was reflective of Commerce's focus on ensuring a successful census in 2020. On April 23, 2019, we sent an updated priority recommendation letter to the Commerce Secretary that included five new recommendations from our recent work and also reflected the department's progress on implementing past recommendations.

We believe that attention to these recommendations is essential for a cost-effective enumeration. The recommendations included implementing reliable cost estimation and scheduling practices in order to establish better

---

[45] The 15 priority recommendations for the 2020 Census cover the period from November 2009 to July 2017.

control over program costs, as well as taking steps to better position the Bureau to develop an internet response option for the 2020 Census.

In addition to our recommendations, to better position the Bureau for a more cost-effective enumeration, on March 18, 2019, we met with OMB, Commerce, and Bureau officials to discuss the Bureau's progress in reducing the risks facing the census. We also meet regularly with Bureau officials and managers to discuss the progress and status of open recommendations related to the 2020 Census, which has resulted in Bureau actions in recent months leading to closure of some recommendations.

We are encouraged by this commitment by Commerce and the Bureau in addressing our recommendations. Implementing our recommendations in a complete and timely manner is important because it could improve the management of the 2020 Census and help to mitigate continued risks.

## CONCLUSION

In conclusion, while the Bureau has made progress in revamping its approach to the census, it faces considerable challenges and uncertainties in implementing key cost-saving innovations and ensuring they function under operational conditions; managing the development and testing of its IT systems; ensuring the cybersecurity of its systems and data; and developing a quality cost estimate for the 2020 Census and preventing further cost increases. For these reasons, the 2020 Census is a GAO high-risk area.

Regarding cybersecurity, the Bureau's involvement of DHS to improve its cybersecurity posture, including cyber threat briefings and vulnerability assessments, is a positive step forward. However, the Bureau's corrective actions to address its high-risk and very high-risk security weaknesses are frequently delayed—often for months—which increases the risk that these weaknesses could be exploited to cause harm to the agency's systems. In addition, the Bureau's process for addressing DHS's cybersecurity recommendations has shortcomings, which increases the risk that the underlying deficiencies identified by DHS may be exploited to gain access to the Bureau's systems and sensitive data.

Going forward, continued management attention and oversight will be vital for ensuring that risks are managed, preparations stay on track, and the Bureau is held accountable for implementing the enumeration, as planned. Without timely and appropriate actions, the challenges previously discussed could adversely affect the cost, accuracy, schedule, and security of the enumeration. We will continue to assess the Bureau's efforts and look forward to keeping Congress informed of the Bureau's progress.

## RECOMMENDATIONS FOR EXECUTIVE ACTION

We are making the following two recommendations to Commerce:

The Secretary of Commerce should direct the Director of the Census Bureau to direct the Census Bureau's CIO to take steps to ensure that identified corrective actions for cybersecurity weaknesses are implemented within prescribed time frames. (Recommendation 1)

The Secretary of Commerce should direct the Director of the Census Bureau to direct the Bureau's CIO to implement a formal process for tracking and executing appropriate corrective actions to remediate cybersecurity weaknesses identified by DHS, and expeditiously address the identified deficiencies. (Recommendation 2)

Chairman Serrano, Ranking Member Aderholt, and Members of the Subcommittee, this completes our prepared statement. We would be pleased to respond to any questions that you may have.

In: Key Government Reports.
Editor: Ernest Clark

ISBN: 978-1-53616-001-7
© 2019 Nova Science Publishers, Inc.

*Chapter 4*

# DATA ACT: PILOT EFFECTIVELY TESTED APPROACHES FOR REDUCING REPORTING BURDEN FOR GRANTS BUT NOT FOR CONTRACTS[*]

## *United States Government Accountability Office*

### ABBREVIATIONS

CAP       Cross-Agency Priority
CDER      Common Data Element Repository
DATA Act  Digital Accountability and Transparency Act of 2014
FAR       Federal Acquisition Regulation
FFR       Federal Financial Report
FFATA     Federal Funding Accountability and Transparency Act of 2006

---

[*] This is an edited, reformatted and augmented version of United States Government Accountability Office; Report to Congressional Addressees, Publication No. GAO-19-299, dated April 2019.

| GSA | General Services Administration |
| HFC | Hydrofluorocarbon |
| HHS | Department of Health and Human Services |
| NOA | Notice of Award |
| OFFM | Office of Federal Financial Management |
| OFPP | Office of Federal Procurement Policy |
| OMB | Office of Management and Budget |
| PMA | President's Management Agenda |

# WHY GAO DID THIS STUDY

The DATA Act required OMB or a designated federal agency to establish a pilot program to develop recommendations for reducing recipient reporting burden for federal grantees and contractors. The grants portion of the pilot tested six ways to reduce recipient reporting burden while the procurement portion focused on testing a centralized reporting portal for submitting reporting requirements. This chapter follows a 2016 GAO review on the design of the pilot.

This chapter assesses the extent to which (1) the pilot met the statutory requirements set out in the DATA Act, (2) the grants portion of the pilot demonstrated changes in reporting burden, and (3) the procurement portion demonstrated changes in reporting burden. GAO reviewed statutory requirements, pilot plans, agency data and reports and interviewed OMB staff and officials from HHS and GSA.

# WHAT GAO RECOMMENDS

GAO recommends that the Director of OMB ensure that information is collected regarding how centralized reporting of procurement requirements might reduce recipient reporting burden—including input from stakeholders such as contractors through an iterative and ongoing process—to inform

OMB's planned expansion of the Central Reporting Portal. OMB neither agreed nor disagreed with the recommendation but provided technical comments, which GAO incorporated as appropriate.

## WHAT GAO FOUND

In response to requirements of the Digital Accountability and Transparency Act of 2014 (DATA Act), the Office of Management and Budget (OMB) led implementation of a pilot program, known as the Section 5 Pilot, aimed at developing recommendations for reducing recipient reporting burden for federal grantees and contractors.

The pilot program met many, but not all, of its statutory requirements. For example, the act required OMB to issue guidance to agencies for reducing reporting burden for federal award recipients (including both grantees and contractors) based on the pilot's findings. OMB partially met this requirement because the guidance it issued only applied to grants.

The pilot program consisted of two parts, which differed considerably in both design and results: The grants portion, administered by the Department of Health and Human Services (HHS), examined six approaches for reducing grantee reporting burden and found positive results related to reductions in reporting time as well as reduced duplication. HHS incorporated ongoing stakeholder input during the pilot, and its findings contributed to government-wide initiatives related to federal reporting and reducing grantee-reporting burden.

The procurement (contracts) portion of the pilot, led by OMB with assistance from the General Services Administration (GSA), did not collect sufficient evidence to determine whether centralizing procurement reporting through a single web-based portal would reduce contractor reporting burden—a key objective of the pilot. The pilot planned to test the portal by collecting weekly Davis-Bacon wage data from a minimum of 180 contractors, potentially resulting in thousands of submissions over a year. However, in the end, the pilot did not result in any Davis-Bacon data due to lack of contractor participation and the absence of iterative and ongoing stakeholder engagement. Subsequently, OMB expanded the pilot to include hydrofluorocarbon (HFC) reporting but received only 11 HFC submissions. (See Figure) In addition, HFC reporting was not suited for assessing changes in reporting burden because it was a new requirement and thus no comparative data existed. OMB plans to expand its use of the portal for additional procurement reporting requirements but still does not have information from stakeholders that could help inform the expansion.

Congressional Addressees:

In fiscal year 2017, the federal government awarded $675 billion in grants to state and local governments and $500 billion in contracts. Recipients of these grants and contracts are required to report federal spending and a range of other information to comply with applicable laws and regulations. Grant recipients and federal contractors face challenges related to duplicative and burdensome reporting when complying with these requirements. Using standardized data and processes can reduce federal reporting burden and increase the accuracy of data reported.

The Digital Accountability and Transparency Act of 2014 (DATA Act) required the Office of Management and Budget (OMB) and the Department of the Treasury to establish standardized government-wide financial data standards.[1] In addition, the DATA Act added section 5 to the Federal Funding Accountability and Transparency Act of 2006 (FFATA), which provided an opportunity for simplifying reporting for federal contracts, awards, and subawards.[2] Toward that end, the act required OMB, or a federal agency designated by OMB, to establish a pilot program to test potential approaches for reducing reporting burden for federal award recipients—both grantees and contractors (procurement). OMB was also charged with developing evidence-based recommendations and guidance to federal

---

[1] Pub. L. No. 113-101, § 3. 128 Stat. 1146, 1148-1149 (May 9, 2014). The DATA Act amended the Federal Funding Accountability and Transparency Act of 2006 (FFATA). Pub. L. No. 109-282, 120 Stat. 1186 (Sept. 26, 2006), codified at 31 U.S.C. § 6101 note. We refer to language added to FFATA by the DATA Act as DATA Act requirements.

[2] See FFATA, § 5(b). In this report, we refer to the pilot required by this provision as the "Section 5 Pilot."

agencies for eliminating unnecessary duplication in financial reporting, and for reducing compliance costs for federal award recipients based on the pilot findings.

The DATA Act includes a provision for us to review its implementation. This chapter assesses the extent to which (1) the Section 5 Pilot met the statutory requirements of the act, (2) the grants portion of the Section 5 Pilot demonstrated changes in federal award recipients' reporting burden, and (3) the procurement portion of the Section 5 Pilot demonstrated changes in federal award recipients' reporting burden.

To address these objectives, we assessed pilot activities by reviewing the requirements for the pilot contained in the DATA Act as well as pilot plans and data from agencies involved in administering and executing the pilot. These agencies included the Department of Health and Human Services (HHS), OMB's Offices of Federal Financial Management (OFFM) and Federal Procurement Policy (OFPP), and the General Services Administration (GSA).

We determined that the pilot data we reviewed were reliable for the purposes of our work by reviewing the data, tracing them back to underlying agency source documents, and interviewing relevant agency staff. We also reviewed OMB documents including a report to Congress and two memorandums to federal agencies based on the findings of the pilot. We interviewed OMB staff as well as HHS and GSA officials responsible for implementing the Section 5 Pilot. Additional details regarding our objectives, scope, and methodology are provided in appendix I.

We conducted this performance audit from November 2017 to April 2019 in accordance with generally accepted government auditing standards. Those standards require that we plan and perform the audit to obtain sufficient, appropriate evidence to provide a reasonable basis for our findings and conclusions based on our audit objectives. We believe that the evidence obtained provides a reasonable basis for our findings and conclusions based on our audit objectives.

# BACKGROUND

Signed into law on May 9, 2014, the DATA Act required OMB, or an agency it designated, to establish a pilot program to facilitate the development of recommendations for (1) standardized reporting elements across the federal government, (2) elimination of unnecessary duplication in financial reporting, and (3) reduction of compliance costs for recipients of federal awards. To meet these requirements, OMB established a pilot program with two components—one that focused on federal grants and another on federal contracts (procurement).

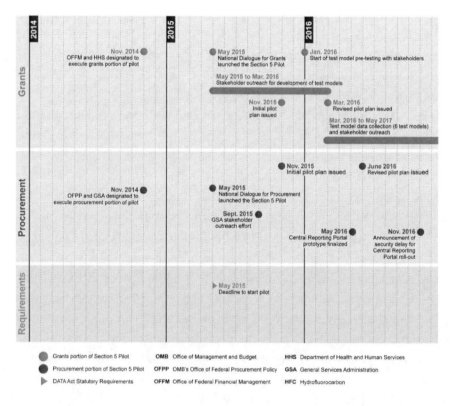

Figure 1. (Continued).

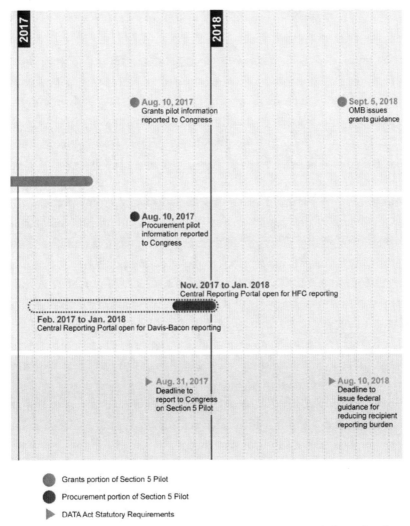

Source: GAO Analysis of Public Law 113-101, 128 Stat. 1146 and information from the OMB, HHS, and GSA. | GAO-19-299.

Figure 1. Timeline of Section 5 DATA Act Pilot Activities and Requirements.

OMB designated HHS as the executing agency of the grants portion of the Section 5 Pilot with oversight from OFFM.

OFPP was responsible for designing and leading the procurement portion of the pilot focusing on reporting of Federal Acquisition Regulation

(FAR) procurement requirements.[3] OFPP collaborated with the Chief Acquisitions Officers' Council and GSA on specific aspects of implementation including the development of the Central Reporting Portal, a reporting tool which is intended to centralize FAR reporting. See Figure 1 for a timeline of the activities undertaken by the grants and procurement portions of the pilot as well as deadlines required by the act.

As part of our ongoing oversight of the DATA Act's implementation, we have monitored OMB's efforts to meet its statutory requirements related to the Section 5 Pilot. In April 2016, we reported on the design plans for the Section 5 Pilot.[4] We found that HHS's design for the grants portion of the pilot was generally on track to meet statutory requirements and partially adhered to leading pilot design practices. However, we also reported that the procurement portion was not on track to meet requirements, and that its plans did not follow leading pilot design practices. In response to a recommendation in our report, OMB revised its plan for the procurement portion to better reflect leading practices for pilot design identified in our April 2016 report. These changes included more fully documenting its data collection plans and including a sampling plan to meet diversity requirements for pilot participants.

According to OMB staff, the ongoing work and related grants guidance resulting from the Section 5 Pilot reflects a broader strategy for reducing federal recipient reporting burden that is outlined in the President's Management Agenda (PMA). Released in March of 2018, and led by the Executive Office of the President and the President's Management Council, PMA is a strategy to modernize how federal agencies deliver mission outcomes and provide services in three key areas: (1) modern information

---

[3] The FAR provides uniform acquisition policies and procedures for use by all executive agencies. These agencies are required to follow the FAR. They enforce its rules, including reporting requirements, through contracts with individual contractors. The plan for the procurement portion of the pilot refers to these as "FAR reporting requirements." In addition, OMB uses this term in its August 2017 Report to Congress on the status of the Section 5 Pilot. For consistency, this report will follow the same approach.

[4] See GAO, *DATA Act: Section 5 Pilot Design Issues Need to Be Addressed to Meet Goal of Reducing Recipient Reporting Burden*, GAO-16-438 (Washington, D.C.; Apr. 19, 2016).

technology; (2) data, accountability, and transparency; and (3) the workforce for the 21st Century.[5]

Several Cross-Agency Priority (CAP) goals include PMA's milestones and activities. These CAP goals identify opportunities for multiple agencies to collaborate on government-wide efforts and report on goal progress quarterly. Two of these, CAP Goals 5 and 8, include strategies for reducing federal award recipient reporting burden.[6] OMB staff told us that some of the findings from the Section 5 Pilot and recommendations from their subsequent report to Congress informed the focus of these CAP goals.

For example, according to OMB staff, the grants portion of the Section 5 Pilot focused on identifying how changes in grants data collection and grant management may reduce federal recipient reporting burden. PMA CAP Goal 8 is described as building on these efforts by shifting the focus toward the life cycle of grants management and standardizing grants management activities using agile technology.

# SECTION 5 PILOT MET MANY BUT NOT ALL STATUTORY REQUIREMENTS

We determined that the Section 5 Pilot fully met three of the DATA Act's statutory requirements, substantively met one, and partially met two others.[7] The Section 5 Pilot fully met the following statutory requirements: (1) that pilot data collection cover a 12-month reporting cycle[8]; (2) timely

---

[5] President's Management Council and Executive Office of the President, *President's Management Agenda: Modernizing Government for the 21st Century* (Washington, D.C.: 2018).

[6] See *PMA CAP Goal 5: Sharing Quality Services* and *CAP Goal 8: Results-Oriented Accountability for Grants, available at* http://www.performance.gov/CAP/CAP_goal_5.html and http://www.performance.gov/CAP/ CAP_goal_8.html.

[7] We determined that a requirement was "substantively met" when actions taken by OMB or its designated agency did not fully adhere to a specific aspect of a requirement but were consistent with and generally achieved the broader goal or objective involved.

[8] We concluded that the Section 5 Pilot, as a whole, met this requirement. For example, the six test models of the grants portion of the pilot collected data between March 2016 and May 2017, thereby covering a full 12-month reporting cycle. Although the procurement portion of the pilot was open for data collection for at least 12 months (from February 2017 to February

issuance of OMB's report to Congress in August of 2017 to select congressional committees;[9] and (3) that the report to Congress contain a discussion of any needed legislative actions as well as recommendations related to automating and streamlining aspects of federal financial reporting to reduce the reporting burden of federal award recipients.[10]

We found that the pilot also substantively met the requirement that the pilot program include a combination of federal award recipients and an aggregate value of awards of not less than $1 billion but not more than $2 billion. Although the $122 billion in grants included in the pilot greatly exceeded the upper bound, this was principally a result of the decisions by OFFM and HHS to pilot different test models for reducing reporting burden, and to include a wide range of different types of grants. The total value of grant awards exceeded the amount envisioned by the act.[11]

OMB's August 2017 report stated that the decision to go beyond the minimum requirement of testing one approach was made in the interest of achieving the DATA Act's objective to identify ways to reduce reporting burden as well as the effect this decision would have on the aggregate value of grants sampled.[12] We believe that the pilot substantively met this requirement and did not identify any negative effects related to the larger aggregate value of grants, contracts, and subawards included in the grants portion of the pilot. We found that the approach followed by OMB and HHS furthered the broader objective identified by this section of the act.

---

2018), actual data collection occurred only during a 3-month period. However, since the data that were collected—relating to reporting on hydrofluorocarbons—are only required to be submitted annually, we concluded that this also covered a 12-month data cycle.

[9] Office of Management and Budget, *Report to Congress: DATA Act Pilot Program* (Aug. 10, 2017).

[10] According to OMB staff, the report to Congress did not identify any required legislative actions because the findings of the pilot did not indicate that any such actions were needed. However, the report did include three government-wide recommendations for OMB and agencies to streamline federal financial reporting and reduce the reporting burden of federal award recipients. We determined that this met the reporting requirement.

[11] For more information on each test model see the text box titled "High-Level Summaries of DATA Act Section 5 Pilot Grants Test Models," as well as appendix II.

[12] Office of Management and Budget, *Report to Congress: DATA Act Pilot Program* (Aug. 10, 2017).

| Statutory Requirement | Assessment |
|---|---|
| **The pilot program must:** | |
| • Collect data during a 12-month reporting cycle; and | ● |
| • Include a combination of federal award recipients (grantees and contractors) and an aggregate value of awards not less than $1B but not more than $2B.[a] | ◐ |
| **Congressional reporting requirements:** | |
| • OMB must issue a report to select Congressional committees no later than 90 days after the date on which the pilot terminates (Issue report by August 31, 2017) | ● |
| **The report must include:** | |
| • A description of the data collected, the usefulness of the data provided, and the cost to collect the data from participants; and | ◖ |
| • A discussion of any legislative actions required and recommended for consolidating aspects of federal financial reporting to reduce the costs to recipients of federal awards, automating aspects of federal financial reporting to increase efficiency to reduce the costs to recipients of federal awards, simplifying the reporting requirements for recipients of federal awards, and improving financial transparency | ● |
| **Government-wide implementation requirements:** | |
| • Not later than one year after the date on which the Director of OMB submits the report (August 10, 2018), the Director of OMB shall issue guidance to the head of federal agencies as to how the government-wide financial data standards established shall be applied to the information required to be reported by entities receiving federal awards to:<br> ○ reduce the burden of complying with reporting requirements; and<br> ○ simplify the reporting process, including by reducing duplicative reports [b] | ◖ |

● Requirement Fully Met

◐ Requirement Substantively Met[a]

◖ Requirement Partially Met

Source: GAO Analysis of Public Law 113-101, 128 Stat. 1146 and information from the Office of Management and Budget (OMB). Department of Health and Human Services (HHS), and the General Services Administration (GSA). | GAO-19-299.

[a]We use "substantively met" when actions taken by OMB or its designated agency did not fully adhere to a specific aspect of a requirement but generally achieved the broader goal or objective involved.

[b]OMB was required to issue guidance to agencies 1 year after the issuance of its August 2017 report to Congress. Therefore, the guidance should have been issued by August 10, 2018.

Figure 2. Assessment of Section 5 Pilot against Statutory Requirements.

In addition, we determined that the pilot partially met two of the act's requirements. The first of these requirements concerns the act's requirement that OMB's report to Congress include a description of the data collected, the usefulness of the data provided, and the cost to collect pilot data from participants. The report that OMB issued to Congress in August 2017 included information on the first two of these but only partly addressed the third. Specifically, it contained cost information for only the grants portion of the pilot, stating that the cost associated with executing this portion during fiscal years 2015 through 2017 was more than $5.5 million. The report did not contain any cost information on the procurement portion of the pilot.[13]

The DATA Act also required that OMB issue guidance to agencies for reducing reporting burden for federal award recipients—including both grantees and contractors—but the guidance subsequently issued only pertained to the grants community. We determined that OMB only partially met this requirement. On September 5, 2018, OMB issued M-18- 24: *Strategies to Reduce Grant Recipient Reporting Burden*. Among other things, this memorandum contained guidance to federal agencies making the SF-424B form optional based on findings from the grants portion of the pilot.[14] Form SF-424B is used by grantees to document assurances regarding their compliance with a wide range of rules and regulations. Figure 2 summarizes our assessment.

## THE GRANTS PORTION OF THE PILOT IDENTIFIED SEVERAL WAYS TO REDUCE REPORTING BURDEN AND PROVIDED SUPPORT FOR GOVERNMENT-WIDE STREAMLINING EFFORTS

### All Six Grant Test Models Reported Evidence of Reducing Burden, Increasing Accuracy, or Both

As the agency designated by OMB to execute the grants portion of the Section 5 Pilot, HHS developed and analyzed six "test models" to determine if adopting the proposed changes would contribute to the pilot program's

---

[13] In June 2018, OFPP staff told us that they estimated the cost of the procurement pilot to be approximately $1.5 million and referred us to GSA for supporting information. GSA, which was responsible for the development of the central reporting portal, provided documentation for approximately $742,000 of funding related to the development of the Central Reporting Portal.

[14] OMB Memorandum M-18-24 (Sept. 5, 2018).

objectives of reducing reporting burden and duplication. These test models examined a variety of grant reporting issues that HHS had identified as presenting challenges. All but one of the test models, the Common Data Element Repository (CDER) Library 2, based their findings on data collected from grantees.

---

**High-Level Summaries of DATA Act Section 5 Pilot Grants Test Models**

- CDER Library 1 test model assessed the extent to which an online and searchable library containing data element definitions for grant reporting could enable grantees to fill out forms consistently and easily.[15]
- CDER Library 2 test model assessed the extent of duplication across grant forms within the federal government. This test model provided information on potential changes in data element definitions and updates to grant forms that would comply with the DATA Act and standardized reporting elements.
- Consolidated Federal Financial Report test model assessed the extent to which submitting federal financial data once, through a single system, could reduce burden for both grant recipients and the federal government, and streamline the grants closeout process.
- Single Audit test model assessed the extent to which combining or eliminating duplicative financial reporting on single audit forms could reduce grant recipients reporting burden.
- Notice of Award (NOA) test model assessed the extent to which a consolidated and standardized Notice of Award coversheet could impact reporting burden by allowing grant recipients to locate required reporting data in one place.

Learn Grants test model assessed the extent to which a publicly available website on Grants.gov with information on grant reporting requirements could improve the grants community's knowledge of the grant life cycle process.[16]

Source: OMB Grants Pilot Test Plans | GAO-19-299.

---

[15] See https://repository.usaspending.gov/cder_library/.
[16] See https://www.grants.gov/web/grants/learn-grants.html.

The text box above provides high-level summaries of each of the six models. Additional details on the approach followed for each model, as well as reported results, can be found in appendix II.

## Table 1. Reported Results for Grants Test Models of the Section 5 Pilot

| Test Model | Effect reported on: | | |
|---|---|---|---|
| | Time[a] | Duplication[b] | Accuracy[c] |
| **CDER Library 1** | | | |
| Hypothesis: If grant recipients are provided with definitions of data elements through CDER Library, then they will be able to accurately complete forms in a timely manner. | √ | — | √ |
| **CDER Library 2** | | | |
| Hypothesis: If duplication across forms can be identified using CDER Library, then agencies can update or reduce forms to reduce grant recipient burden. | — | √ | — |
| **Consolidated Federal Financial Report (FFR)** | | | |
| Hypothesis: If grant recipients can enter complete FFR information systematically through one entry point instead of multiple different avenues, and that information could be shared electronically from that point forward, then grant recipient burden will be reduced and data accuracy will be improved. | √ | — | √ |
| **Single Audit** | | | |
| Hypothesis: If grant recipients do not have to report the same information on duplicative forms, then grant recipients' burden will be reduced. | √ | √ | √ |
| **Notice of Award (NOA)** | | | |
| Hypothesis: If grant recipients have a standardized NOA for federal awards, then grant reporting burden may be reduced for recipients by standardizing access to data needed to populate information collections. | √ | — | √ |
| **Learn Grants** | | | |
| Hypothesis: If grant recipients are supplied with grants lifecycle information in one website, then they will have increased access to grants resources and knowledge of the grants lifecycle process. | — | — | √ |

Source: GAO Summary of data from OMB and HHS. | GAO-19-299.

Legend: √ = Test model reported having a positive effect on reducing burden on dimension indicated. — = Test model did not report having a positive effect on reducing burden on dimension indicated.

Note:

[a]"Time" refers to a reduction of the amount of time awardees spent on fulfilling specific grant reporting requirements.

[b]"Duplication" refers to a reduction in duplicative items found across tested forms.

[c]"Accuracy" refers to an improvement in the accuracy of reporting submitted by awardees.

According to data provided by HHS, five of the six test models showed evidence of decreasing grantee reporting burden either by reducing the time required to meet existing reporting requirements, streamlining those requirements, by eliminating duplication, or both. In addition, several test models reported increases in the accuracy of grantee reporting.

For example, the Consolidated Federal Financial Report test model, which examined the effect of submitting Federal Financial Report data through one rather than multiple systems, found that 64 percent of participants reported that they believed a single system resulted in a reduction in the time needed to fulfill reporting requirements, and 65 percent reported that that they believed it would improve the accuracy of the information they submitted. See Table 1 for a summary of the types of effects on time, duplication, or accuracy for each test model identified throughout the grants portion of the Section 5 Pilot.

HHS incorporated iterative stakeholder input throughout the execution of the grants portion of the Section 5 Pilot. HHS used feedback from stakeholders involved in HHS efforts to streamline grants reporting. Throughout the pilot, HHS consulted with various partner organizations to gather input and feedback from the broader grant community to refine the test models, solicit pilot participation, and collect data on the test models.

## OMB Used Findings from the Grants Portion of the Pilot to Support Recommendations and Government-Wide Guidance for Reducing Grantee Reporting Burden

OMB's August 2017 report to Congress on the findings of the Section 5 Pilot contained three broad recommendations and stated that OMB plans to take action on these recommendations. These recommendations covered (1) standardizing core data elements, (2) eliminating duplication through auto-population of data, and (3) leveraging information technology open data standards to develop new tools across the federal government. We found that evidence from the grant test models supported all three recommendations for streamlining federal reporting discussed in the report. For example, OMB recommended that its staff standardize core data elements used for managing federal financial assistance awards based on reductions in administrative burden experienced in the CDER Library 1 test model. In another example, four test models supported OMB's recommendation for increased use of data auto-population from existing federal data sources as a way to reduce duplication in reporting.[17]

Findings from the grants portion of the Section 5 Pilot also provided support for government-wide efforts to streamline reporting and reduce recipient reporting burden. These include OMB's memorandum M-18-24: *Strategies to Reduce Grant Recipient Reporting Burden*, which discusses efforts to automate and centralize grant management processes. Among other things, M-18-24 requires that federal agencies evaluate the systems and methods currently used to collect information from grant recipients to eliminate duplicative data requests. OMB staff confirmed that M-18-24 incorporates findings from some of the test models of the grants portion of the pilot such as the Single Audit test model, which examined reducing duplicative reporting of grant recipients' data. The efforts to reduce duplicative reporting in M-18-24 also align with OMB's recommendation in its August 2017 report to Congress to eliminate unnecessary duplication in reporting by leveraging information technology that can auto-populate from existing data sources.

In addition, OMB staff told us that findings from the grants portion of the pilot contributed to broader, government-wide initiatives related to federal reporting. For example, according to OMB staff, the three recommendations from the August 2017 report to Congress are reflected in CAP Goal 8 of the President's Management Agenda, which focuses on results-oriented accountability for grants. These OMB staff also told us that findings from the grants portion of the pilot informed two CAP Goal 8 strategies. For example, the CAP Goal 8 grants management strategy

---

[17] The four test models were CDER Library 2, Consolidated Federal Financial Report, Single Audit, and Notice of Award. OMB's report to Congress described how these four test models demonstrated reductions in burden by enabling grantees to submit data once, in one location, for use multiple times in multiple places.

focuses on standardizing grants management business processes and data. OMB developed a comprehensive taxonomy for core grants management data standards that is currently available for public comment. In addition, a second strategy focuses on incorporating a risk-based performance management approach to metrics in grant award operations to determine low-risk and high-value federal awards. CAP Goal 8 also states plans to streamline the 2019 Single Audit Compliance Supplement to focus on requirements that inform grant award performance.[18]

## PROCUREMENT PORTION OF PILOT DID NOT RESULT IN SUFFICIENT OR APPROPRIATE DATA TO ASSESS CHANGES IN CONTRACTORS' BURDEN REDUCTION

### Lack of Contractor Participation and the Absence of Iterative and Ongoing Stakeholder Engagement Limited the Ability of Procurement Pilot to Achieve its Objectives

Unlike the grants portion of the pilot, the procurement portion did not result in data collection that could be used for an evidence-based assessment of ways to reduce reporting burden. OMB's Office of Federal Procurement Policy (OFPP) sought to assess five test models that, according to the report to Congress, were essential to centralized procurement reporting.[19] However, the pilot did not fully test any of the hypotheses associated with those test models. The reasons for not testing the hypotheses included a lack of contractor participation and a lack of iterative and ongoing stakeholder

---

[18] Office of Management and Budget, *Federal Register: Draft Federal Grants Management Data Standards for Feedback,* accessed January 17, 2019, http://www.govinfo.gov/content/pkg/FR-2018-11-16/pdf/2018-24927.pdf.

[19] The procurement and grants portions of the Section 5 Pilot used the term "test model" somewhat differently. The grants portion test models represented separate topics, often quite different from each other, where approaches to reducing reporting burden were tested. The procurement portion used the term to describe different processes or steps related to testing the usefulness of the Central Reporting Portal.

participation and engagement throughout the course of the pilot. See appendix III for additional information regarding the various procurement test models, associated hypotheses, and additional details regarding our assessment.

The procurement portion of the pilot focused entirely on the development and testing of a central reporting portal to consolidate FAR reporting requirements. According to OFPP staff, the pilot intended to eventually identify ways to centralize a wide range of reporting requirements that contractors currently meet through decentralized methods. Contractors must report many types of information depending on the contract. Toward that end, OFPP, with the assistance of GSA, created a procurement reporting website called the Central Reporting Portal. To test the efficacy of this portal for reducing burden, OFPP initially decided to examine how well it handled a specific FAR reporting requirement—the reporting of payroll data in accordance with the Davis-Bacon Act.[20] According to pilot plans, Davis-Bacon reporting requirements were selected because they were identified by contractors as "pain points" during initial stakeholder outreach conducted in 2014 and 2015. OFPP planned to collect and analyze 1 year of weekly Davis-Bacon wage reporting data from at least 180 contractors through the Central Reporting Portal to identify how centralized reporting might reduce contractor reporting burden.

However, during the 12-month procurement data collection period, no contractors agreed to submit their Davis-Bacon data as part of the pilot.

---

[20] The Davis-Bacon Act requires contractors and subcontractors working on federally funded contracts in excess of $2,000 to pay at least locally prevailing wages to laborers and mechanics. The act covers both new construction and the alteration or repair of existing public buildings and works. Pub. L. No. 71-798, 46 Stat. 1494 (1931), as amended; *codified at* 40 U.S.C. §§ 3141–3148. The Department of Labor sets prevailing wage rates for various job categories in a local area on the basis of periodic surveys it conducts of contractors, unions, public officials, and other interested parties. Congress has extended this requirement beyond projects funded directly by the federal government by including Davis-Bacon Act prevailing wage provisions in numerous related laws under which federal agencies assist construction projects through grants, loans, guarantees, and insurance. Examples of related laws include the Federal-Aid Highway Acts, the Housing and Community Development Act of 1974, and the Federal Water Pollution Control Act. In addition to paying no less than locally prevailing wages, contractors for construction projects that are subject to the Davis-Bacon Act must pay their workers weekly and submit weekly certified payroll records. OFPP's pilot plans were to test whether a centralized portal would simplify this reporting process.

Consequently, OFPP did not collect any wage data. Despite OFPP stating in its plans and reiterating to us as late as September 2017 that it expected to be able to secure at least 180 pilot participants, only one contractor expressed interest in reporting its Davis-Bacon information using the portal.[21] This contractor withdrew from the pilot before submitting any data through the Central Reporting Portal. OFPP staff told us they were aware of the potential for low pilot participation for Davis-Bacon reporting when pilot testing began in February 2017 because contractors already had established processes for fulfilling the highly complex Davis-Bacon reporting requirements, and pilot participation was optional. According to GSA contracting staff, the one contractor who initially expressed interest ultimately decided not to participate because the format in which the contractor tracked and reported payroll data was incompatible with that used by the pilot portal, resulting in additional burden.

However, it was not until August 2017—approximately 7 months into its year-long data collection period—that specific steps were taken to address the fact that the procurement portion of the pilot had not collected any data from Davis Bacon contractors. During this period OFPP did not conduct pilot outreach activities with the contractors, who were key to successful implementation of the pilot. OFPP staff told us that at the time of the pilot launch they learned that contractors were interested in having the Central Reporting Portal be able to communicate with third-party payroll reporting systems to automate reporting. OFPP staff said that although they are exploring this possibility, it was not a capability that was included as part of the pilot. Had this type of feedback on stakeholder needs been obtained sooner, OMB could have explored the feasibility of adding this capability to the portal or engaged in communication with stakeholders to develop alternate approaches that might have persuaded more contractors to participate.

---

[21] OFPP's plan for the procurement portion of the pilot contains the goal of collecting 1 year (52 weeks) of weekly Davis-Bacon wage reporting data from 180 pilot participants.

The usefulness of iterative and ongoing communication is recognized by the *Standards for Internal Control in the Federal Government*.[22] Those standards state that management should use quality information to achieve its objectives, and that management should collect quality information by engaging with stakeholders through iterative and ongoing processes and in a timely manner. In this case, key stakeholders include relevant agencies, contracting officials, and contractors using the system. OFPP's plan for the procurement portion of the pilot recognized the importance of stakeholder engagement stating that, to include a diverse group of recipients in the pilot, they should identify eligible participants for the pilot, conduct outreach to identify participants, and repeat this process as necessary until they achieved the sample necessary to test the Central Reporting Portal.[23] However, as previously stated, no contractors agreed to submit their Davis-Bacon data as part of the pilot. Therefore, OFPP did not repeat this process until the pilot obtained the necessary sample size. Such interactions could have provided important information on contractors' needs and concerns that OFPP could have used to inform their decisions regarding the pilot's implementation.

## Expansion of Procurement Pilot to Include Hydrofluorocarbon Reporting Had Limitations

In November 2017, OFPP expanded the type of data accepted by the pilot to include hydrofluorocarbon (HFC) reporting, a new FAR reporting requirement. However, this choice had limitations in its suitability for providing useful data for testing the hypotheses of the five procurement test models. Unlike Davis-Bacon reporting, where contractors submit weekly reports, HFC is an annual reporting requirement for contractors that emit HFC gases over a certain threshold.[24] The Central Reporting Portal is the

---

[22] GAO, *Standards for Internal Control in the Federal Government*, GAO-14-704G, (Washington, D.C. September 2014).

[23] This information is from OMB's Procurement Pilot Plan and was reproduced in OMB's *Report to Congress*, p. 62.

[24] n certain contracts, contractors are required to report the amount of HFCs or refrigerant blends containing HFC—such as refrigerants, fire suppressants, and other products that may contain

only location where contractors can submit HFC reporting.[25] For the purposes of the pilot, the Central Reporting Portal accepted HFC submissions from November 2017 through February 2018.

During the pilot, 11 HFC annual reports were submitted to the portal (see figure 3). As a result of the small number of reports collected, OMB collected much less data than it had initially expected to receive to test the capabilities of the Central Reporting Portal. If the procurement portion of the pilot had been executed as planned, it could have theoretically resulted in 9,360 Davis-Bacon submissions for analysis.[26] A larger data set of contractors' experiences using the Central Reporting Portal could have informed OMB's decision-making process through analysis of more, and potentially more varied data.

| 2017 | | | | | | | | | | | 2018 | Total Submissions |
|---|---|---|---|---|---|---|---|---|---|---|---|---|
| Feb. | Mar. | Apr. | May | June | July | Aug. | Sep. | Oct. | Nov. | Dec. | Jan. | |
| **Davis-Bacon Submissions** | | | | | | | | | | | | |
| 0 | 0 | 0 | 0 | 0 | 0 | 0 | 0 | 0 | 0 | 0 | 0 | 0 |
| **Hydrofluorocarbon (HFC) Submissions** | | | | | | | | | | | | |
| ▨ | ▨ | ▨ | ▨ | ▨ | ▨ | ▨ | ▨ | ▨ | 8 | 1 | 2 | 11 |

▨ Number of Davis-Bacon submissions
# Number of HFC submissions
▨ HFC data not collected

Source: GAO analysis of Central Reporting Portal data submission documents from general Services Administration (GSA). | GAO-19-299.

Figure 3. Davis-Bacon and HFC Data Submissions to the Central Reporting Portal Made during the Procurement Portion of the Section 5 Pilot.

---

ozone-depleting substances—that normally each contain 50 or more pounds of HFC or refrigerant blends containing HFC in equipment and appliances delivered to the federal government. Contractors are to track this information annually for the federal fiscal year (October 1 to September 30) and report it by November 30 each year during performance of the contract and at the end of the contract. 48 C.F.R. §§ 23.804, 52.223- 11, 52.223-12.

[25] Despite this considerable change in circumstances, OFPP staff told us that they did not amend or create additional plans to reflect the testing of HFC reporting. The procurement plans submitted to us in 2016 stated that future pilot expansion would include HFC reporting.

[26] This figure represents OFPP's target number of participants (180) multiplied by a full year of weekly reports (52). This fully realized scenario assumes participation of all 180 contractors for every week during the year, however, even much more modest participation would have produced a sizable data set. For example, had the pilot been able to attract one quarter of its target number of contractors (45) and if each contractor reported data for only half of the year (26 weeks), it would still have resulted in 1,170 data submissions.

In addition to the small number of submitted HFC annual reports, the decision to switch to using HFC data had another limitation. These data could not be used to examine changes in reporting burden as a result of using the Central Reporting Portal. This is because HFC reporting was a new reporting requirement, and as such, it did not have an established reporting process to use as a point of comparison to assess changes in reporting burden. The objective of the procurement pilot was to assess how centralized reporting can reduce reporting burden. This objective could not be achieved without data on the existing reporting burden.

## OMB's Recommendations for Streamlining Reporting Were Not Supported by Findings from the Procurement Portion of the Pilot

Evidence from the procurement portion of the pilot did not support OMB's government-wide recommendations for reducing reporting burden in its August 2017 report to Congress. As previously stated, OMB's report to Congress included three recommendations that focused on (1) standardizing core data elements, (2) eliminating duplication by using data auto-population, and (3) leveraging information technology open standards to develop new tools. As support for the first recommendation, the report stated that results from the procurement pilot test models demonstrated that standard data elements—coupled with uniform data adoption—and the ability to centrally collect and share information reduces administrative burden. Since the procurement portion of the pilot did not gather or analyze any pilot data from the Davis-Bacon participants, OMB did not assess the extent to which the ability to centrally collect data actually reduces burden. Recommendation two stated that support from the procurement test model demonstrated that recipient burden is reduced when identical data can be entered once in one place and reused. However, the HFC data collection process did not reuse data when capturing information and did not have the ability to auto-populate data.

HFC data collection was the only part of the procurement portion of the pilot that collected information that could have been used to inform this recommendation. According to OFPP staff, the Davis-Bacon portion of the portal had the capability to auto-populate data. However, no Davis-Bacon data were collected that would have allowed quantification of the effects of reusing data on reporting burden. OMB stated that support for the third recommendation included data and information collected from the pilot. Although there was some consultation with stakeholders during initial planning and design of the procurement portion of the pilot and the early development of the portal, the pilot did not actually collect any data from either Davis-Bacon contractors or through the HFC portion of the pilot in the data gathering and analysis portion of the pilot related to this recommendation. In August 2018, OMB announced plans to expand the use of the Central Reporting Portal for FAR reporting, stating that the portal allows contractors to report data to one central location.[27] OFPP staff told us that they are considering centralizing a third FAR requirement using the portal in the future but have not yet determined what that will be. As discussed above, the procurement portion of the pilot did not collect sufficient data to test the effect of the portal on reporting burden. In addition, the plan for the procurement portion states that OFPP intended to analyze feedback on pilot data collection and, depending on that feedback, decide whether to expand the pilot to other FAR reporting requirements. However, the pilot did not collect any such feedback to inform its determination to expand the Central Reporting Portal in the future. As a result, OFPP has limited information regarding issues that could affect expanded use of the Centralized Reporting Portal. In the absence of such information, it is difficult for OFPP to determine whether continued or expanded use of the Central Reporting Portal will reduce reporting burden, and which additional FAR requirements, if any, to include.

---

[27] Office of Management and Budget, *M-18-23: Shifting From Low-Value to High-Value Work.*

## CONCLUSION

### OMB Plans to Expand Use of the Central Reporting Portal to Streamline Reporting of FAR Requirements

To reduce the burden and cost of reporting for recipients of federal funds, Congress included specific provisions in the DATA Act to encourage OMB to take a deliberate and evidence-based approach toward developing guidance for federal agencies in this area. The Section 5 Pilot offered OMB a valuable opportunity—namely, to test a variety of methods and techniques at a small scale before applying them more widely. Such a process may enhance the quality, credibility, and usefulness of evaluations in addition to helping to ensure that time and resources are used more effectively. Similar to what we found when we analyzed the design of the Section 5 Pilot in 2016, our review of its implementation and the results it produced found differences between the grant and procurement portions.

OMB and HHS designed and executed a robust grants portion of the pilot that tested several different approaches for reducing the reporting burden experienced by federal grant recipients. The resulting findings were used to develop OMB's government-wide recommendations, and to inform two subsequent goals in the 2018 President's Management Agenda related to reducing recipient reporting burden.

In contrast, OMB did not fully implement the procurement portion of the pilot consistent with its plans. The procurement portion did not collect data to test the hypotheses associated with any of its five test models, and therefore could not provide empirical support for either OMB's government-wide recommendations or guidance related to reducing reporting burden. Among the factors responsible for this were the lack of Davis-Bacon contractor participation and OMB's inability to find a suitable alternative. OMB has announced its intention to expand centralized reporting for FAR requirements across government. In the absence of timely information regarding the needs and concerns of stakeholders, OMB faces the risk of experiencing implementation challenges similar to those it experienced during the pilot. Although the use of a centralized reporting portal could ultimately prove useful for reducing burden, the lack of information from stakeholders—including the contractors who would use it—raises concerns about the future success of plans for expanding the Central Reporting Portal.

## RECOMMENDATION FOR EXECUTIVE ACTION

The Director of OMB should ensure that information is collected regarding how centralized reporting of procurement requirements might reduce recipient reporting burden—including input from stakeholders such as contractors through an iterative and ongoing process—to inform OMB's planned expansion of the Central Reporting Portal.

## AGENCY COMMENTS AND OUR EVALUATION

We provided a draft of this chapter to OMB, HHS, and GSA for review and comment. HHS and GSA informed us that they had no comments. OMB provided technical comments, which we incorporated as appropriate. OMB neither agreed nor disagreed with our recommendation.

We are sending copies of this chapter to the appropriate congressional committees, The Secretary of Health and Human Services, The Acting Director of OMB, the Administrator of GSA, and other interested parties.

Michelle Sager Director
Strategic Issues

## List of Congressional Addressees

The Honorable Ron Johnson
Chairman
The Honorable Gary Peters

Ranking Member
Committee on Homeland Security and Governmental Affairs
United States Senate

The Honorable Elijah E. Cummings
Chairman

The Honorable Jim Jordan
Ranking Member
Committee on Oversight and Reform
House of Representatives

The Honorable Gerald E. Connolly
Chairman

The Honorable Mark Meadows
Ranking Member
Subcommittee on Government Operations
Committee on Oversight and Reform
House of Representatives

The Honorable Thomas R. Carper
United States Senate

The Honorable Robert Portman
United States Senate

The Honorable Mark Warner
United States Senate

# APPENDIX I: OBJECTIVES, SCOPE, AND METHODOLOGY

This chapter assesses the extent to which (1) the Section 5 Pilot met the statutory requirements of the act, (2) the grants portion of the Section 5 Pilot demonstrated changes in federal award recipients' reporting burden, and (3) the procurement portion of the Section 5 Pilot demonstrated changes in federal award recipients' reporting burden.

To assess the extent to which the pilot met statutory requirements we reviewed section 5 of the Federal Funding Accountability and Transparency Act of 2006, as amended by the Digital Accountability and Transparency Act of 2014, to determine the legal requirements set forth in the act pertaining to establishing, designing, and executing the Section 5 Pilot.[28] We compared these requirements to documents from the Office of Management and Budget (OMB) and designated agencies. These documents included pilot plans for the grants and procurement portions of the pilot, OMB's August 2017 report to Congress, M-18-23: *Shifting from Low-Value to High-Value Work* and M-18-24: *Strategies to Reduce Grant Recipient Reporting Burden*.[29] We also interviewed staff from agencies involved in administering and executing the pilot on how they carried out their responsibilities. These agencies included the Department of Health and Human Services (HHS), OMB's Offices of Federal Financial Management (OFFM) and Federal Procurement Policy (OFPP), and the General Services Administration (GSA).

To assess the extent to which the grants portion of the Section 5 Pilot demonstrated changes in federal award recipients' reporting burden, we reviewed HHS' plans. We analyzed the plans compared to information collected from the various test models throughout the pilot. The data we assessed included survey data and analyses.

---

[28] FFATA, § 5(b). Section 3 of the DATA Act amended or added several sections to FFATA, including FFATA's section 5, which contains the requirement for the Section 5 Pilot.

[29] Office of Management and Budget, *M-18-24: Strategies to Reduce Grant Recipient Reporting Burden* (Washington, D.C.: Sept. 5, 2018); *M-18-23: Shifting From Low-Value to High-Value Work* (Washington, D.C.: Aug. 27, 2018); and *Report to Congress: DATA Act Pilot Program* (Aug. 10, 2017).

We also assessed whether statements on changes in grantees' reporting burden made in OMB's August 2017 report to Congress were supported by documentation. We did this by verifying the statements against supporting information. We determined that the pilot data we reviewed were reliable for the purposes of our work by reviewing the data, tracing them back to underlying agency source documents, and interviewing relevant agency staff. We also interviewed OFFM staff and HHS officials on how the grants portion of the pilot was executed.

To assess the extent to which the procurement portion of the pilot demonstrated changes in reporting burden, we reviewed OMB's plans and compared them to actions OMB took to execute the pilot. We compared OMB's actions to execute the procurement portion of the pilot against criteria identified in *Standards for Internal Control in the Federal Government*.[30] We viewed a demonstration of the Central Reporting Portal tool for reporting Davis-Bacon and hydrofluorocarbon (HFC) submissions. GSA developed the portal and OFPP provided oversight for the portal's development.

We also reviewed documentation including HFC reporting submissions made through the portal. In addition, we interviewed OFPP staff, GSA officials responsible for administering the portal, and three contracting officials from GSA who were assigned to participate in the Davis-Bacon component of the procurement portion of the pilot regarding their actions related to implementing the procurement portion of the pilot.

We conducted this performance audit from November 2017 to April 2019 in accordance with generally accepted government auditing standards. Those standards require that we plan and perform the audit to obtain sufficient, appropriate evidence to provide a reasonable basis for our findings and conclusions based on our audit objectives. We believe that the evidence obtained provides a reasonable basis for our findings and conclusions based on our audit objectives.

---

[30] GAO, *Standards for Internal Control in the Federal Government*, GAO-14-704G, (Washington, D.C. September 2014).

# APPENDIX II: DESCRIPTION OF TEST MODELS FROM GRANTS PORTION OF THE SECTION 5 PILOT

This appendix provides detailed information regarding the test models from the grants portion of the Section 5 Pilot.

## The Common Data Element Repository Library 1 Test Model

The Common Data Element Repository (CDER) Library is an online repository for federal grants-related data standards, definitions, and context. The library is intended to be an authorized source for data elements and definitions for use by the federal government and for recipients reporting grant information.

- Hypothesis: If grant recipients are provided with definitions of data elements through the CDER Library, then they will be able to accurately complete forms in a timely manner.
- Methodology: The Department of Health and Human Services (HHS) divided test model participants into two groups to read a scenario based on the grants lifecycle and complete a data collection tool. The first group used the CDER Library to complete the data collection tool while the second group used all other available sources to complete the data collection tool. After completion of the data collection tool, test model participants filled out a survey about their experiences using the CDER Library.
- Test Model Metrics: Accuracy and completeness of captured data within a period of time and survey results.
- Example of Test Model Results: On average, test model participants that completed a data collection tool using the CDER Library scored 11 percent higher in the accuracy of information requested and, on average, spent 6 fewer minutes when completing the tool.
- Number of Test Model Participants: Fifty-nine.

## The Common Data Element Repository Library 2 Test Model

The CDER Library 2 Test Model focused on identifying duplication in grant forms and data elements across the federal government based on the data standards, definitions, and context within the CDER Library 1.

- Hypothesis: If duplication across forms can be identified using the CDER Library, then agencies can update or reduce forms to reduce grant recipient burden.
- Methodology: HHS conducted an internal analysis of SF-424 form families, using the CDER Library, to identify duplication in data elements to determine which forms could be consolidated.[31]
- Test Model Metrics: Number of duplicative fields within form families and across forms for selected federal entities
- Example of Test Model Results: The internal analysis conducted by HHS identified 371 instances of data element duplication across 10 agency grant funding applications when using standardized data elements from the CDER Library 1.
- Number of Test Model Participants: Not Applicable; the CDER 2 Library Test model did not collect information from test model participants because the test model was an internal document review. The CDER Library 2 test model tested the utility of the data element definitions within the CDER Library 1.

## The Consolidated Federal Financial Report Test Model

The Consolidated Federal Financial Report Test Model focused on examining the potential early validation of consolidated CFFR data and potential future streamlining of the close-out process by allowing the submission of Federal Financial Report (FFR) data in one system, rather than in multiple entry systems.

---

[31] The SF-424 is a standardized form required for use as a cover sheet for submission of pre-applications and applications and related information under discretionary grant programs.

- Hypothesis: If grant recipients can enter complete FFR information systematically through one entry point instead of multiple different avenues and that information could be shared electronically from that point forward, then grant recipient burden will be reduced and data accuracy will be improved.
- Methodology: HHS surveyed Administration for Children and Families grant recipients on their experience submitting a consolidated FFR via HHS's Payment Management System, and grantees on their perceptions of the process for using a consolidated FFR through facilitated discussions.[32]
- Test Model Metrics: Survey results.
- Example of Test Model Results: Sixty-four percent of the CFFR test model participants reported that submitting their FFR through a single system would result in reduced reporting time. In addition, 65 percent of the CFFR test model participants believed using the payment management system for submitting FFR data would improve the accuracy of the information they submitted.
- Number of Test Model Participants: One-hundred fifteen tested the pilot environment and 30 participated in the facilitated discussions.

## The Single Audit Test Model

The Single Audit Test Model consisted of (1) an audit and opinions on the fair presentation of the financial statements and the Schedule of Expenditures of Federal Awards; (2) gaining an understanding of and testing internal control over financial reporting and the entity's compliance with laws, regulations, and contract or grant provisions that have a direct and material effect on certain federal programs (i.e., the program requirements);

---

[32] The FFR, reported on the Standard Form 425, is used for reporting grant expenditures for recipients of federal assistance.

and (3) an audit and an opinion on compliance with applicable program requirements for certain federal programs.[33]

The Single Audit Test Model focused on reducing reporting of data on duplicative forms.

- Hypothesis: If grant recipients do not have to report the same information on duplicative forms—for example, the SEFA compared to the Single Audit Report Package and Data Collection Form—then grant recipients' burden will be reduced.
- Methodology: HHS collaborated with the Office of Management and Budget's Office of Federal Financial Management and the Department of Commerce Federal Audit Clearinghouse (FAC) to create a pilot environment for test model participants to submit key portions of a modified Standard Form—Single Audit Collection.[34] HHS conducted two focus groups with test model participants subject to the Single Audit. The first focus group discussed and completed a survey on the new form. The second group, a sample of test model participants who are subject to perform a Single Audit submitted the existing form in the FAC pilot environment, completed a separate data collection form similar to the new form, and completed a survey on the effectiveness and burden of the new form.
- Test Model Metrics: Focus group feedback and survey results.
- Example of Test Model Results: All test model participants with access to the Single Audit's pilot environment believed the upload feature for reporting requirements could decrease duplication in required grant reporting.

---

[33] Congress passed the Single Audit, as amended, 31 U.S.C. ch. 75, to promote, among other things, sound financial management, including effective internal controls, with respect to federal awards administered by nonfederal entities. The Single Audit Act requires states, local governments, and nonprofit organizations expending $750,000 or more in federal awards in a year to obtain an audit in accordance with the requirements set forth in the act.

[34] The Single Audit collects financial data from entities that expend $750,000 or more in federal funds during the annual reporting period using the Single Audit Data Collection Form, also known as the Standard Form—Single Audit Collection.

- Number of Test Model Participants: Thirteen tested the pilot environment and 123 participated in facilitated discussions.

## THE NOTICE OF AWARD TEST MODEL

This model focused on the feasibility of developing a standardized Notice of Award (NOA) to reduce reporting burden and facilitate access to standardized data needed to populate Single Audit information collection.[35]

- Hypothesis: If grant recipients have a standardized NOA for federal awards, then grant-reporting burden may be reduced for recipients by standardizing access to data needed to populate information collections.
- Methodology: HHS divided test model participants into two groups and completed a data collection tool. The first group completed the data collection tool using three standardized NOAs, while the second group completed the data collection tool using three non-standardized NOAs. After completion of the data collection tool, test model participants self-reported their respective times to complete the data collection tool. They also filled out a survey about the standardized NOA's impact on reporting burden and provided input on elements to include in a standardized NOA.
- Test Model Metrics: Self-reported form completion time, accuracy, and survey results.
- Example of Test Model Results: Test model participants with access to the standardized NOA coversheets spent an average of 3 minutes less when completing the test model's data collection tool.
- Number of Test Model Participants: One-hundred four.

---

[35] The NOA is a document that contains information that grant recipients need to perform routine administrative operations. The data elements included in the NOA are standardized under the Uniform Guidance at 2 CFR 200. However, NOAs often differ in format and content across agencies, as well as departments within agencies.

## The Learn Grants Test Model

The Learn Grants Test Model is a website on Grants.gov that summarizes and provides links to new and important grants information such as policies, processes, funding, and other information needed throughout the grants life cycle. The website intended to make it easier for stakeholders to find, learn about, and apply for federal grants and promote the standardization of grants terminology and data.

- Hypothesis: If grant recipients are supplied with grants life cycle information in one website, then they will have increased access to grants resources and knowledge of the grants life cycle process.
- Methodology: HHS developed a grants knowledge quiz from information on the Learn Grants website. HHS administered the knowledge quiz to test model participants in two phases. First, test model participants completed the knowledge quiz using existing knowledge and without the Learn Grants website. Next, test model participants completed the knowledge quiz with access to the Learn Grants website. HHS compared the results from both knowledge quizzes. After completion of the knowledge quiz, test model participants completed a survey on the usefulness of the Learn Grants website and its impact on increasing knowledge quiz scores.
- Test Model Metrics: Knowledge quiz accuracy and survey results on the usefulness of Learn Grants website.
- Example of Test Model Results: Test model participants experienced an average 10 percent (one quiz point) increase in their grant knowledge quiz scores when using the Learn Grants website. New grantees who participated in the test model also reported that the Learn Grants website provided useful grants information.
- Number of Test Model Participants: Fifty-seven.

# APPENDIX III: ASSESSMENT OF TEST MODELS IN THE PROCUREMENT PORTION OF THE SECTION 5 PILOT

## Table 2. Assessment of Test Models in the Procurement Portion of the Section 5 Pilot

| Procurement Test Model and Hypothesis | GAO's Assessment | Assessment Rationale |
|---|---|---|
| **1. Standardize the process for submission of Federal Acquisition Regulation (FAR) data** <br> **Hypothesis:** <br> A uniform submission process for FAR required post-award reports will reduce contractor burden and cost. | Hypothesis not tested. | **Original plan (Davis-Bacon):** <br> The Office of Management and Budget's Office of Federal Procurement Policy (OFPP) planned to test this hypothesis by gathering data on the time it takes to submit reporting data through the Central Reporting Portal and outside of the portal, with self-reported data from contractors. According to OFPP, data were not collected due to a lack of participation in the Davis-Bacon portion of pilot. <br> **Revised Strategy (Hydrofluorocarbon):** <br> This hypothesis could not be tested through hydrofluorocarbon (HFC) reporting because it was a reporting requirement without an existing reporting method through which to compare reporting burden. |
| **2. Verify that FAR standards address needs Hypothesis:** <br> Verification of FAR standards for post award reporting will confirm the value of existing data standards and reduce variations that will, in turn, reduce contractor burden and cost. | Hypothesis not tested. | **Original plan (Davis-Bacon):** <br> OFPP planned to execute this test model through focus groups. According to OFPP, no focus groups were conducted. <br> **Revised Strategy (HFC):** <br> This hypothesis could not be tested through HFC reporting because it was a reporting requirement without an existing reporting method through which to compare reporting burden. |
| **3. Prepopulate data into the Central Reporting Data** <br> **Hypothesis:** | Hypothesis not tested. | **Original Strategy (Davis-Bacon):** <br> OFPP planned to test this hypothesis by gathering data on the time it takes to submit reporting data through the Central Reporting Portal and outside of the portal, with self-reported data from contractors. |

# Table 2. (Continued)

| Procurement Test Model and Hypothesis | GAO's Assessment | Assessment Rationale |
|---|---|---|
| If contractors do not have to report the same information to different locations then contractor burden will be reduced | | According to OFPP, data were not collected due to a lack of participation in the Davis-Bacon portion of pilot.<br><br>**Revised Strategy (HFC):**<br>This hypothesis could not be tested through HFC reporting because it was a reporting requirement without an existing reporting method through which to compare reporting burden |
| **4. Consolidate data collection and access (proof of concept)**<br>**Hypothesis:**<br>If contractors can enter FAR-required reporting data systematically through one entry point instead of multiple different avenues, and that information can be shared electronically with appropriate individuals, then contractor burden will be reduced and data access improved. | Hypothesis not tested. | **Original plan (Davis-Bacon):**<br>OFPP planned to test this hypothesis by gathering data on the time it takes to submit reporting data through the Central Reporting Portal and outside of the portal, with self-reported data from contractors. OMB also planned to conduct guided discussions. According to OFPP, data were not collected due to a lack of participation in the Davis-Bacon portion of pilot.<br><br>**Revised Strategy (HFC):**<br>This hypothesis could not be tested through HFC reporting because it was a reporting requirement without an existing reporting method with which to compare reporting burden. |
| **5. Central Reporting Portal can Interface with other reporting systems Hypothesis:**<br>If interfaces can be built to support access to other reporting systems, contractor burden will be reduced. | Hypothesis not tested, but metric associated with test model was met.a | **Original plan (Davis-Bacon):**<br>According to OFPP staff, the Davis-Bacon part of the Central Reporting Portal was able to provide prepopulating of data by interfacing with other reporting systems or drop down menus for all reporting fields. However, it could not demonstrate that such prepopulation resulted in a reduction of contractor burden.<br><br>**Revised Strategy (HFC):**<br>This is not applicable for HFC reporting which is reported through open fields. |

Source: GAO Analysis of OFPP's Procurement Pilot Project Plan, OMB's August 2017 report to Congress, and Interviews with OMB staff | GAO-19-299

[a] Although OFPP did not actually test the hypothesis associated with this test model, it did meet the metric that it had associated with the test model in its pilot plan. That metric is to develop prepopulating capabilities in the Central Reporting Portal by interfacing with other reporting systems.

# VETERANS

In: Key Government Reports.
Editor: Ernest Clark

ISBN: 978-1-53616-001-7
© 2019 Nova Science Publishers, Inc.

*Chapter 5*

# MILITARY SPOUSE EMPLOYMENT: PARTICIPATION IN AND EFFORTS TO PROMOTE THE MY CAREER ADVANCEMENT ACCOUNT PROGRAM*

## *United States Government Accountability Office*

The Honorable James M. Inhofe
Chairman

The Honorable Jack Reed
Ranking Member
Committee on Armed Services
United States Senate

The Honorable Adam Smith
Chairman

---

* This is an edited, reformatted and augmented accessible version of the United States Government Accountability Office Report, Publication No. GAO-19-320R, dated April 9, 2019.

The Honorable Mac Thornberry
Ranking Member
Committee on Armed Services
House of Representatives

For many of the approximately 612,000 spouses of active duty servicemembers, the special conditions of military life may make it difficult to start or maintain a career.[1] Military spouses may have to move frequently to keep families together when servicemembers are relocated, or they may have to bear a larger share of family responsibilities. The My Career Advancement Account (MyCAA) program is one approach the Department of Defense (DOD) has taken to help military spouses improve their employment opportunities. The MyCAA program provides up to $4,000 in tuition assistance for education or training for eligible spouses of servicemembers.[2] The use of MyCAA funds is restricted to the attainment of certificates, licenses, or associate's degrees in a portable career field, which is defined by DOD and the Department of Labor as one that is high-growth, high-demand and most likely to have job openings in military duty locations.

The John S. McCain National Defense Authorization Act for Fiscal Year 2019 includes a provision for GAO to review participation in and awareness of the MyCAA program.[3] This chapter examines (1) what is known about participation rates among military spouses who are eligible for the MyCAA program, and (2) how DOD promotes awareness of and participation in the MyCAA program.

To address the first objective, we reviewed information on the number of spouses who received tuition assistance through MyCAA from annual DOD military family readiness reports for fiscal years 2011 through 2016,

---

[1] The cited number of spouses of active duty servicemembers is from fiscal year 2017.

[2] To be eligible for the program, spouses must have successfully completed high school and be married to active duty servicemembers in paygrades E-1 to E-5, W-1 to W-2, and O-1 to O-2. Paygrades are administrative classifications used primarily to standardize compensation across military services. Numbers represent pay grades within different pay categories: "E" for enlisted, "W" for warrant officers, and "O" for commissioned officers.

[3] Pub. L. No. 115-232, § 574 (2018).

the years for which DOD reported MyCAA data. We also obtained data from DOD on military personnel and on the MyCAA program to determine the percentage of spouses who received tuition assistance under MyCAA for fiscal year 2017, the most recent data available at the time of our review. To understand potential reasons for trends in MyCAA participation, we interviewed DOD officials and reviewed 2015 data from its Survey of Active Duty Spouses (ADSS), the most recent available at the time of our review.[4] We assessed the reliability of these data by conducting data checks, reviewing documentation, and interviewing knowledgeable DOD officials and researchers. We found these data to be sufficiently reliable to generally describe participation in the MyCAA program and have included caveats regarding what the data on the number of potentially eligible spouses represent and other limitations, as appropriate.

To address the second objective, we reviewed DOD's MyCAA outreach materials and analyzed all of the pages on the MyCAA website as of February 2019 using an automated web-scraping program, which extracts and analyzes website data. We assessed the website's content against relevant standards on information quality of federal websites.[5] We interviewed DOD officials about the agency's efforts to inform eligible spouses about the MyCAA program and promote participation in it. We also interviewed representatives from three military family advocacy organizations that we judgmentally selected on the basis of relevant research the organizations conducted on spouse employment; recommendations from other advocacy organizations; or involvement in DOD's Spouse Ambassador Network, which is composed of a variety of groups that are active in military spouse communities.

We conducted this performance audit from September 2018 to April 2019 in accordance with generally accepted government auditing standards. Those standards require that we plan and perform the audit to obtain

---

[4] DOD administered the survey from December 2014 through May 2015. DOD mailed paper surveys in February 2015 to those who did not respond via the web. The survey asks if respondents had used MyCAA tuition assistance in the past.

[5] https://digital.gov/resources/checklist-of-requirements-for-federal-digital-services/ accessed December 6, 2018.

sufficient, appropriate evidence to provide a reasonable basis for our findings and conclusions based on our audit objectives. We believe that the evidence obtained provides a reasonable basis for our findings and conclusions based on our audit objectives.

## RESULTS IN BRIEF

DOD data show that the number of military spouses receiving tuition assistance through the MyCAA program has declined more than 40 percent, from about 38,000 spouses in fiscal year 2011 to about 21,000 in fiscal year 2017. Further, as of fiscal year 2017, about 7 percent of eligible spouses participated in the program, compared to about 10 percent in fiscal year 2011. Various factors may have contributed to the decline. For example, DOD officials said that external trends such as decreases in the number of active duty forces and improvements in the labor market may have contributed to declines in enrollment. Further, estimates from DOD survey data show that some eligible spouses did not participate in MyCAA because of personal or family obligations or because they needed education or training not covered under the program.

DOD officials also attributed declining participation to a lack of program awareness, which is consistent with 2015 DOD survey estimates that about half of eligible spouses who had not used MyCAA were not aware of the program. DOD officials said that to increase MyCAA program awareness, they developed new content for DOD websites, hosted webinars for military spouses, created e-newsletters, sent hard-copy mailers, and posted information on various DOD social media accounts.

However, we found that some MyCAA outreach materials contained inaccurate website information as of early February 2019. During its review of our draft report, DOD updated these materials to include corrected website information as of March 2019. Nonetheless, spouses may still be deterred from participating in the program due to technical difficulties in accessing the website. As of January 2019, DOD officials said they are taking steps to address technical difficulties with accessing the MyCAA website.

## BACKGROUND

Through MyCAA, up to $4,000 in tuition assistance is available to spouses of servicemembers within certain paygrades.[6] Specifically, spouses of active duty servicemembers in paygrades E1 to E-5, W-1 to W-2, and O-1 to O-2 are eligible for the program. The use of MyCAA tuition assistance is restricted to the attainment of certificates, licenses, or associate's degrees for portable careers, and funds cannot be used for bachelor's or advanced degrees. To request MyCAA tuition assistance, spouses must first develop an education and training plan.[7] This plan is reviewed and approved by a career coach. Examples of approved career fields for MyCAA include medical assistants and other occupations in the health care industry. After the plan is approved, spouses can request tuition assistance on a course-by-course basis, no earlier than 60 days prior to the start of the course.[8]

As part of a DOD effort to understand the value of the program and identify options for improving it, the RAND Corporation (RAND) studied MyCAA. In its 2015 report, RAND recommended ways that DOD could

---

[6] We previously reported that since the program's inception in 2009, there have been several changes to its eligibility criteria and benefits. Previously, the MyCAA program was open to any spouse of an active duty servicemember, and they could receive up to $6,000 in tuition funds for any continuing education, including bachelor's and advanced degrees. See GAO, *Military Spouse Employment Programs: DOD Can Improve Guidance and Performance Monitoring*, GAO-13-60 (Washington, D.C.: December 13, 2012). As of October 2010, DOD (1) changed the eligibility criteria to target the program to spouses of servicemembers within certain paygrades, (2) reduced the benefit amount to $4,000, and (3) restricted the funds' use to the attainment of associate's degrees, certificates, and licenses, and not for bachelor's or advanced degrees. According to a DOD policy document, these criteria help ensure fiscal sustainability.

[7] The Military Community and Family Policy office within DOD is responsible for MyCAA program operations. Career coaches, through the Military OneSource call center, assist spouses with completing MyCAA applications and individual career plans.

[8] According to DOD officials, spouses cannot request tuition assistance more than 60 days before the start of a course because course catalogues may not be updated or correct prior to this time period, and this policy also helps the career coaches manage their workload.

address potential barriers to using the program, such as by promoting MyCAA on an ongoing basis.[9]

## PARTICIPATION IN MYCAA HAS DECLINED SINCE FISCAL YEAR 2011

According to DOD's annual military family readiness reports and program data, the number and percentage of eligible spouses receiving MyCAA tuition assistance has declined since fiscal year 2011 (see fig. 1). Specifically, about 21,000 spouses received MyCAA tuition assistance in fiscal year 2017, a more than 40 percent decline from the reported number of spouses who received assistance in fiscal year 2011 (about 38,000), though enrollment did not change substantially from fiscal years 2015 to 2017.

Further, the percentage of eligible spouses who received MyCAA tuition assistance also declined over this time period.[10] However, this decline in the percentage of eligible spouses who participated was less than the decline in the total number of spouses receiving assistance.

According to DOD data, of the approximately 302,000 spouses of service members in MyCAA eligible paygrades in fiscal year 2017, about 7 percent received tuition assistance through the program, similar to the rate for fiscal years 2014 through 2016.[11] In comparison, about 10 percent of eligible spouses received tuition assistance in fiscal year 2011. DOD

---

[9] According to DOD officials, spouses cannot request tuition assistance more than 60 days before the start of a course because course catalogues may not be updated or correct prior to this time period, and this policy also helps the career coaches manage their workload.

[10] We refer to civilian spouses who are married to servicemembers in paygrades eligible for MyCAA as "eligible spouses," though this group may include spouses who are ineligible for the program based on other factors, such as exhaustion of benefits.

[11] This number does not include spouses who are active duty servicemembers themselves as they would not be eligible to participate in the MyCAA program. Additionally, data on spouses of active duty servicemembers do not include those married to National Guard or reserve servicemembers who are activated on Title 10 orders, or in an active duty status, though those spouses could potentially be eligible to participate in MyCAA.

officials said there has been a decline in use of other family benefit programs as well.

Based on information we obtained from DOD officials, DOD survey data, and representatives from military family advocacy organizations, reasons why eligible spouses may not participate in MyCAA include:

- Broad external trends: DOD officials said that trends, such as a decline in the number of active duty forces and improvements in the labor market that may encourage spouses to pursue employment instead of education, may contribute to decreases in MyCAA enrollment.[12]

- *Family responsibilities:* DOD officials said that spouses may open a MyCAA account but not complete the application requirements because, for example, of changes in family circumstances, such as having a child or transferring to another location. According to DOD estimates from the 2015 ADSS, of the eligible spouses who were aware of MyCAA but did not use it, about 40 percent reported they had limited time due to personal or family obligations.[13] Representatives from two military family advocacy organizations we spoke with said that spouses who are busy with childcare may not have time to pursue education or to focus on their career.

---

[12] According to DOD demographic reports, in fiscal year 2011 there were about 1.4 million active duty servicemembers, of whom 726,500 had spouses. In fiscal year 2017, there were nearly 1.3 million active duty servicemembers, of whom 612,127 had spouses.

[13] We requested estimates from DOD of 2015 survey responses for a subpopulation of respondents not currently in the military and married to servicemembers in eligible paygrades (E-1 to E-5, W-1 to W-2, or O-1 to O-2). The estimates from DOD presented in this report were subject to both nonsampling and sampling errors. Nonsampling errors are those that may be introduced in the results due to the practical difficulties of conducting a survey. For example, survey respondents may have difficulties interpreting a particular question or make errors when selecting responses to a survey question, and study staff may not detect and correct errors during data entry or analysis, all of which can introduce unwanted variability into the survey results. Sampling errors measure the uncertainty introduced into the estimates because not every member of the population was surveyed and are expressed as a margin of error. The margins of error for all estimates presented in this report are +/- 5 percentage points or fewer. In a prior study, RAND analyzed data from the 2012 iteration of this survey for a subpopulation of civilian spouses who were married to servicemembers in eligible paygrades. In its analysis of 2012 ADSS data, RAND estimated that about half of eligible spouses who did not use MyCAA reported that they had limited time due to personal or family obligations.

- *Education covered by MyCAA:* According to 2015 ADSS estimates, about one-third of eligible spouses who were aware of the program but did not use it reported that they needed education, training, or testing that was not covered by MyCAA. Representatives from two military family advocacy organizations we spoke with said one potential barrier to using MyCAA is that tuition assistance cannot be used towards obtaining a bachelor's degree.

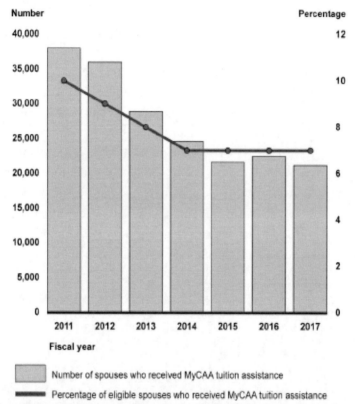

Source: GAO analysis of Department of Defense (DOD) annual reports to Congress on the agency's plans for military family readiness for fiscal years 2011 through 2015. MyCAA program data, and Defense Enrollment Eligibility Reporting System (DEERS) data. | GAO-19-320R.

Figure 1. Number and Percentage of Eligible Military Spouses Who Received Tuition Assistance through the My Career Advancement Account (MyCAA) Program, Fiscal Years 2011 through 2017.

**Data table for Figure 1. Number and Percentage of Eligible Military Spouses Who Received Tuition Assistance through the My Career Advancement Account (MyCAA) Program, Fiscal Years 2011 through 2017**

| | Number of spouses who received MyCAA tuition assistance | Percentage of eligible spouses who received MyCAA tuition assistance |
|---|---|---|
| 2011 | 38,000 | 10 |
| 2012 | 36,000 | 9 |
| 2013 | 28,898 | 8 |
| 2014 | 24,644 | 7 |
| 2015 | 21,638 | 7 |
| 2016 | 22,438 | 7 |

Note: Data on the number who receive tuition assistance are tracked based on the number of spouses who are approved for tuition assistance. According to DOD officials, these data may change over time depending on the completion of approved coursework. For example, if a spouse was approved for tuition assistance but did not attend school, they would be removed from the count of spouses who received tuition assistance that year. For fiscal years 2011 through 2015, the figure presents the values contained in publicly available reports. Values for fiscal years 2016 and 2017 are based on program data GAO obtained from DOD. Data on the number of eligible spouses represent civilian spouses of active duty servicemembers in MyCAA eligible paygrades (E-1 to E-5; W-1 to W-2; and O-1 to O-2), though this group may include spouses who are ineligible for MyCAA based on other factors, such as exhaustion of benefits. Additionally, these data do not include spouses of National Guard or reserve servicemembers who are activated on Title 10 orders, or in an active duty status, though those spouses could be eligible to participate in MyCAA.

- *Paygrade eligibility:* Representatives from three military family advocacy organizations said that a servicemember may not remain in an eligible paygrade long enough for their spouse to take advantage of the program. Similarly, according to 2015 ADSS estimates, about 10 percent of eligible spouses who were aware of the program but did not use it believed that they would not be eligible long enough to use MyCAA.[14]

---

[14] In addition to MyCAA, there are other programs that provide educational services for military spouses. For example, spouses may be eligible for benefits under the Post-9/11 GI Bill, which includes tuition for postsecondary courses. For more information on programs that provide educational services to servicemembers and their families, see GAO, *Military and Veteran*

- *Lack of awareness:* DOD officials also attributed declining MyCAA participation to a lack of awareness of the program. This is consistent with 2015 ADSS estimates which indicated that about a quarter of eligible spouses used MyCAA, and of those who had not used the program at any time, about half were unaware of it.[15]

## DOD HAS A STRATEGY TO INCREASE AWARENESS OF MYCAA AND HAS TAKEN STEPS TO ADDRESS INACCURATE INFORMATION AND WEBSITE ACCESSIBILITY ISSUES THAT COULD HINDER PARTICIPATION

DOD officials described several regular outreach efforts to increase awareness of the MyCAA program. In its 2015 study, RAND recommended that DOD promote MyCAA on a continuing basis because about half of eligible spouses who did not use the program were not aware of the program.[16] DOD officials told us that in response to this gap in awareness, they produced content for DOD websites, hosted webinars with military spouses, created e-newsletters, sent hard-copy mailers, and posted information on various DOD social media accounts (for an example of this outreach, see fig. 2).

Additionally, career coaches at a DOD call center are responsible for helping military spouses develop career plans and referring them to appropriate services to address challenges to enrolling in MyCAA. DOD

---

*Support: Detailed Inventory of Federal Programs to Help Servicemembers Achieve Civilian Employment*, GAO-19-97R (Washington, D.C.: January 17, 2019).

[15] In its study of 2012 ADSS data, RAND estimated that one in five eligible spouses used the MyCAA program in the previous year and, of those who did not use it, approximately half were unaware of MyCAA.

[16] RAND Corporation, *Advancing the Careers of Military Spouses.* In addition, RAND released a report in 2016 that suggested performance indicators for the Spouse Education and Career Opportunities program. See RAND Corporation, *The Military Spouse Education and Career Opportunities Program: Recommendations for an Internal Monitoring System* (Santa Monica, CA: 2016).

officials also said they coordinate with stakeholder groups who work with military spouses. For example, DOD officials told us they meet quarterly with the Spouse Ambassador Network. DOD shares information on MyCAA through various events, such as workshops and hiring events at military installations. Information is also shared during quarterly webinars with career counselors at the installations.

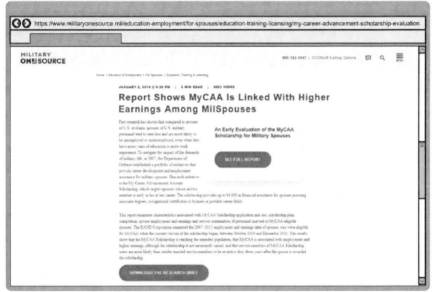

Source: https://www.militaryonesource.mil/education-employment/for-spouses/education-training-licensing/my-career-advancement-scholarship-evaluation. Accessed Jan. 8, 2019. | GAO-19-320R.

Figure 2. Excerpt of Department of Defense Blog Post Promoting the My Career Advancement Account (MyCAA) Program.

To expand on its ongoing efforts to increase program awareness, DOD drafted a formal communication strategy in October 2018 for its MyCAA outreach, which was in its initial implementation phase at the time of our review. This strategy proposes ways to tailor communications to various segments of the program's intended audience. For example, communications directed toward military spouses who are early in their careers will highlight the pursuit of licenses, certificates, or associate's degrees as a useful start to an education or career plan. The strategy also seeks to increase awareness among the stakeholder groups that have a role in connecting military spouses to resources. These include the Spouse Ambassador Network, schools, career coaches, installation-based employment readiness specialists, and spouses with experience navigating military life, among others.

However, we found that some of DOD's outreach materials contained inaccurate website information and that the MyCAA website can be difficult to access. For example, DOD distributes a Frequently Asked Questions document for MyCAA which, at the time of our review, referred users to an inactive link for enrolling in the program. DOD officials told us this was because DOD changed the address of the MyCAA website in July 2018 as part of a move to a cloud platform and had not updated all of the corresponding documents. Officials said they update their outreach materials every year or when there is a major program change. However, as of early February 2019, the Frequently Asked Questions document and nine additional MyCAA outreach materials had not been updated to reflect the new website address.[17] As a result, military spouses who had relied on that information may have encountered an obstacle to successfully enrolling in the program. During its review of our draft report, DOD updated these materials to include corrected website information as of March 2019.[18]

The MyCAA website has also experienced technical difficulties, which may affect the website's accessibility and deter eligible military spouses from enrolling. DOD officials said that the MyCAA website's identification verification system experienced 13 outages from June through November 2018. The MyCAA website also experienced technical issues from July through mid-August 2018 as the agency implemented software upgrades and

---

[17] Using an automated web scraping program, which extracts and analyzes website data, we examined all of the pages on the MyCAA website at https://mycaa.militaryonesource.mil. On the 40 pages of the site, we found 8 pdf documents, including the Frequently Asked Questions document, which listed an inaccurate web address for the program. In addition, DOD officials provided us with 2 additional outreach documents that contained an inactive link.

[18] We reviewed DOD's updates in March 2019 and found that the outreach materials that we previously identified as having inaccurate website information no longer contain the inactive link. Moreover, according to DOD officials, DOD's communication strategy seeks to keep MyCAA outreach materials current through regular updates.

moved the website to a cloud platform. DOD officials told us that as a result, some spouses were unable to register for Fall 2018 classes and enrollment in MyCAA declined. In addition, the website may be difficult to access from certain devices. According to DOD officials, about 30 percent of those who visit the MyCAA website access it via a mobile device. However, we had difficulty accessing the website from mobile devices. For example, we received an error message that the connection to the site may not be private (see fig. 3).

Source: https://mycaa.militaryonesource.mil. (Images as of Feb. 6, 2019 on a Chrome browser in an Android 9 operating system and on a Safari browser in an iPhone iOS 12 operating system). | GAO-19-320R.

Figure 3. Two Examples of Error Messages When Accessing My Career Advancement Account (MyCAA) Website.

Representatives from one military family advocacy organization we spoke with described receiving a similar error message on other DOD websites that include information on the MyCAA program, and said eligible spouses would likely leave the website rather than take additional steps to access it after receiving this type of message.

DOD has taken steps to address technical difficulties with the website. Specifically, DOD's communication strategy includes potential updates to the MyCAA website's user interface to make it more mobile-friendly. Additionally, for users who receive an error message when attempting to reach the site, DOD provides instructions for installing a special DOD file containing a security certificate to eliminate the error message if they have not clicked through the error message to install the relevant certificate. DOD officials told us that nearly all of the other websites under the purview of the Military Community and Family Policy office use a different type of security certificate so that this special DOD file is not needed. As of January 2019, DOD officials said they are considering using this type of certificate for the MyCAA site as well.

## AGENCY COMMENTS

We provided a copy of this draft report to the Department of Defense for review and comment. These comments are reproduced in enclosure I. In our draft report, we recommended that DOD update the MyCAA outreach materials to include the program's current website address. During the agency's review of our draft report, DOD agreed with this recommendation and updated the MyCAA outreach materials. We subsequently reviewed the outreach materials in March 2019 and confirmed DOD corrected the materials. As a result of the agency's actions, we removed the recommendation from our report.

We are sending copies of this chapter to the appropriate congressional committees, the Secretary of the Department of Defense, and other interested parties.

Chelsa Gurkin
Acting Director Education,
Workforce, and Income Security

# ENCLOSURE I: COMMENTS FROM THE DEPARTMENT OF DEFENSE

OFFICE OF THE ASSISTANT SECRETARY OF DEFENSE
1500 DEFENSE PENTAGON
WASHINGTON, D.C. 20301-1500

MAR - 5 2019

MANPOWER AND
RESERVE AFFAIRS

Ms. Chelsa Gurkin
Acting Director, Education, Workforce, and Income Security
U.S. Government Accountability Office
441 G Street, N.W.
Washington, DC 20548

Dear Ms. Gurkin:

This is the Department of Defense (DoD) response to the GAO Draft Report, GAO-19-320R, "MILITARY SPOUSE EMPLOYMENT: Participation in and Efforts to Promote the My Career Advancement Account Program," dated February 8, 2019 (GAO Code 103026). The Office of the Secretary of Defense is committed to implementing the GAO recommendation to update the My Career Advancement Account (MyCAA) outreach materials, including the Frequently Asked Questions, and the current address of the program's website.

Supporting military spouse education and career opportunities is a top priority of my office. We have developed a robust communication strategy for the MyCAA program, to include regular updates to associated outreach materials. Consistent with our communication strategy and GAO's recommendation, all MyCAA outreach materials are now current. We will continue to ensure that military spouses are aware of our resources and that those resources are easily accessible. We appreciate the GAO's work to review the MyCAA program and offer actionable recommendations.

Our response to the draft GAO report is enclosed.

Sincerely,

Ann G. Johnston
Deputy Assistant Secretary of Defense
(Military Community and Family Policy)

**GAO DRAFT REPORT DATED FEBRUARY 8, 2019**
**GAO-19-320R (GAO CODE 103026)**

**"MILITARY SPOUSE EMPLOYMENT: PARTICIPATION IN AND EFFORTS TO PROMOTE THE MY CAREER ADVANCEMENT ACCOUNT PROGRAM"**

**DEPARTMENT OF DEFENSE COMMENTS**
**TO THE GAO RECOMMENDATION**

**RECOMMENDATION 1:** The Secretary of Defense should update the MyCAA outreach materials, including the Frequently Asked Questions, to include the current address of the program's website.

**DoD RESPONSE:** The Department of Defense concurs with GAO's recommendation to update the MyCAA outreach materials, including the Frequently Asked Questions, to include the current address of the program's website. The updates have been completed and all MyCAA outreach materials are now current.

In: Key Government Reports.
Editor: Ernest Clark

*Chapter 6*

# VETERANS HEALTH ADMINISTRATION: PAST PERFORMANCE SYSTEM RECOMMENDATIONS HAVE NOT BEEN IMPLEMENTED[*]

## *United States Government Accountability Office*

### ABBREVIATIONS

| | |
|------|------|
| SAIL | Strategic Analytics for Improvement and Learning |
| VA   | Department of Veterans Affairs |
| VHA  | Veterans Health Administration |

---

[*] This is an edited, reformatted and augmented version of United States Government Accountability Office; Report to Congressional Requesters, Publication No. GAO-19-350, dated April 2019.

# WHY GAO DID THIS STUDY

VHA anticipates that it will provide care to more than 7 million veterans in fiscal year 2019. The majority of veterans using VHA health care services receive care in one or more of the 172 medical centers or at associated outpatient facilities. VHA collects an extensive amount of data that can be used to assess and manage the performance of medical centers. Many measures are publicly reported on VA web pages, allowing veterans the ability to compare medical centers' quality of care.

GAO was asked to assess VHA's management of medical center performance. This chapter examines (1) the tools VHA uses to assess medical center performance; (2) VHA's use of medical center performance information to assess medical center directors; and (3) the extent to which VHA has evaluated the effectiveness of the SAIL system.

GAO reviewed VHA policies, guidance, and performance information for medical centers and their associated directors. GAO also interviewed officials from VHA as well as from four VA medical centers, selected for variation in performance and geographic location.

# WHAT GAO RECOMMENDS

GAO recommends that the Under Secretary for Health: (1) assess recommendations from previous evaluations of SAIL for implementation; and (2) implement, as appropriate, recommendations resulting from the assessment. VA concurred with GAO's recommendations and identified actions it is taking to implement them.

# WHAT GAO FOUND

Department of Veterans Affairs' (VA) Veterans Health Administration (VHA) officials told GAO they primarily use the Strategic Analytics for

Improvement and Learning (SAIL) system to assess VA medical center performance. SAIL includes 27 quality measures in areas such as acute care mortality and access to care. VHA officials use SAIL to calculate and assign each medical center an annual star rating of 1 (lowest) to 5 (highest) stars as an assessment of overall quality. For the 146 medical centers that received star ratings in fiscal year 2018, the distribution of star ratings was as follows: 6 percent, 1 star; 24 percent, 2 stars; 38 percent, 3 stars; 19 percent, 4 stars; and 12 percent, 5 stars. Although the specific medical centers within each star-rating category could change from year to year, GAO found that the fiscal year 2018 star ratings for 110 of the 127 medical centers (87 percent) that received star ratings in fiscal year 2013 did not differ by more than 1 star from their fiscal year 2013 rating.

GAO found that VHA's appraisal process for assessing medical center director performance relies heavily on medical center performance information, including SAIL. For example, the most heavily weighted appraisal element (40 percent of the overall rating) is made up entirely of medical center performance information.

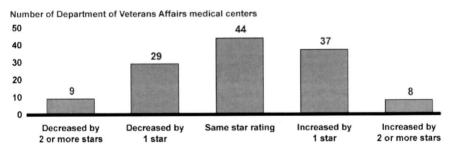

Source: Veterans Health Administration (VHA). | GAO-19-350.

Changes in VHA Strategic Analytics for Improvement and Learning Star Ratings, Fiscal Year 2013 Compared to Fiscal Year 2018.

SAIL was evaluated in 2014 and 2015, but VHA has not assessed the recommendations from those evaluations, or taken action on them. The evaluations, which found issues related to the validity and reliability of SAIL and its star ratings for measuring performance and fostering accountability, together included more than 40 recommendations for improving SAIL. The findings are similar to concerns expressed by officials GAO interviewed from VHA, networks, and medical centers about SAIL's effectiveness and how it is currently being used to assess medical center performance. VHA officials told GAO the findings and recommendations of the previous SAIL evaluations were not assessed because the evaluation reports were not widely distributed within VHA due to leadership turnover, as well as attention that was diverted to other concerns such as extensive wait times for medical appointments. Without ensuring that the recommendations resulting from these previous evaluations are assessed and implemented as appropriate, the identified deficiencies may not be adequately resolved, and VHA's ability to hold officials accountable for taking the necessary actions may be diminished.

April 30, 2019

The Honorable Johnny Isakson
Chairman

The Honorable Jon Tester
Ranking Member
Committee on Veterans' Affairs
United States Senate

The Honorable Mark Takano
Chairman

The Honorable Phil Roe
Ranking Member
Committee on Veterans' Affairs
House of Representatives

The Honorable Derek Kilmer
House of Representatives

The Department of Veterans Affairs' (VA) Veterans Health Administration (VHA) anticipates that it will provide care to more than 7 million veterans in fiscal year 2019. The majority of veterans utilizing VHA health care services receive care in one or more of VA's 172 medical centers or their associated outpatient facilities. VHA collects an extensive amount of data that can be used to assess and manage the performance of its medical centers, including data on patient outcomes, access to care, and the patient experience. Many measures are publicly reported and summarized on VA web pages, allowing veterans the ability to review and compare medical centers' quality of care. VHA's Strategic Analytics for Improvement and Learning (SAIL) system consolidates, summarizes, and provides tools for interpreting medical center performance information. VHA designed SAIL to provide internal benchmarking of medical center performance and to promote high quality health care delivery across its system of regional networks and medical centers.[1]

We and others have expressed concerns about VHA's management of its health care system, including VHA's ability to effectively provide and monitor access to quality and timely health care to veterans. These concerns contributed to our decision to add VA health care to our High-Risk List in 2015, and to its continued inclusion in our 2017 and 2019 updates.[2] You asked us to assess VHA's management of network and medical center performance as part of a broad-based management review of VHA.[3] This chapter examines:

---

[1] Each of VHA's 18 regional Veterans Integrated Service Networks is responsible for managing and overseeing medical centers within a defined geographic area.

[2] GAO maintains a high-risk list to focus attention on government agencies and programs that it identifies as high risk due to their greater vulnerabilities to fraud, waste, abuse, and mismanagement or the need for transformation to address economy, efficiency, or effectiveness challenges. See GAO, *High-Risk Series: An Update*, GAO-15-290 (Washington, D.C.: Feb. 11, 2015); GAO, *High-Risk Series: Progress on Many High-Risk Areas, While Substantial Effort Needed on Others*, GAO-17-317 (Washington, D.C.: Feb. 15, 2017); and GAO, *High-Risk Series: Substantial Efforts Needed to Sustain Progress on High-Risk Areas*, GAO-19-157SP (Washington, D.C.: Mar. 6, 2019).

[3] We have previously issued several reports examining specific aspects of VHA's management. For a complete list of our previous work in this area, see the "Related GAO Products" page at the end of this report.

1) the tools VHA uses to assess and manage medical center performance;
2) VHA's use of medical center performance information to assess the performance of its network and medical center directors; and
3) the extent to which VHA has evaluated the effectiveness of the SAIL system.

To examine the tools VHA uses to assess and manage medical center performance, we reviewed VHA policies and related documents that describe performance measures and other information VHA officials use to assess, monitor, compare, and manage performance across its medical centers. Additionally, we interviewed officials from VHA's Office of Reporting, Analytics, Performance, Improvement and Deployment, who are responsible for determining and reporting on medical center performance. We also reviewed documents and interviewed officials from four VA medical centers to obtain information on the tools they use to monitor and manage performance: Nebraska-Western Iowa Health Care System (Omaha, Neb.); New York Harbor Health Care System (New York, N.Y.); Tennessee Valley Healthcare System (Nashville and Murfreesboro, Tenn.); and VA Central California Health Care System (Fresno, Calif.). We selected these medical centers for variation in geographic location, medical center complexity level, quality (indicated by SAIL star ratings for fiscal years 2016 and 2017), and directors' individual performance ratings.[4] We also interviewed officials from the four regional networks that oversee these four selected medical centers. Information obtained from these selected networks and medical centers cannot be generalized. Our scope was focused on examining the tools used to assess medical center performance as a whole;

---

[4] VHA categorizes medical centers according to complexity level, which is determined on the basis of the characteristics of the patient population, clinical services offered, educational and research missions, and administrative complexity. There are three complexity levels with level 1 representing the most complex facilities and level 3 the least complex. Level 1 is further subdivided into categories 1a, 1b, and 1c.

VHA uses data from SAIL to assign each VA medical center an annual star rating of 1 (lowest) to 5 (highest) stars to demonstrate overall quality.

we did not specifically examine all tools that can be used to monitor and assess performance for specific programs or health conditions.

To examine VHA's use of medical center performance information to assess the performance of its network and medical center directors, we reviewed relevant VHA documents, including the performance plan templates used to evaluate network and medical center directors for fiscal years 2016 through 2018. In addition, we interviewed officials from the VA and VHA offices that oversee human resource efforts and executive performance management—VA's Corporate Senior Executive Service Management Office and VHA's office of Workforce Management and Consulting. We also interviewed officials from the networks and medical centers in our review to obtain their perspectives on VHA's performance assessment process.

To determine the extent to which VHA has evaluated the effectiveness of the SAIL system, we reviewed prior reports on VHA quality of care data, including SAIL.[5] We also interviewed officials from VHA's Office of Reporting, Analytics, Performance, Improvement and Deployment; Health Information Management; Office of Internal Audit and Risk Assessment; and the Assistant Deputy Under Secretary for Health for Integrity. In addition, we interviewed officials from our selected networks and medical centers to obtain their perspectives on SAIL's effectiveness in assessing medical center performance. We evaluated VHA's actions in the context of relevant federal standards for internal control.[6]

We conducted this performance audit from October 2017 to April 2019 in accordance with generally accepted government auditing standards.

---

[5] See GAO, *VA Health Care Quality: VA Should Improve the Information It Publicly Reports on the Quality of Care at Its Medical Facilities*, GAO-17-741 (Washington, D.C.: Sept. 29, 2017); and VA Office of Inspector General, *Evaluation of the Quality, Safety, and Value Program in Veterans Health Administration Facilities Fiscal Year 2016* (Washington, D.C: Mar. 31, 2017).

[6] GAO, *Standards for Internal Control in the Federal Government*, GAO-14-704G (Washington, D.C.: September 2014). Internal control is a process affected by an entity's oversight body, management, and other personnel that provides reasonable assurance that the objectives of an entity will be achieved.

Those standards require that we plan and perform the audit to obtain sufficient, appropriate evidence to provide a reasonable basis for our findings and conclusions based on our audit objectives. We believe that the evidence obtained provides a reasonable basis for our findings and conclusions based on our audit objectives.

# BACKGROUND

## Medical Center Performance: SAIL

VHA began using the SAIL system in 2012 to measure, evaluate, and benchmark the quality, efficiency, and productivity of medical centers, and to highlight successful strategies of high-performing medical centers. SAIL includes 29 performance measures (27 quality measures and two measures of overall efficiency and capacity) in areas such as acute-care mortality, access to care, and employee satisfaction. (See appendix I for the full list of SAIL measures). SAIL is a diagnostic tool that allows VHA to assess medical centers' performance relative to their peers, and determine how much absolute improvement they have made in the past year based on relevant clinical data.

VHA publishes SAIL results quarterly to provide information to network and medical center officials regarding improvement opportunities at each medical center.[7] SAIL data are also available on VHA's intranet site. VHA staff can view a wide range of detailed information about their medical center, compare performance to other medical centers, and (for those staff with medical-record-level access) view information on patients with a particular medical condition.

---

[7] VHA officials told us that complete results for SAIL's 29 performance measures are not available for up to several months after the end of each quarter.

## Network and Medical Center Director Performance Appraisal Process

VHA conducts annual performance appraisals for all network and medical center officials. The appraisal process begins when officials from VHA's office of Workforce Management and Consulting transmit a performance plan template to the network directors. The template identifies performance priorities and expectations for the upcoming appraisal period and criteria to be used to measure performance outcomes and ratings for each performance element. Network directors use the template to develop performance plans that include targets and time frames—the schedule of when performance targets are to be achieved during the year—with each of the medical center directors in their network. According to VA policy, performance plans resulting from the template should be finalized within 30 days of the start of the appraisal period. After expectations have been set for a medical center director, the director, in turn, sets performance expectations for the department heads within the medical center.

## VHA PRIMARILY USES SAIL AND ITS ASSOCIATED STAR RATINGS TO ASSESS AND MANAGE MEDICAL CENTER PERFORMANCE

## VHA Primarily Uses SAIL and Its Star Ratings to Assess Medical Center Performance

VHA officials told us they primarily use the SAIL system to assess the performance of medical centers. Specifically, VHA uses SAIL data to calculate and assign each medical center an annual star rating of 1 (lowest) to 5 (highest) stars as an assessment of overall quality.

SAIL documentation states that the goal of the star ratings is for low-performing medical centers to learn from the best practices of high-performing ones, although all medical centers have the opportunity to improve. VHA applies a weighting and calculation methodology to each of SAIL's 27 quality measures to determine a single composite score for each medical center. The scores are then ranked and grouped by percentile and the associated medical centers are assigned initial star ratings based on their relative ranking. For example, the lowest performing 10 percent of medical centers as determined by SAIL's 27 quality measures are assigned a 1-star rating, and the next lowest performing 20 percent of medical centers are assigned a 2-star rating. (See Figure 1).

After the initial star rating is determined by SAIL measures each year, VHA officials can make changes to the rating if a medical center meets certain conditions. For example, SAIL documentation states that a medical center that initially received a 5-star rating will be reduced to a 4- star rating if it has a high mortality rate.

In addition, VHA officials told us they can decide to increase a 1-star medical center's rating to a 2-star rating if the medical center outperforms the bottom 10 percent of U.S. hospitals in certain criteria as measured by external systems such as the Centers for Medicare & Medicaid Services' *Hospital Compare* website.[8] We found that the percentage of medical centers that received a final 1- star rating ranged from 4 percent to 10 percent from fiscal years 2013 through 2018. VHA officials publish the final annual star ratings for each medical center both internally and externally. See Figure 2 for the number of medical centers that received each final star rating for fiscal years 2013 through 2018.

---

[8] *Hospital Compare* publicly posts health care quality measures for VA medical centers as well as non-VA hospitals that participate in Medicare, enabling veterans and others the opportunity to compare the performance of non-VA hospitals and VA medical centers on a common set of quality measures.

A VHA official also told us that extenuating circumstances may also be considered in some cases, such as with the medical centers in Puerto Rico and Houston, Texas after both areas were affected by severe hurricanes in 2017.

Source: Veterans Health Administration (VHA). | GAO-19-350.

Note: VHA primarily uses SAIL to assess and manage VA medical center performance on 29 performance measures (27 quality measures and two measures of overall efficiency and capacity). VHA applies a weighting and calculation methodology to each of SAIL's 27 quality measures to determine a single composite score for each medical center annually. The scores are then ranked and grouped by percentile and the associated medical centers are assigned initial star ratings based on their relative ranking.

Figure 1. Strategic Analytics for Improvement and Learning (SAIL) Initial Star-Rating Distribution for Department of Veterans Affairs (VA) Medical Centers.

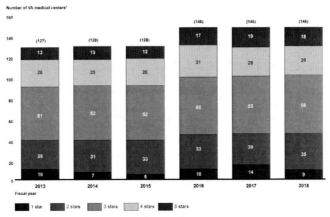

Source: Veterans Health Administration (VHA). | GAO-19-350.

Note: VHA primarily uses SAIL to assess and manage VA medical center performance on 29 performance measures (27 quality measures and two measures of overall efficiency and capacity). VHA assigns each medical center an initial star rating of 1 (lowest) to 5 (highest) stars to represent overall quality of care, based on each medical center's performance on the 27 SAIL quality measures. The scores are then ranked and grouped by percentile and the associated medical centers are assigned initial star ratings based on their relative ranking. VHA officials told us they can decide to increase a 1-star or decrease a 5-star medical center's initial star rating when determining the final star rating if the medical center meets specified conditions.

[a]VHA officials told us that the number of VA medical centers published in SAIL results does not match the total number of VA medical centers because the way a medical center is defined for SAIL differs from the way it is defined for VA site classification.

Figure 2. Number of Department of Veterans Affairs (VA) Medical Centers by Strategic Analytics for Improvement and Learning (SAIL) Final Star Rating, Fiscal Years 2013 through 2018.

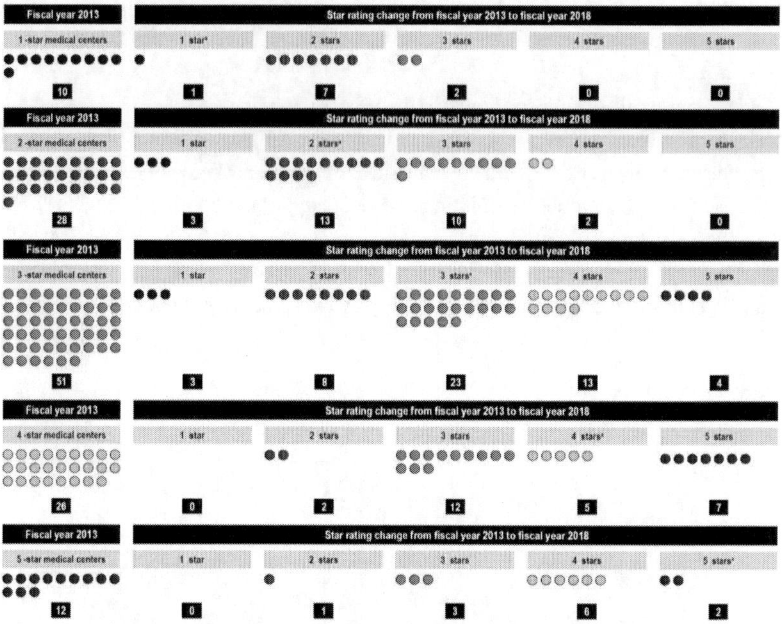

Source: Veterans Health Administration (VHA). | GAO-19-350.

Notes: VHA primarily uses SAIL to assess and manage VA medical center performance on 29 performance measures (27 quality measures and two measures of overall efficiency and capacity). VHA assigns each medical center an initial star rating of 1 (lowest) to 5 (highest) stars to represent overall quality of care, based on each medical center's performance on the 27 SAIL quality measures. The scores are then ranked and grouped by percentile and the associated medical centers are assigned initial star ratings based on their relative ranking. VHA officials told us they can decide to increase a 1-star or decrease a 5-star medical center's initial star rating when determining the final star rating if the medical center meets specified conditions.

Our analysis included the 127 VA medical centers that received star ratings in both fiscal years 2013 and 2018.

[a]No change from fiscal year 2013 star rating.

Figure 3. Strategic Analytics for Improvement and Learning (SAIL) Final Star Ratings for Department of Veterans Affairs (VA) Medical Centers in Fiscal Year 2013 Compared to Fiscal Year 2018.

Although the specific medical centers within each star-rating category could change from year to year, we found that the fiscal year 2018 star ratings for 110 of the 127 medical centers (87 percent) that received star ratings in fiscal year 2013 did not differ by more than 1 star from their fiscal year 2013 star rating. For example, eight of the 10 1-star medical centers in fiscal year 2013 received either a 1- or 2-star rating in fiscal year 2018. (See Figure 3). In addition, 44 of the 127 medical centers had the same rating in fiscal year 2018 as they did in fiscal year 2013. At the end of the 6-year period of our review, only one medical center differed by more than 2 stars from its fiscal year 2013 star rating, decreasing from 5 stars to 2.

## VHA Uses Tools from the SAIL System to Manage Medical Center Performance

VHA officials told us they use SAIL tools on VHA's intranet when conducting site visits to medical centers and for other performance management efforts. The SAIL system includes several performance management tools that present data in greater detail than SAIL's quarterly data release and enable officials to identify areas for improvement. VHA, network, and medical center officials we interviewed mentioned three in particular:

- Opportunity matrix – This matrix shows how a medical center ranks compared to others on all SAIL performance measures based on quarterly data. Each performance measure is labeled by quintile, with the first quintile comprising the top 20 percent of medical centers and the fifth quintile comprising the bottom 20 percent. Officials told us they use this tool to focus improvement efforts by examining specific measures for which a medical center needs improvement.
- Geometric control charts – These charts, referred to as G-Charts, allow officials to monitor on a daily basis what VHA considers to be rare occurrences. For example, one G-Chart allows VHA to monitor patient safety indicators that contain information on occurrences of specific medical conditions, such as cardiac arrest,

pneumonia, and sepsis. Medical center officials can use these charts to examine the occurrence of events over time, analyze patient-level data, and quickly detect changes in the frequency of these events. Other events that the charts allow VHA to monitor include inpatient complications and deaths.

- Symphony action triggers – Symphony is an online tool that tracks over 100 performance measures daily, related to medical center access, outcomes, and productivity, and includes an early warning system to notify network and medical center officials of results that require attention. Officials can use Symphony to view patient-level information to understand the details of particular events and determine solutions.

VHA officials also told us that they use these tools to manage medical center performance as part of their ongoing support of lower performing medical centers. Specifically, officials who oversee SAIL identify lower performing medical centers using SAIL and conduct site visits as part of VHA's Strategic Action for Transformation initiative. This initiative utilizes a four-tiered, escalating approach based on the severity of concern at a medical center. In order of increasing severity, the four levels are watch, high-risk, critical, and VA receivership. One-star medical centers are automatically placed on the high-risk list, along with some 2-star medical centers with decreasing performance. If performance continues to decrease, medical centers are considered critical, and can be escalated to VA "receivership," at which point VHA officials may step in to correct ongoing problems and replace network or medical center leadership officials. As of January 2019, VHA officials told us no medical center had entered VA receivership since the initiative began.[9] VHA officials told us that they may also conduct site visits or hold calls with medical center leadership by request, although their focus is on lower performing medical centers.

In addition to the SAIL tools, which report data on performance measures across the entire medical center, VHA officials told us that they

---

[9] VHA officials told us that, as of January 2019, 19 medical centers were on the watch list, 10 were on the high risk list, and one was on the critical list.

may also use other data sources as part of medical center performance management. For example, several program offices—such as primary care, mental health, and surgery—have dashboards that track performance and quality of care specific to those offices. In addition, VA's Inpatient Evaluation Center focuses on mortality data, including estimates of expected patient mortality.

## VHA'S APPRAISAL PROCESS FOR ASSESSING NETWORK AND MEDICAL CENTER DIRECTORS' PERFORMANCE RELIES HEAVILY ON MEDICAL CENTER PERFORMANCE INFORMATION

We found that VHA relies heavily on medical center performance information to assess the performance of its network and medical center directors. VA's *Senior Executive Service Part V. Performance Appraisal System handbook* states that directors are assessed using five appraisal elements established by the Office of Personnel Management: (1) Results Driven, (2) Leading People, (3) Leading Change, (4) Business Acumen, and (5) Building Coalitions.[10] The five elements are included in VHA's performance plan template, which forms the basis for network and medical center directors' performance plans. The handbook designates a relative weight for each element used to calculate a director's rating. (See Figure 4). The handbook states that a director is rated in each element on a scale of level 1 to level 5, with 5 being the highest level. Each rating is then multiplied by the weight for its corresponding element, and the results are added to generate a summary score. According to the handbook, the

---

[10] VA adopted the Office of Personnel Management's government-wide SES performance appraisal system in fiscal year 2012 and modified it, as permitted by the Office of Personnel Management, to address VA-unique requirements. See VA, *Senior Executive Service, Part V. Performance Appraisal System,* VA Handbook 5027/2 Part V (Washington, D.C.: Nov. 6, 2014).

summary score is used to identify potential recipients of pay increases and monetary awards.

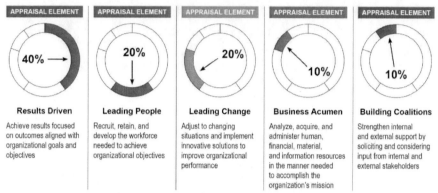

Source: Department of Veterans Affairs (VA). | GAO-19-350.

Note: For network directors, performance information is based on the aggregate performance of all VA medical centers in the network.

Figure 4. VA Network and Medical Center Directors' Performance Plan Template Elements and Associated Weights, Fiscal Year 2018.

The most heavily weighted appraisal element in the handbook, Results Driven, represents 40 percent of a director's overall performance and is based entirely on medical center performance information. Specifically, for fiscal year 2018, SAIL results comprised 25 percent of the overall rating and included measures such as patient mortality, length of stay, and readmissions. Other medical center performance information comprised the remaining 15 percent of the overall rating. (See Figure 5).

Medical center performance information is also used when assessing directors' performance across other appraisal elements. For example, in VHA's fiscal year 2018 performance plan template, the Leading Change appraisal element included the implementation of suicide prevention initiatives, using medical center performance in the SAIL mental health domain as criteria. In addition, the Leading People element included performance information from VA's All Employees' Survey, which included medical center staff.[11]

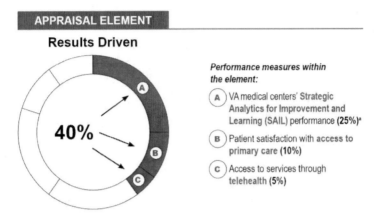

Source: Department of Veterans Affairs (VA). | GAO-19-350.

[a]The Veterans Health Administration (VHA) primarily uses SAIL to assess and manage VA medical center performance on 29 performance measures (27 quality measures and two measures of overall efficiency and capacity). For network directors, performance information is based on the aggregate performance of all VA medical centers in the network.

Figure 5. Components of "Results Driven" Performance Appraisal Element for VA Network and Medical Center Directors, Fiscal Year 2018.

Although medical center performance information plays a prominent role in the performance assessment process, VHA officials told us that there are other considerations that may result in medical center directors receiving a rating that is higher than that indicated by the star rating of the medical center. For example, VHA officials told us that when calculating a medical center director's rating for the Results Driven element, they consider whether the medical center's overall performance improved or deteriorated compared to the previous year's performance.[12] These officials also stated

---

[11] VA developed its annual All Employees' Survey in 2001 to assess workforce satisfaction and organizational climate.

[12] For medical center directors, VHA officials determine the rating for the Results Driven appraisal element, and the network director determines the rating for the other four appraisal elements, according to VHA officials. For network directors, VHA officials determine the ratings for all five appraisal elements.

that they take into consideration the length of a director's tenure, such as cases where a director started at a low-performing medical center partway through the rating year and would not have had sufficient time to improve the medical center's performance from the previous year.

In our review, we also found that the release of VHA's performance plan template is often delayed, which can limit its effectiveness as a means of assessing directors' performance. Specifically, in fiscal years 2016, 2017, and 2018, VHA released the performance plan template to network directors in November or December, close to the end of the first quarter of the performance appraisal period.[13] Directors at two of the medical centers in our review expressed frustration with the delay and not having a full year to meet performance expectations, but directors at the two other medical centers stated that they find the process clear and are able to anticipate performance expectations. Officials from VHA's office of Workforce Management and Consulting, which sends out the template, told us that they have been working in recent years to shorten the template's development and review process within VHA; however, the delays may continue because of late changes from VA or the Office of Personnel Management. In our December 2016 review of human resource management practices at VHA, we also reported on delays in the release of VHA's performance plan template.[14] We reported that the delay limited medical center officials' ability to use the template as a tool to align expectations and performance, which is inconsistent with leading practices on employee performance management. We recommended that VHA accelerate its efforts to develop a modern, credible, and effective performance management system, including the timely release of the performance plan template. VA partially concurred with our recommendation and has made limited progress in implementing it. As of December 2018, this recommendation remains open and we reiterate the need for VHA to implement it.

---

[13] For fiscal year 2019, VHA released a draft performance plan template on December 4, 2018, pending additional guidance from VA. VHA incorporated VA's guidance (sent January 25, 2019) into the template and sent a revised version on January 29, 2019, to network directors.

[14] GAO, *Veterans Health Administration: Management Attention Is Needed to Address Systemic, Long-standing Human Capital Challenges,* GAO-17-30 (Washington, D.C., Dec. 23, 2016).

## VHA HAS NOT ASSESSED FOR IMPLEMENTATION PREVIOUS RECOMMENDATIONS MADE TO ENSURE SAIL'S EFFECTIVENESS IN ASSESSING MEDICAL CENTER PERFORMANCE

Although SAIL is used in the assessment of both medical centers' and directors' performance, VHA officials have not assessed and implemented as appropriate the recommendations from previous evaluations of the SAIL system to ensure its effectiveness. This is inconsistent with federal standards for internal control, which state that management should remediate identified internal control deficiencies on a timely basis.[15] This remediation may include assessing the results of reviews to determine appropriate actions, and, once decisions are made, completing and documenting corrective actions on a timely basis.

VHA officials told us that since it was established in 2012, there have been two evaluations of SAIL:[16]

- The first evaluation was an internal review, which VHA officials told us was completed in February 2014 and submitted to the director of VHA's Office of Analytics and Business Intelligence and reviewed by the then Under Secretary for Health and Principle Deputy Under Secretary for Health. The internal review, which had 22 recommendations, found issues related to the validity and reliability of SAIL as a tool for measuring performance and fostering accountability. For example, it included a recommendation that VHA no longer use aggregate star ratings for accountability, or for presenting medical center quality and efficiency information to stakeholders. Rather, the recommendation called for VHA to work to identify valid and reliable approaches for presenting this information.

---

[15] GAO-14-704G.

[16] In addition to the two evaluations, VHA officials also discussed potential SAIL measure changes and weights with subject matter experts in health policy and research in April 2014.

- The second evaluation was an external review, which VHA officials told us was submitted to the Office of the Principal Deputy Under Secretary for Health in April 2015.[17] The external review included 19 recommendations for short- and long-term improvements to SAIL, such as a recommendation to examine the potential for misclassifying medical centers—i.e., assigning star ratings that do not reflect medical centers' pattern of performance on the underlying measures. The review noted two ways such misclassification could occur: (1) two medical centers with summary scores that are close together could receive different star ratings, or (2) two medical centers with widely different summary scores could receive the same star rating.

The findings of the previous SAIL evaluations are similar to concerns that officials from the four networks and four medical centers in our review expressed about SAIL's effectiveness, including whether the star ratings were an accurate reflection of medical center performance. For example,

- officials from one medical center told us that, because the mortality measure has a higher weight relative to other SAIL measures, it can amplify the importance of a small difference between medical centers. As a result, a 1-star medical center may appear to be performing much more poorly on this measure than it is in practice; and
- officials from two medical centers told us that the length-of-stay measure may not be an accurate reflection of quality of care, as there are valid clinical reasons why some veterans need a longer length of stay that may not be reflected in the diagnostic and procedure codes for that stay. Therefore, the difference in performance on the length of stay measure between two medical centers may be the result of

---

[17] Booz Allen Hamilton, *Spectrum TOPR 0075: Veterans Health Administration (VHA) Strategic Analytics for Improvement and Learning (SAIL) Assessment.* (McLean, Va.: Apr. 24, 2015). The total cost of the review was about $325,000.

how data were entered into the medical record and coded, rather than actual differences in quality of care.[18]

In addition, VHA officials also expressed concerns about SAIL and how it is currently being used to assess medical center performance. For example, VHA officials who oversee SAIL told us it was designed to be an internal performance improvement tool, but is now also being used as a performance accountability tool. The external review included a recommendation that VHA consider whether the primary purpose of SAIL is improvement or accountability, as SAIL would need to be redesigned to do both. One VHA official told us that SAIL is being used in punitive ways through the Strategic Action for Transformation initiative.

For example, at one medical center, officials told us that they received a letter from VHA's Executive in Charge about the medical center's low performance only a few months after its star level increased from 1 to 2 stars. Officials said the letter warned them that medical center leadership could be removed if performance does not improve. Medical center officials described this as counterproductive for their improvement efforts, as it was demoralizing while not identifying any specific areas for improvement.

VHA officials confirmed that, other than their routine reviews to determine the need for annual adjustments to SAIL measures and other minor adjustments to the system, they have not assessed or implemented as appropriate the recommendations from the internal and external SAIL evaluations. In addition, although the Under Secretary for Health received a response to the internal review's recommendations from an individual program office, VHA officials told us no action was taken on the response or to formally assess the recommendations from the internal review.[19]

---

[18] Medical coding involves using the available clinical information in patient medical records to assign numerical codes from the *International Classification of Diseases, Tenth Revision* coding system, referred to as ICD-10. This coding system is used by health care providers to classify all diagnoses, symptoms, and procedures recorded in conjunction with hospital care in the United States.

[19] VHA officials told us the response was provided by officials within VHA's Office of Operational Analytics and Reporting, and expressed their agreement or disagreement with the recommendations from the internal review.

Officials noted that two reasons for the lack of action taken to assess recommendations for implementation were leadership turnover and attention diverted to other issues, such as concerns about extended wait times for medical appointments at VHA medical facilities.[20] In addition, officials stated that the evaluations were not widely distributed within VHA. As a result, officials we spoke with from several VHA offices were unaware that SAIL had ever been evaluated. To address the federal internal control standard for timely remediation of identified deficiencies, federal agencies assign responsibility and authority for carrying out and documenting corrective actions.[21]

VHA officials told us they did not formally assign responsibility to an office to assess recommendations from previous evaluations of SAIL. As a result, when the officials who received both evaluations left VHA, there were no other individuals or offices responsible for ensuring that recommendations were acted on.

VHA officials who oversee SAIL told us that they are planning to use the 2015 external review as part of their plans to make changes to SAIL and its measures. However, there is no documentation available describing the planned changes to SAIL or how those planned changes will incorporate the results of the external review. If changes made to SAIL run counter to the evidence, it could potentially diminish the integrity of the system to effectively evaluate performance.

## CONCLUSION

VHA primarily uses the SAIL system to assess and compare the performance of medical centers. Veterans can also view SAIL data to

---

[20] In 2014, a series of events called into question the ability of veterans to gain timely access to care from VHA medical facilities. Reviews by us, the VA Office of Inspector General, and others substantiated allegations of extended wait times for veteran appointments at VHA medical facilities. We found that VHA employees responsible for scheduling medical appointments at certain facilities engaged in inappropriate practices to make wait times appear more favorable.

[21] GAO-14-704G.

compare medical center performance when making health care decisions. Officials from the networks and medical centers in our review expressed concerns about how SAIL is being used and whether star ratings are an accurate reflection of medical center quality. SAIL has been evaluated twice, and both evaluations have found similar concerns with SAIL. However, VHA has yet to use the results of those evaluations to address identified concerns and make evidence-based improvements to the SAIL system. Specifically, VHA has not taken action to ensure that officials assess the recommendations from SAIL evaluations, document their decisions, and implement recommendations as appropriate. If changes to SAIL are implemented without this assessment of existing evaluations, VHA may make changes that run counter to the evidence, potentially diminishing the integrity of the system to effectively evaluate performance.

## RECOMMENDATIONS

We are making the following two recommendations to VA:

- The Under Secretary for Health should assess recommendations from two previous evaluations of SAIL. This assessment should include the documentation of decisions about which recommendations to implement and assignment of officials or offices as responsible for implementing them. (Recommendation 1)
- The Under Secretary for Health should implement, as appropriate, recommendations resulting from the assessment of the two previous SAIL evaluations. (Recommendation 2)

## AGENCY COMMENTS

We provided VA with a draft of this chapter for review and comment. VA provided written comments, which are reprinted in appendix II. In its written comments, VA concurred with both of the report's recommendations, and identified actions it is taking to implement them.

We are sending copies of this chapter to the appropriate congressional committees, the Secretary of Veterans Affairs, the Under Secretary for Health, and other interested parties.

Debra A. Draper
Director, Health Care

## APPENDIX I: VHA STRATEGIC ANALYTICS FOR IMPROVEMENT AND LEARNING (SAIL) PERFORMANCE MEASURES

| Domain | Number of measures | Measure | Desired Direction of Measure |
|---|---|---|---|
| Acute care Mortality | 2 | In-Hospital risk adjusted mortality (SMR) | Lower |
| | | 30-day risk adjusted mortality (SMR30) | Lower |
| Avoidable Adverse Events | 2 | Risk adjusted complication Index | Lower |
| | | Healthcare associated infections | Lower |
| Length of stay and Utilization Management | 3 | Severity adjusted average length of stay (ALOS) | Lower |
| | | %Acute admission reviews met InterQual criteria | Higher |
| | | %Acute continued stay reviews met InterQual criteria | Higher |
| Performance Measures | 3 | Inpatient core measures mean percentage (ORYX) | Higher |
| | | HEDIS outpatient core measure mean percentage (chart abstract) | Higher |
| | | HEDIS outpatient core measure mean percentage (population based) | Higher |
| Patient Experience | 5 | HCAHPS score (patient rating of hospital) | Higher |
| | | Rating of primary care provider | Higher |
| | | Rating of specialty care provider | Higher |
| | | Care Transition (inpatient) | Higher |
| | | Stress discussed (PCMH) | Higher |

| Domain | Number of measures | Measure | Desired Direction of Measure |
|---|---|---|---|
| Employee Satisfaction | 2 | Best Places to Work score | Higher |
| | | Registered nurse turnover rate | Lower |
| Care Transitions | 2 | ACSC hospitalizations | Lower |
| | | Hospital-wide all conditions 30-day readmission rate | Lower |
| Access | 5 | Timely Appointment, Care and Information –PCMH | Higher |
| | | Timely Appointment, Care and Information –SC | Higher |
| | | Same Day Appointment When Needed – PCMH | Higher |
| | | Call center speed in picking up calls | Lower |
| | | Telephone abandonment rate | Lower |
| Mental Health | 3 | Mental health population coverage | Higher |
| | | Mental health continuity of care | Higher |
| | | Mental health experience of care | Higher |
| Efficiency/ Capacity | 2 | Stochastic frontier analysis (= 1/SFA) | Higher |
| | | Physician Capacity | Lower |

Source: Veterans Health Administration (VHA) SAIL Fact Sheet. | GAO-19-350.

Notes: The information in this table is reprinted verbatim from VHA's SAIL Fact Sheet. See Office of Reporting, Analytics, Performance, Improvement, & Deployment, *Strategic Analytics for Improvement and Learning (SAIL) Fact Sheet,* September 25, 2018.

The acronyms VHA used in the table are as follows: SMR=standard mortality ratio; HEDIS=Healthcare Effectiveness Data and Information Set; HCAHPS= Hospital Consumer Assessment of Healthcare Providers and Systems; PCMH=patient-centered medical home; ACSC=ambulatory care sensitive conditions; SC=specialty care.

# APPENDIX II: COMMENTS FROM THE DEPARTMENT OF VETERANS AFFAIRS

THE SECRETARY OF VETERANS AFFAIRS
WASHINGTON

April 9, 2019

Ms. Debra A. Draper
Director, Health Care
U.S. Government Accountability Office
441 G Street, NW
Washington, DC 20548

Dear Ms. Draper:

 The Department of Veterans Affairs (VA) has reviewed the Government Accountability Office (GAO) draft report: *VETERANS HEALTH ADMINISTRATION: Past Performance System Recommendations Have Not Been Implemented* (GAO-19-350).

 The enclosure contains the actions to be taken to address the draft report recommendations.

 VA appreciates the opportunity to comment on your draft report.

    Sincerely,

    *Robert L. Wilkie*

    Robert L. Wilkie

Department of Veterans Affairs (VA) Comments to
Government Accountability Office (GAO) Draft Report
***VETERANS HEALTH ADMINISTRATION: Past Performance System
Recommendations Have Not Been Implemented***
(GAO-19-350)

**Recommendation 1:** **The Under Secretary for Health should assess recommendations from two previous evaluations of SAIL. This assessment should include the documentation of decisions about which recommendations to implement and assignment of officials or offices as responsible for implementing them.**

**VA Comment:** Concur. The Veterans Health Administration (VHA) Office of Reporting, Analytics, Performance Improvement and Deployment (RAPID) will take the following actions to assess recommendations from two previous evaluations of Strategic Analytics for Improvement and Learning (SAIL):

1. Review prior recommendations from SAIL evaluations for relevance and appropriateness. The responsible entities are RAPID and the VHA National Leadership Council.

2. Establish a governance process for future iterations of SAIL that is linked to the larger strategic priorities of VHA including the implementation of the VA Maintaining Internal Systems and Strengthening Integrated Outside Networks (MISSION) Act, and implements appropriate recommendations from prior evaluations of SAIL. The responsible entities are RAPID and the VHA National Leadership Council.

3. After implementing a new governance process for SAIL and revising the framework for VHA performance accountability, conduct a formative evaluation (including quantitative measure validation and qualitative assessment of its effectiveness for performance management) to determine if the revised SAIL approach is meeting agency goals. The responsible entities are RAPID; the VHA National Leadership Council; and the Office of Discovery, Education and Affiliate Network.

VHA has taken actions to implement the recommendations from two previous external evaluations of SAIL in 2014 and 2015 to include:

- Clarifying for all stakeholders the purpose of the Measurement System: SAIL remains an improvement and learning system and the focus of its use in senior executive appraisal includes both of those emphases. We achieve those functions through: (a) establishing dedicated teams of improvement specialists and data and subject matter experts throughout the agency to assist low-performing hospitals; (b) providing tools for our health system leaders to track star rating (relative performance against other sites) and absolute

  improvement (size of change in their own performance); (c) hosting SAIL webinars twice a month that are open to all field users, allowing anyone in the agency to learn from subject matter experts across VA.

Continually updating Measures and Weighting: All domains and metrics, as well as their weights, have been reviewed and updated regularly (minimum annually), with inputs from partner program offices, field users, VA Central Office senior leadership, and the SAIL workgroup. We note that the efficiency domain has changed to efficiency/capacity domain to include physician capacity metrics based on accepted benchmarks of clinical productivity.

- Measure Hierarchy: The domain and metric weighting scheme have incorporated inputs from partner offices and stakeholders. The measure hierarchy has evolved overtime to reflect policy priorities (e.g., mental health care); clinical program areas (e.g., primary care and specialty care); and domains that serve frontline care (e.g., inpatient acute care outcome, care transition outcome, outpatient care outcome, and patient perception); and service providers (e.g., registered nurse turnover, mental health care provider survey, and physician capacity). Factor analysis was conducted to assess alternative grouping of metrics and various dashboard and analytic tools have been developed and linked on SAIL for users to conduct analyses by their program area.
- Scoring/star rating: We have conducted analysis to assess performance of various scales of star rating and found, contrary to recommendations from the 2015 review, a three-stars system does not perform better than a five-stars system. Given that the Centers for Medicare and Medicaid Services (CMS) also used a five-stars system – because CMS' technical expert panel felt it provided a better differentiation of performance and a ladder of progress, VHA felt it was appropriate to continue this approach. RAPID incorporated a recommendation from the VHA National Leadership Council to promote a one-Star VA facility to a two-Stars if it outperforms one-Star Medicare Hospitals based on comparable metrics. Finally, to ensure VHA is comparing medical centers with similar clinical missions, RAPID created complexity groupings (fixed stratification) built upon how VHA classifies facility complexity. For example, large, urban, teaching VA medical centers are compared with each other, and not star-rated by comparisons with smaller facilities with more limited services. Please note that CMS has been criticized for the lack of such stratification within the five-star methodology it uses for Hospital Compare.
- Collaborating program offices for SAIL have many avenues to solicit comments and questions from across the organization, which our staff, managers, and

leadership are not hesitant to use. These include a Help Desk feature on the SAIL reporting site; separate Help Desk features on each of the SAIL component measure domains (which are staffed by subject matter experts who respond personally); and frequent discussion of SAIL and its components during the VHA National Leadership Council meetings and the meetings of its component governance boards. RAPID also has the means to collect confidential feedback about the usefulness of reporting tools (i.e. SAIL is one tool, but there are many reporting tools that support SAIL). For anonymous feedback of concerns about the integrity of SAIL, RAPID encourages the use of the Office of the Inspector General (OIG) hotline, and RAPID works closely with the OIG on such matters. Target Completion Date: December 31, 2019.

**Recommendation 2: The Under Secretary for Health should implement, as appropriate, recommendations resulting from the assessment of the two previous SAIL evaluations.**

**VA Comment:** Concur. RAPID will establish a process to implement this recommendation and take the following actions in parallel with addressing Recommendation 1 to assess recommendations from two previous evaluations of SAIL:

1. Review prior recommendations from SAIL evaluations for relevance and appropriateness. (Responsible entities: RAPID and the VHA National Leadership Council.)

2. Establish a governance process for future iterations of SAIL that is linked to the larger strategic priorities of VHA, including the implementation of the MISSION Act, and implement appropriate recommendations from prior evaluations of SAIL The responsible entities are RAPID and the VHA National Leadership Council.

3. After implementing a new governance process for SAIL and revising the framework for VHA performance accountability, conduct a formative evaluation (including quantitative measure validation and qualitative assessment of its effectiveness for performance management) to determine if the revised SAIL approach is meeting agency goals. The Responsible entities are the VHA National Leadership Council, Office of Discovery, Education and Affiliate Network, and RAPID. Target Completion Date: December 31, 2019.

In: Key Government Reports.  ISBN: 978-1-53616-001-7
Editor: Ernest Clark  © 2019 Nova Science Publishers, Inc.

*Chapter 7*

# VETERANS HEALTH CARE: VA NEEDS TO ADDRESS CHALLENGES AS IT IMPLEMENTS THE VETERANS COMMUNITY CARE PROGRAM<sup>*</sup>

*Sharon M. Silas*

## WHY GAO DID THIS STUDY

In June 2018, Congress passed the VA MISSION Act of 2018, which requires VA to establish a permanent community care program. VA plans to consolidate the Choice Program and its other VA community care programs into one community care program—the VCCP. This legislation helps address some of the challenges faced by the Choice Program and VA's other community care programs. VA's implementation of the VCCP can benefit from the lessons learned under the Choice Program. Ignoring these lessons

---

\* This is an edited, reformatted and augmented version of United States Government Accountability Office; Testimony Before the Committee on Veterans' Affairs, U.S. Senate, Accessible Version, Publication No. GAO-19-507T, dated April 10, 2019.

learned increases VA's risk for not being able to ensure that all veterans receive timely access to care in the community and that community providers are reimbursed in a timely manner.

This testimony focuses on lessons learned from the Choice Program, including recommendations GAO has made to VA to help ensure (1) veterans' timely access to care under the VCCP (2) effective monitoring of veterans' access to care under the VCCP, and (3) timely payments to community providers under the VCCP. This testimony is based on GAO reports on the Choice Program that were issued in June 2018 and September 2018.

## WHAT GAO RECOMMENDS

GAO has made 12 recommendations to VA to improve its management and oversight of the Choice Program and the VCCP. VA generally agreed with all but one of GAO's recommendations. GAO continues to believe that all of the recommendations are warranted. As of April 2019, these recommendations have not been implemented.

## WHAT GAO FOUND

The Department of Veterans Affairs' (VA) Veterans Choice Program (Choice Program) allows eligible veterans to obtain health care services from providers not directly employed by VA (community providers). The program is largely managed by third party administrators (TPA), who are responsible for establishing provider networks, scheduling veterans' appointments, and paying providers. GAO has identified the following challenges to the Choice Program that VA needs to address as it implements its new Veterans Community Care Program (VCCP).

## Factors That Adversely Affected Veterans' Timely Access to Care

GAO found that numerous factors adversely affected veterans' timely access to care through the Choice Program. These factors included (1) administrative burden caused by complexities of referral and appointment scheduling processes; (2) poor communication between VA and its medical facilities; and (3) inadequacies in the networks of community providers established by the TPAs, including an insufficient number, mix, or geographic distribution of community providers. VA has taken steps intended to help address these factors, however, some have not been fully addressed. In June 2018, GAO made five recommendations to VA, including that VA establish a system that will facilitate care coordination and exchanges of information among VA medical facilities, VA clinicians, TPAs, community providers, and veterans. VA agreed or agreed in principle with all five recommendations, but has not yet implemented them.

## Unavailable and Unreliable Data

GAO found that VA cannot systematically monitor the timeliness of veterans' access to Choice Program care because it lacks complete, reliable data to do so. The data limitations GAO identified included a lack of data on the timeliness of accepting referrals and opting veterans in to the program, inaccurate data on clinically indicated dates (which are used to measure the timeliness of care), and unreliable data on the timeliness of urgent care. In June 2018, GAO made five recommendations to VA, including that VA implement mechanisms to allow VA to systematically monitor the amount of time taken to prepare referrals, schedule appointments, and complete appointments. VA agreed with four of the five recommendations, but has not yet implemented them.

## Untimely Payments to Community Providers

GAO identified three key factors that affected timeliness of payments to community providers under the Choice Program. These factors included (1) VA's untimely payments to TPAs, which in turn extended the length of time TPAs took to pay providers' claims; (2) Choice Program reimbursement requirements, which led to claim denials; and (3) inadequate provider education on filing claims. GAO found that VA has taken actions to address the factors, such as amending certain reimbursement requirements. However, two of these factors have not been fully addressed. In September 2018, GAO made two recommendations to VA, including that VA collect data on and monitor compliance with its requirements pertaining to customer service for community providers. VA agreed with the recommendations, but has not yet implemented them.

Chairman Isakson,

Ranking Member Tester, and Members of the Committee:

I am pleased to be here today to discuss the challenges the Department of Veterans Affairs (VA) has faced in implementing the Veterans Choice Program (Choice Program) that VA needs to address as it plans and implements its new community care program.[1]

In June 2018, the VA MISSION Act of 2018 was enacted and required VA to establish a permanent community care program. VA plans to consolidate the Choice Program and its other VA community care programs into one community care program—the Veterans Community Care Program (VCCP).[2]

---

[1] The Veterans Access, Choice, and Accountability Act of 2014 created the Choice Program as a temporary program to address problems with veterans' timely access to care at VA medical facilities. Under the Choice Program, when eligible veterans face long wait times, lengthy travel distances, or other challenges accessing care at VA medical facilities, they may obtain health care services from community providers—that is, providers who are not directly employed by VA. Pub. L. No. 113-146, 128 Stat. 1754 (2014). The Choice Program's authority sunsets on June 6, 2019.

[2] Pub. L. No. 115-182, tit. I, 132 Stat. 1393 (2018).

This legislation helps address some of the challenges faced by VA in ensuring timely access to care through the Choice Program and VA's other community care programs.

My testimony today focuses on lessons learned from the Choice Program, including recommendations we have made to VA to help ensure

1. veterans' timely access to care under the VCCP,
2. effective monitoring of veterans' access to care under the VCCP, and
3. timely payments to community providers under the VCCP.

My remarks are based on our work examining the Choice Program; specifically, our reports issued in June 2018 and September 2018 and recommendations therein.[3] These reports provide details on our scope and methodology. We conducted all of the work on which this statement is based in accordance with generally accepted government auditing standards. Those standards require that we plan and perform the audit to obtain sufficient, appropriate evidence to provide a reasonable basis for our findings and conclusions based on our audit objectives. We believe that the evidence obtained provides a reasonable basis for our findings and conclusions based on our audit objectives.

## BACKGROUND

The Veterans Access, Choice, and Accountability Act of 2014 provided up to $10 billion in funding for veterans to obtain health care services from community providers through the Choice Program when veterans faced long wait times, lengthy travel distances, or other challenges accessing care at

---

[3] See GAO, *Veterans Choice Program: Improvements Needed to Address Access-Related Challenges as VA Plans Consolidation of Its Community Care Programs*, GAO-18-281 (Washington, D.C.: June 4, 2018) and GAO, *Veterans Choice Program: Further Improvements Needed to Help Ensure Timely Payments to Community Providers*, GAO-18-671 (Washington, D.C.: Sept. 28, 2018).

VA medical facilities.[4] The temporary authority and funding for the Choice Program was separate from other previously existing programs through which VA has the option to purchase care from community providers. Legislation enacted in April, August, and December of 2017 and June 2018 extended the Choice Program and provided an additional $9.4 billion for the Veterans Choice Fund.[5] Authority for the Choice Program will sunset on June 6, 2019.[6]

## Responsibilities of the Choice Program's Third Party Administrators

In October 2014, VA modified its existing contracts with two contractors— referred to as third party administrators (TPA)—that were administering another VA community care program to add certain administrative responsibilities associated with the Choice Program. For the Choice Program, each of the two TPAs—Health Net and TriWest—was responsible for managing networks of community providers who deliver care in a specific multi-state region. Specifically, the TPAs were responsible for establishing networks of community providers, scheduling appointments with community providers for eligible veterans, and paying community providers for their services.

---

[4] Pub. L. No. 113-146, §§ 101, 802, 128 Stat. 1754, 1755-1765, 1802-1803 (2014).

[5] An Act to amend the Veterans Access, Choice, and Accountability Act of 2014 to modify the termination date for the Veterans Choice Program, and for other purposes, Pub. L. No. 115-26, § 1, 131 Stat. 129 (2017). VA Choice and Quality Employment Act of 2017, Pub. L. No. 115-46, § 101, 131 Stat. 958, 959 (2017) (providing an additional $2.1 billion for the Veterans Choice Fund); An Act to amend the Homeland Security Act of 2002 to require the Secretary of Homeland Security to issue Department of Homeland Security-wide guidance and develop training programs as part of the Department of Homeland Security Blue Campaign, and for other purposes, Pub. L. No. 115-96. Div. D, § 4001, 131 Stat. 2044, 2052-53 (2017) (providing an additional $2.1 billion for the Veterans Choice Fund) and Pub. L. No. 115-182, tit. V, § 510, 132 Stat. 1393,__ (2018) (providing an additional $5.2 billion for the Veterans Choice Fund).

[6] Pub. L. No. 115-182, tit. I, § 143, 132 Stat. 1393, __ (2018), amending section 101(p) of the Veterans Access, Choice, and Accountability Act of 2014, Pub. L. No. 113-146, 128 Stat. at 1763.

Health Net's contract for administering the Choice Program ended on September 30, 2018, with TriWest continuing to administer the Choice Program in its region and the region previously administered by HealthNet until the program ends.

## Process for Choice Program Appointment Scheduling

Through policies and standard operating procedures for VA medical facilities and contracts with the TPAs, VA established processes for referring and scheduling appointments through the Choice Program: one process for time-eligible veterans and another for distance-eligible veterans.[7] Table 1 provides an overview of the appointment scheduling process that applies when a veteran is referred to the Choice Program because the veteran is time-eligible—that is, the next available medical appointment with a VA clinician is more than 30 days from the veteran's preferred date or, in the absence of such a date, the date the veteran's physician determines he or she should be seen.

When veterans reside more than 40 miles from a VA medical facility or meet other travel-related criteria, VA uses the appointment scheduling process it developed for distance-eligible veterans. The process for distance-eligible veterans differs from that for time-eligible veterans in that VA medical facilities do not prepare a referral and send it to the TPA.

Instead, distance-eligible veterans contact the TPA directly to request Choice Program care.

---

[7] For the purposes of this statement, the terms "time-eligible" and "distance-eligible" refer to the Choice Program processes used to schedule veterans' appointments. VA uses the time-eligible appointment scheduling process when the services needed are not available at a VA medical facility or are not available within allowable wait times. We did not evaluate VA's determination that veterans for whom services were unavailable were eligible for the Choice Program. VA uses the distance-eligible appointment scheduling process when veterans reside more than 40 miles from a VA medical facility or meet other travel-related criteria. Data we obtained from the TPAs indicate that VA and the TPAs used the time-eligible appointment scheduling process about 90 percent of the time from fiscal year 2015 through fiscal year 2016 (the first 2 years of the Choice Program's implementation).

**Table 1. Process for Veterans to Obtain Department of Veterans Affairs (VA) Choice Program Care if They Are Time-Eligible**

| Steps of the Choice Program scheduling process | Completed by VA medical facility staff | Completed by Choice Program third party administrator (TPA) staff | Completed by the veteran |
|---|---|---|---|
| A VA clinician determines the veteran needs care. | Responsible | | |
| VA medical facility staff confirm the veteran's eligibility for Choice Program care and begin contacting the veteran to offer a referral to the Choice Program. The veteran agrees to be referred to the Choice Program. | Responsible | | Responsible |
| VA medical facility staff compile relevant clinical information (including a description of the specific services and type of medical specialist the veteran needs) and submit the veteran's referral to the TPA. | Responsible | | |
| TPA staff review the veteran's Choice Program referral to ensure it contains information needed to proceed with appointment scheduling and accept the referral if the information is sufficient. | | Responsible | |
| TPA staff contact the veteran by telephone to confirm that he or she wants to opt in to the Choice Program. If the veteran is not reached by telephone, the TPA sends a letter requesting that the veteran contact the TPA to opt in to the program. | | Responsible | |
| If the veteran opts in to the Choice Program, TPA staff create an authorization and begin efforts to schedule an appointment with a community provider. | | Responsible | |

| Steps of the Choice Program scheduling process | Completed by VA medical facility staff | Completed by Choice Program third party administrator (TPA) staff | Completed by the veteran |
|---|---|---|---|
| TPA staff schedule an appointment with a community provider. The authorization (which contains relevant clinical information, a description of authorized services, and a period of validity) is sent to the community provider. The veteran is informed of the date and time of the appointment. | | Responsible | |
| The veteran attends the initial appointment with the Choice Program community provider. | | | Responsible |

Legend: = responsibility for process step.
Source: GAO analysis of VA documents. | GAO-19-507T.
Note: VA uses the time-eligible appointment scheduling process when the services needed are not available at a VA medical facility or are not available within allowable wait times.

## Choice Program Claim Processing and Payment

VA's Choice Program TPA processes claims it receives from community providers for the care they deliver to veterans and pays providers for approved claims. Figure 1 provides an overview of the steps the TPA follows for processing claims and paying community providers.

To be reimbursed for its payments to providers, the TPA in turn submits electronic invoices—or requests for payment—to VA. The TPA generates an invoice for every claim it receives from community providers and pays. VA reviews the TPA's invoices and either approves or rejects them. Invoices may be rejected, for example, if care provided was not authorized. Approved invoices are paid, whereas rejected invoices are returned to the TPA. Under the Prompt Payment Act, VA is required to pay its TPAs within 30 days of receipt of a clean Choice Program invoice.[8]

---

[8] 31 U.S.C. § 3903(a)(1); 5 C.F.R. part 1315.

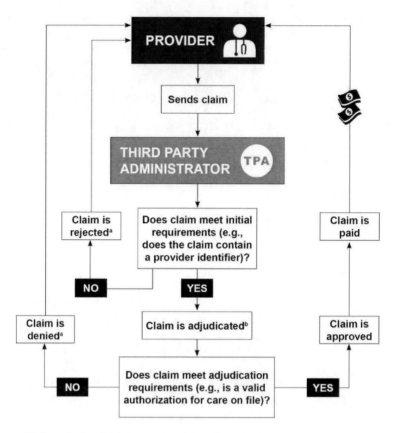

Source: GAO analysis of third party administrator (TPA) information. GAO-19-507T.

[a]According to TPA officials, rejected claims are claims returned up front to providers due to, for example, the use of invalid claim forms and missing provider identification numbers. Denied claims are claims that contain the necessary data elements but do not pass required claim processing steps, which, for example, verify the veteran's eligibility for the Veterans Choice Program, that a valid authorization for care is on file, and that the claim is not a duplicate.

[b]Claim adjudication refers to the process of reviewing a claim and making the decision to approve or deny it. Claims being adjudicated are either classified as clean or non-clean claims. Clean claims are claims that contain all required data elements, while non-clean claims are those claims that are missing required data elements that the TPA must obtain before the claim is paid.

Figure 1. Steps the TPA Follows to Process and Pay Claims from Community Providers for Care Delivered Under the Veterans Choice Program.

## VA's Planned Veterans Community Care Program

The VA MISSION Act of 2018, among other things, requires VA to establish a permanent community care program no later than 1 year after passage of the Act (June 6, 2019) and authorizes VA to utilize a TPA for claims processing. VA refers to the consolidated program as the VCCP. In December 2016, prior to enactment of the VA MISSION Act of 2018, VA issued a request for proposals for contractors to help administer the VCCP. The VCCP will be similar to the current Choice Program in certain respects. For example, under the VCCP, TPAs will be responsible for establishing regional networks of community providers and processing and paying those providers' claims. However, unlike the Choice Program, under the VCCP, VA is planning to have medical facilities—not the TPAs—generally be responsible for scheduling veterans' appointments with community providers. VA awarded contracts for administering the VCCP in three of six regions on December 28, 2018. As of April 3, 2019, VA had not yet awarded contracts for the remaining three regions.

Generally, all veterans enrolled in the VA health care system would be able to qualify for care through the VCCP when (1) VA does not offer the care or service required by the veteran; (2) the veteran resides in a state without a full-service VA medical facility; (3) the veteran would have been eligible under the 40-mile criterion of the Choice Program before June 6, 2018; (4) VA cannot provide the veteran with care and services that comply with its designated access standards; or (5) the veteran and the veteran's referring clinician agree that it is in the best interest of the veteran to receive care in the community. In January 2019, VA proposed new access standards for the VCCP based on average drive times and wait times:

- For primary care, mental health, and non-institutional extended care services, VA is proposing a 30-minute average drive time standard.
- For specialty care, VA is proposing a 60-minute average drive time standard.
- VA is proposing appointment wait-time standards of 20 days for primary care, mental health care, and non-institutional extended

care services, and 28 days for specialty care from the date of request with certain exceptions.[9]

Eligible veterans who cannot access care within those standards would be able to choose between eligible community providers and care at a VA medical facility. VA expects to issue the final regulation establishing access standards for the VCCP by June 2019.

## VA Needs to Address Various Factors That Adversely Affected Veterans' Access to Care through the Choice Program to Help Ensure Timely Care under the VCCP

**Table 2. GAO Recommendations for Addressing Factors Adversely Affecting Veterans' Access to Care and the Implementation Status of These Recommendations**

| GAO recommendation | Implementation status |
|---|---|
| The Under Secretary for Health should (1) establish oversight mechanisms to ensure that VA is collecting reliable data on the reasons that VA medical facility or third party administrator (TPA) staff are unsuccessful in scheduling veterans' appointments through the Veterans Community Care Program (VCCP), and (2) demonstrate that it has corrected any identified deficiencies.[a] | VA agreed with our recommendation and stated that it has developed a mechanism for capturing unsuccessful scheduling attempts. According to VA, this mechanism will be incorporated into its new Health Share Referral Manager system, which VA expects will be fully implemented across all VA medical facilities by September 2019. The exact oversight mechanism and ability to identify and correct deficiencies are still being established. |
| The Secretary of Veterans Affairs should ensure that the contracts for the VCCP include performance metrics that will allow VA to monitor average driving times between veterans' homes and the practice locations of community providers that participate in the TPAs' networks. | VA agreed with our recommendation and stated that its Veterans Community Care Network contract request for proposals includes performance metrics that will allow VA to monitor average driving times between veterans' homes and the practice locations of community providers that participate in the TPAs' networks. |

---

[9] 84 Fed. Reg. 5629 (Feb. 22, 2019).

| GAO recommendation | Implementation status |
|---|---|
| The Secretary of Veterans Affairs should establish a system for the VCCP to help facilitate seamless, efficient information sharing among VA medical facilities, VA clinicians, TPAs, community providers, and veterans. Specifically, this system should allow all of these entities to electronically exchange information for the purposes of care coordination | VA agreed with our recommendation and stated that its new Health Share Referral Manager system, which VA expects will be fully implemented across all medical facilities by September 2019, will be a key component of an overall system that will facilitate information sharing among medical facilities, VA clinicians, TPAs, community providers, and veterans. VA expects to implement this recommendation by September 2019. |
| The Under Secretary for Health should conduct a comprehensive evaluation of the outcomes of the two appointment scheduling pilots it established at the Alaska and Fargo VA Health Care Systems (where VA medical facility staff, rather than TPA staff, are responsible for scheduling veterans' Choice Program appointments), which should include a comparison of the timeliness with which VA medical facility staff and TPA staff completed each step of the Choice Program appointment scheduling process, as well as the overall timeliness with which veterans received appointments. | VA agreed with our recommendation. VA's new Health Share Referral Manager system, which VA expects will be fully implemented across all medical facilities by September 2019, will enable VA to assess the timeliness of appointment scheduling. VA expects to implement this recommendation by October 2019. |
| The Under Secretary for Health should issue a comprehensive policy directive and operations manual for the VCCP and ensure that these documents are reviewed and updated in a timely manner after any significant changes to the program occur. | VA agreed in principle with this recommendation and stated that the VA Office of Community Care will consider whether new policy directives are needed after the VCCP has been implemented and interim challenges to implementation have been resolved. |

Source: GAO-18-281 and GAO analysis of Department of Veterans Affairs (VA) information. | GAO-19-507T.

[a]The report in which we made these recommendations, refers to the VCCP as the consolidated community care program VA plans to implement, because the name of the program had not yet been announced. See GAO, *Veterans Choice Program: Improvements Needed to Address Access-Related Challenges as VA Plans Consolidation of Its Community Care Programs*, GAO-18-281 (Washington, D.C.: June 4, 2018).

In June 2018, we reported that numerous factors adversely affected veterans' timely access to care through the Choice Program and could affect implementation of the VCCP.[10] These factors included the following: (1) administrative burden caused by complexities of VA's referral and appointment scheduling processes; (2) poor communication between VA and its medical facilities; and (3) inadequacies in the networks of community providers established by the TPAs, including an insufficient number, mix, or geographic distribution of community providers. VA has taken steps to help address these factors; however, not all access factors have been fully addressed. For example, to help address administrative burden and improve the process of coordinating veterans' Choice Program care, VA established a secure e-mail system and a mechanism for TPAs and community providers to remotely access veterans' VA electronic health records. However, these mechanisms only facilitate a one-way transfer of necessary information. They do not provide a means by which VA medical facilities or veterans can view the TPAs' step-by-step progress in scheduling appointments or electronically receive medical documentation associated with Choice Program appointments.

We made five recommendations to VA to address the factors that adversely affected veterans' access to Choice Program care. VA agreed or agreed in principle with all five recommendations. Our recommendations and the steps, if any, VA has taken in response to these recommendations are described in Table 2.

## VA Needs Complete and Reliable Data to Effectively Monitor Veterans' Access to Care under the VCCP

In June 2018, we reported that VA cannot systematically monitor the timeliness of veterans' access to Choice Program care because it lacks complete, reliable data to do so.[11] VA will need to address these data

---

[10] See GAO-18-281.
[11] See GAO-18-281.

limitations in order to effectively monitor the care delivered to veterans through the VCCP. The data limitations we identified included the following:

- A lack of data on the timeliness of accepting referrals and opting veterans in to the program. We found that the data VA uses to monitor the timeliness of Choice Program appointments do not capture the time it takes VA medical facilities to prepare veterans' referrals and send them to the TPAs, nor do they capture the time spent by the TPAs in accepting VA medical facilities' referrals and opting veterans in to the Choice Program. VA had implemented an interim solution to monitor overall wait times that relies on VA medical facility staff consistently and accurately entering unique identification numbers on VA clinicians' requests for care and on Choice Program referrals, a process that is prone to error.
- Inaccuracy of clinically indicated dates. We found that clinically indicated dates (used to measure the timeliness of care) are sometimes changed by VA medical facility staff before they send Choice Program referrals to the TPAs, which could mask veterans' true wait times. We found that VA medical facility staff entered later clinically indicated dates on referrals for about 23 percent of the 196 authorizations we reviewed.[12] It is unclear if VA medical facility staff mistakenly entered incorrect dates manually, or if they inappropriately entered later dates when the VA medical facility was delayed in contacting the veteran, compiling relevant clinical information, and sending the referral to the TPA.
- Unreliable data on the timeliness of urgent care. We found that VA medical facilities and TPAs do not always categorize Choice Program referrals and authorizations in accordance with the

---

[12] We manually reviewed a random, non-generalizable sample of 196 Choice Program authorizations. The authorizations were created for veterans at 6 selected VA medical facilities who were referred to the program between January and April of 2016, the most recent period for which data were available when we began our review. The sample of authorizations included 55 for routine care, 53 for urgent care, and 88 that the TPAs returned without scheduling appointments.

contractual definition for urgent care. According to the contracts, a referral is to be marked as "urgent," and an appointment is to take place within 2 business days of the TPA accepting it, when a VA clinician has determined that the needed care is (1) essential to evaluate and stabilize the veteran's condition, and (2) if delayed would likely result in unacceptable morbidity or pain. We reviewed a sample of 53 urgent care authorizations and determined that about 28 percent of the authorizations were originally marked as routine care authorizations but were changed to urgent by VA medical facility or TPA staff, in an effort to administratively expedite appointment scheduling.

**Table 3. GAO Recommendations for Improving the Timeliness and Accuracy of Data on Veterans' Wait Times for Care and the Implementation Status of These Recommendations**

| GAO recommendation | Implementation status |
|---|---|
| The Under Secretary for Health should establish an achievable wait-time goal for the Veterans Consolidated Community Care Program (VCCP) that will permit VA to monitor whether veterans are receiving VA community care within time frames that are comparable to the amount of time they would otherwise wait to receive care at VA medical facilities.[a] | VA agreed with our recommendation and has proposed wait-time standards for the VCCP. VA stated that, as its new standards are implemented, there will be transparency on the wait times for obtaining an appointment in the community, which will allow providers and veterans to make a more informed decision on where to obtain care based on medical need and timeliness of the appointment. According to VA, VA staff are meeting weekly to review current processes and determine if further updates are needed. VA expects to implement this recommendation by June 2019. |
| The Under Secretary for Health should design an appointment scheduling process for the VCCP that sets forth time frames within which (1) veterans' referrals must be processed, (2) veterans' appointments must be scheduled, and (3) veterans' appointments must occur, which are consistent with the wait-time goal VA has established for the program. | VA agreed with our recommendation and stated that it is developing a decision support tool to help determine how to deliver care in a timely and convenient manner. Among other features, the tool will display both VA clinic availability and the veteran's eligibility for community care, so administrative and clinical staff can work with the veteran to make an informed decision on when and where the requested care could be best delivered. According to VA, VA staff are meeting weekly to review current processes and determine if further updates are needed. VA expects to implement this recommendation by June 2019. |

| GAO recommendation | Implementation status |
|---|---|
| The Under Secretary for Health should establish a mechanism that will allow VA to systematically monitor the average number of days it takes for medical facilities to prepare referrals, for medical facilities or third-party administrators (TPA) to schedule veterans' appointments, and for veterans' appointments to occur, under the VCCP. | VA agreed with our recommendation and stated that it is developing a mechanism to systematically monitor the average number of days it takes for medical facilities to prepare referrals, for medical facilities or TPAs to schedule veterans' appointments, and for veterans' appointments to occur, under the VCCP. According to VA, this mechanism will be incorporated into its new Health Share Referral Manager system, which VA expects will be fully implemented across all VA medical facilities by September 2019. |
| The Under Secretary for Health should implement a mechanism to prevent veterans' clinically indicated dates from being modified by individuals other than VA clinicians when veterans are referred to the VCCP. | VA agreed with our recommendation and stated that its new Health Share Referral Manager system, which VA expects will be fully implemented across all VA medical facilities by September 2019, will interface with the existing consult package that has been modified to allow a VA clinician to enter the clinically indicated date while restricting schedulers from making alterations to it. |
| The Under Secretary for Health should implement a mechanism to separate clinically urgent referrals and authorizations from those for which the VA medical facility or the TPA has decided to expedite appointment scheduling for administrative reasons. | VA did not agree with this recommendation and stated there will no longer be a need to separate clinically urgent referrals for care from those that need expediting under the VCCP. However, we maintain that our recommendation is warranted. In particular, we found that VA's data did not always accurately reflect the timeliness of urgent care because both VA medical center and TPA staff inappropriately recategorized some routine care referrals and authorizations as urgent ones for reasons unrelated to the veterans' health conditions. |

Source: GAO-18-281 and GAO analysis of Department of Veterans Affairs (VA) information. | GAO-19-507T.
[a]The report in which we made these recommendations, refers to the VCCP as the consolidated community care program VA plans to implement, because the name of the program had not yet been announced. See GAO, Veterans Choice Program: Improvements Needed to Address Access-Related Challenges as VA Plans Consolidation of Its Community Care Programs, GAO-18-281 (Washington, D.C.: June 4, 2018).

We made five recommendations to VA on improving the completeness and accuracy of data on veterans' wait times for care. VA agreed with four of the five recommendations. Our recommendations and the steps VA has taken in response to these recommendations are described in Table 3.

## FURTHER IMPROVEMENTS ARE NEEDED TO HELP
## ENSURE TIMELY PAYMENTS TO COMMUNITY PROVIDERS

In September 2018, we reported that three key factors affected timeliness of payments to community providers under the Choice Program and that if unaddressed could affect provider payment timeliness for the VCCP.* These factors included the following: (1) VA's untimely payments to TPAs, which in turn extended the length of time TPAs took to pay community providers' claims; (2) Choice Program reimbursement requirements, which led to claim denials; and (3) inadequate provider education on filing claims. We reported that VA has taken some actions to address these factors. For example, VA updated its payment system and related processes to pay TPAs more quickly. According to VA data, as of July 2018, VA was paying at least 90 percent of the TPAs' invoices within 7 days, a significant increase from the 50 percent timely payments VA made to TPAs between November 2014 and September 2016. In addition, VA and the TPAs had taken steps to amend certain reimbursement requirements and improve provider education to help providers resolve claims processing issues.

However, we found that VA has not fully addressed two of these factors. First, with respect to reimbursement requirements, VA does not have complete data allowing it to effectively monitor adherence with its policy for VA medical facilities to perform timely reviews and approvals of secondary authorization requests. Community providers request secondary authorization requests when veterans need health care services that exceed the period or scope of the original authorization. Incomplete data impacted VA's ability to meet the requirement. When VA medical facilities delay these reviews and approvals, community providers may have to delay care or deliver care that is not authorized, which in turn increases the likelihood that the providers' claims will be denied and the providers will not be paid. Second, with respect to provider education on filing claims, VA requires the TPAs to establish a customer call center to respond to calls from veterans

---

* See GAO-18-671.

and non-VA providers. However, VA does not enforce the contractual requirement for responding to calls from community providers and allows the TPAs to prioritize calls from veterans over calls from community providers. Consequently, VA is not collecting data, monitoring, or enforcing compliance with its contractual requirements for the TPAs to provide timely customer service to providers. As a result, VA does not have information on the extent to which community providers face challenges when contacting the TPAs about claims payment issues, which could contribute to the amount of time it takes to receive reimbursement for services.

**Table 4. GAO Recommendations on Improving the Timeliness of Payments to Community Providers and the Implementation Status of These Recommendations**

| GAO recommendation | Implementation status |
|---|---|
| Once VA's new software for managing authorizations has been fully implemented, the Undersecretary for Health should monitor data on secondary authorization request approval decision time frames to ensure VA medical facilities are in adherence with VA policy, assess the reasons for nonadherence with the policy, and take corrective actions as necessary. | VA agreed with our recommendation and stated that it has already taken steps to improve compliance with secondary authorization request approval timeframes.by identifying challenges, agreeing on improvement actions, and providing training. According to VA, its new Health Share Referral Manager system, which VA expects will be fully implemented across all medical facilities by September 2019, will automate secondary authorization request reporting and tracking. According to VA, it will utilize this new system to ensure compliance with secondary authorization request approval time frames. |
| The Undersecretary for Health should collect data and monitor compliance with the Choice Program contractual requirements pertaining to customer service for community providers, and take corrective actions as necessary. | VA agreed with our recommendation and stated that it currently does not have the ability to monitor and assess the performance of customer service operations under the Choice Program contracts. VA has included additional requirements for customer service in the Veterans Community Care Network request for proposals and plans to monitor compliance with these requirements under the Veterans Community Care Program. VA expects to implement this recommendation by December 2019. |

Source: GAO-18-671 and GAO analysis of Department of Veterans Affairs (VA) information. | GAO-19-507T.

To address remaining factors that affect provider payment timeliness, we made two recommendations to VA. VA agreed with both recommendations. Our recommendations and the steps VA has taken in response to these recommendations are described in Table 4.

In summary, consolidating its existing community care programs into the VCCP and launching this new program in June 2019 is a large and complex undertaking, which comes with many risks and challenges for VA. Heeding the lessons learned from its implementation and management of the Choice Program will better position VA to ensure veterans receive timely access to care under the VCCP and avoid past challenges such as delays in scheduling appointments and untimely payments to community providers. Continued oversight of VA's implementation of the VCCP will be critical given the scale of change and the associated risks. We stand ready to assist this Committee with this continued oversight.

Chairman Isakson, Ranking Member Tester, and Members of the Committee, this concludes my prepared statement. I would be pleased to respond to any questions you may have.

# CONTENTS OF EARLIER VOLUMES

# INDEX

## T

## U

## V

## W